Joel Levin

How Judges Reason

The Logic of Adjudication

PETER LANG
New York • San Francisco • Bern
Frankfurt am Main • Berlin • Wien • Paris

Library of Congress Cataloging-in-Publication Data

Levin, Joel.
   How judges reason / Joel Levin.
    p. cm
   Includes bibliographical references and index.
   1. Judicial process. I. Title.
K2100.L48   1992   347'.01—dc20   91-37405
ISBN 0-8204-1549-9   CIP
[342.71]

Die Deutsche Bibliothek-CIP-Einheitsaufnahme

Levin, Joel:
How judges reason / Joel Levin.—New York; Berlin;
Bern; Frankfurt/M.; Paris; Wien: Lang, 1992
   ISBN 0-8204-1549-9

Cover Design by James F. Brisson.

The paper in this book meets the guidelines for permanence and
durability of the Committee on Production Guidelines for
Book Longevity of the Council on Library Resources.

© Peter Lang Publishing, Inc., New York 1992

Printed in the United States of America.

To Mace and Clare, who first
taught me to measure rules by values,
and to Becky, Julius, Luba,
and Morris, who taught them.

Chapter IV originally appeared, in a shorter and somewhat different form, in 33 *Case Western Res. L. Rev.* 208 (1983).

The quotations beginning each chapter are taken from "Law Like Love", reprinted from *W. H. Auden: Collected Poems* (edited by Edward Mendelson, copyright 1940, renewed 1968).

Permission to use these writings was kindly granted by Case Western Reserve Law Review and Random House, Inc. respectively.

Table of Contents

Preface

This is an explanation of how individuals think and reason when they are behaving as judges. The end product of judges' reasoning is often called, somewhat imprecisely, the common law, and its shape and influences are varied and divergent. In some ways, the flow of judicial reasoning is predictable in the way any reasoning system can be predicted. One looks to implication and consistency, and adds rules of inference, elegance, and simplicity. However, there are two significant reasons why judicial reasoning is not only unusual, but complex and difficult to predict.

First, getting legal concepts and lines of precedent straight and in good order is not enough. Justice and fairness always count. Even the basic terminology of the legal system reflects this. There are Justice Departments, ministers of justice, and (architecturally) justice centers, halls of justice, and justice buildings; but there are not rule departments, ministers of legal standards, precedent centers, halls of strict construction of past decisions, or norm buildings. There was a Justice Holmes and Justice Cardozo, but never a Chief of Law-and-Order Holmes or Associate Stare-Decisis-Enforcer Cardozo. If a rule offends fairness, neither consistency nor years of hallowed history bars its reconsideration. For example, under old English law, a debtor buying a house, making 29 years and 11 months of payments on a 30-year mortgage forfeited all monies if the final payment was one day late. So offensive to justice was this rule that an "equity of redemption" was imposed to allow the debtor to keep, at least, his past equity paid.

Second, legal reasoning is irreducibly democratic. The influences of individual judges, and the lawyers and litigants who influence them, count without regard to a decision's improbability, unreasonability, inconsistency, or even stupidity. This is unlike other areas where, for example, my view of quantum mechanics and the view of a Cal Tech physics professor would never be placed on the same footing. If both of us were appointed to a court, however, then at least in one important sense, our decisions would each count, and count significantly (although not necessarily equally).

If understanding a reasoning system is not difficult enough, the additional need to gain insight into the political process and discover some wisdom about justice under law humbles any potential theorist. This book, however modest its contribution, was made possible only because of the insight and wisdom many have shared (or tried to share). John Finnis, Ronald Dworkin, John Mackie, Banks McDowell, H. L. A. Hart, Greg Mullaly, Peter Novik, Derek Parfit, and Joseph Raz contributed such insight and wisdom, and the first four read and suggested improvements to various drafts of the manuscript. Also, Robert Lawry and David Van Zandt read the manuscript and made useful suggestions.

Constructing a theory of judicial reasoning has been a daunting task, and one I would not have undertaken without the early and constant encouragement of Daniel Coquillette. I owe an enormous debt to John Finnis, without whose encouragement, criticism, sagacity and advice the work could not have been completed.

A number of colleagues and former colleagues at my law firm, Nurenberg, Plevin, Heller & McCarthy, have suffered through manuscript drafts and have contributed valuable suggestions and corrections. The same fate befell and similar assistance came from my patient editor at Lang Publishing, Michael Flamini.

Finally, without the support and encouragement of my parents and my wife Susan, the book would not have been possible. No mere thanks here can do justice to that debt.

Introduction

If we, dear, know we know no more
Than they about the law,
If I no more than you
Know what we should and should not do
Except that all agree
Gladly or miserably
That the law is
And that all know this,
If therefore thinking it absurd
To identify Law with some other word

W.H. Auden

This book presents an account of judicial pluralism. Judicial pluralism is a theory of adjudication, that is, a theory of how judges decide cases. It is meant to be descriptive, but neither anecdotal nor sociological. Certainly, not all judges decide cases the same way or even consistently with how they have decided cases in the past. Measuring changes in the conduct of a particular judge or predicting the outcomes of a set of judges might be interesting tasks for a legal sociologist and could be essential for a lawyer advising his or her client. They are not, except incidentally, the concern here.

Rather, we start with the fact that adjudication is carried on in a regular manner, one which appears to vary in outcome from how judges would act if they were not judges. Less cryptically, we can notice a certain judicial demeanor and behavior which separates individuals judging from the same individuals acting elsewhere. These judges appear guided by some discrete set of standards, not unlike participants in a complex game, following abstract principles, and relying on the examination of abstruse texts. Moreover, the rest of society, to some extent, endorses and abets this behavior. Poor judging and wrong decisions receive condemnation, condemnation based on getting things wrong rather than the mere dislike of partisan result. It is this general judging behavior that a theory of adjudication describes.

The term "pluralism," although borrowed from social science, is meant to be used without reference to the social scientific literature.[1] Rather, it refers to what some might think the obvious and others think the ridiculous position that the "correct" outcome of judicial decisions is a function of irreducibly individual conceptions of judicial role. Judicial role here means how a judge, as a judge, ought to decide, as opposed to what the correct decision would be as determined by someone other than the judge *qua* judge. The judge here is local: for a particular society. Role plays something of the part of a catalyst in legal reasoning. It is necessary to develop a structure for determining the method by which decisions should be made, and then it (more or less) drops out. Before beginning an explanation of the reasoning structure, I might offer some of the concerns that motivated the construction of the theory of pluralism in the first place.

It would seem that we could draw an easy contrast between two types of society. The first society, call it civil, has a well developed judiciary interpreting a rich body of law for a peaceful populace. The second society, call it discordant, has competing judiciaries interpreting divergent law for a society on, or over, the brink of civil war. At first glance, it appears that how judges should decide cases—what shall here be called a judicial view—is fairly clear and certainly singular in the civil society; while it is probably fuzzy and pluralistic in the discordant soci-

---

1 In social science, pluralism refers to the existence of different factions or interests in a society and the pressure and influence these factions or interests bring to bear in political decision making. As a political theory, pluralism sees a social order where groups seek to advance their preferences and, by working with other groups and compromising to obtain a greater support, obtain legislation that stabilizes an otherwise fractious community. When given an environment free of restraining coercion, the pluralist process supposedly allows for participatory democracy and inhibits a dictatorship by the majority. Such a theory has, in recent years, been attacked by philosophers as obscure and confused and by social scientists as mistaken and malevolent. See Brian Barry, *Political Argument* (1965); William E. Conolly, *The Terms of Political Discourse* (1974); and Theodore J. Lowi, *The End of Liberalism* (1969).

ety. Established criteria for decision making exist in the civil society, and study at the bar reveals these criteria. Discordant societies—whether at civil, international, or revolutionary war or simply involved in factional or sectarian unrest—possess disputed or inchoate criteria.

This picture of two types of society has a ready attraction. Certainly such matters as property ownership, constitutional law, or treason are just the sort of things which operate differently in the two societies. The only initial difficulty would seem to be one of classification, and that should not generally present any great conceptual difficulty.

However, there is a difficulty; in fact, the usual one. Persons and societies do not operate in any neat and categorically tidy manner. How does one classify Roman-conquered Greece, early Norman England, 19th century China, much of the African continent during colonial and immediately post-colonial times, Basque Spain, Eastern European ghettos, frontier Indian America, or recent Northern Ireland, Jordanian West Bank, Afghanistan or Haiti? Divided or subjugated societies present obvious classification problems. Consider the experience of countries engaging in civil war (*e.g.*, Chinese, American, English, Indian, Nigerian, French Revolution), with one side eventually prevailing. At what point does the society move from discordant to civil?[2] Surely, classification is arbitrary, and the intermediate steps continuous and infinite. If nothing else, peace evaporates, victories dissipate, armistices are circumvented.

Yet even in these situations, societies function; often, as with the Celts, the Anglo-Saxons, and the Normans together in medieval England, for hundreds of uneasy years. Perhaps the

---

2 This problem occurs, among other places, when revolutionary groups take control of a state and attempt to establish legitimacy. Two discussions of this matter, and of some of the problems of drawing lines, can be found in J. M. Eekelaar, "Principles of Revolutionary Legality", and John M. Finnis, "Revolutions and Continuity of Law", both found in *Oxford Essays in Jurisprudence*, second series 22-76 (ed. A. W. B. Simpson, 1973). Cases in this area are legion, but one interesting contrast in Pakistan would include the two cases of *The State v. Dosso* (1959) I *Pakistan L.R.* 849; and *Bhutto v. Chief of Army Staff* (1977) XXIX *Pakistan L.R.* 658.

aberrant case of discord is in fact the paradigm and the civil society is the rarity.

This view was the initial motivation for developing the theory of judicial pluralism. Societies absorb groups with divergent views and still function. More importantly, as it is more far reaching, individuals within societies take on fundamentally different political, economic, religious, social, ethical, and aesthetic beliefs and attitudes. These differences only occasionally lead to civil war, but they do affect positions which determine individual views of adjudication. Because the overlap between similar beliefs is so extensive in the area of adjudication, one can be lulled into believing that a consensus exists when it does not. Similar is hardly equivalent to identical, and common ends are not always the same ends, let alone the same means. When disagreement does arise, and similarity breaks down, the difference between discordant and civil societies dissolves.

Judicial pluralism, then, is a descriptive theory that is unconcerned with whether a society is civil or discordant, or just how civil it is. In that theories of adjudication mask attitudinal differences, large or small, pluralism makes at least the minimal claim of greater descriptive power.

What, then, is being described, or put differently, why bother with the theory of adjudication? The purpose is a general and fundamental one: it allows us to determine which judicial actions are correct, true, appropriate, or accurate. Competing theories of adjudication, such as legal realism, positivism, and rights theory, all provide other explanations than pluralism for how to determine correct answers and analyses. What counts as proper judicial conduct or as the correct products of adjudication matters enormously.

Much of this work involves criticism of competing theories. The purpose is less critical than it is expository. Through an analysis of what is right and wrong with other theories, pluralism can more fully be developed. Chapters I and II discuss the framework of judicial pluralism, with Chapters III, V and VI contrasting the basic principles of that structure with realism, pluralism, and rights theory respectively. A word here might be helpful as to why such a contrast is necessary.

Pluralism might be thought to be relativistic. That is, pluralism allows individual beliefs and attitudes to be reckoned into the model of the proper judicial role. Further, a three part structure of answers, criteria, and justification is developed. At the level of justification, such things as political, moral, and religious preferences count. Because of this double intrusion of non-objective factors, pluralism might appear to be relativistic (or subjectivistic), a trait associated with legal realism. Relativism has been scorned and ridiculed as a theory that holds that judges do what they want, without stricture, guidance or authority. Under relativism, rules and principles have a capricious place and the rule of law is without meaning.

The basic mistake in such criticism is that it assumes a pluralist view means relativism, while a singular (usually consensual) theory means objectivity. The fact that many embrace a particular view hardly objectifies it. Certainly, the paradigm of objectivity—the empirical world and science—does not apply in any transparent way to adjudication. Law is just what individuals think it is, at least to the extent that it is a conventional, contingent, human object. At one time, a breach of a promise to marry was recoverable, as with the breach of any other promise. Today, no one believes such an action could be brought successfully.[3] What changed were people's perceptions about basic social norms. With an attitudinal change came a change in what it is proper for a judge to do.

Of course, naive realism—a belief that judicial reasoning is no more than preferences of individual judges—is obviously mistaken. (It is perhaps more than a little confusing that those associated with the relativist position in law are called "realists", thus here naive realists.) Where such a theory goes wrong is an essential problem for the pluralist to solve. That is the purpose of Chapter III's discussion of the legal realism. Much of the criticism aimed at the legal realists, if valid, would be fatal to the pluralist, and it is thus essential to diffuse that criticism also. Certainly, though, the fact that some preferences and choices

---

3 See, *Buckland v. Buckland*, [1987] 2 All E.R. 300, [1967] 2 W. L. R. 1506 (Pr. & Div.), discussed in Joel Levin and Banks McDowell, "The Balance Theory of Contracts: Seeking Justice in Voluntary Obligations", 29 *McGill L.J.* 24, 70-74 (1983).

enter into the adjudication equation does not mean that no
structure exists, that no demand for consistency can be made,
that no cry of complete inappropriateness can be raised, or that
no means exist for achieving judicial veracity, precision, craftsmanship, aptness, or truth.

Chapter V serves a similar purpose with regard to legal positivists rather than legal realists.   Briefly, positivists rely on
consensus as a way out of discordant societies. The lack of a
descriptive apparatus available to a positivist to explain discordant societies clearly, applies more devastatingly to the ordinary
civil realm positivists claim to be their own. Positivists are anti-
relativists with a vengeance.   Surely, they claim, it cannot be
argued but that it is, *e.g.*, wrong to trespass on another's land,
illegal to rob a bank, essential to have two witnesses to validate a
will, necessary to be eighteen years old to vote. A few interpretations are necessary to fill in the vagaries, but a general
doubt indicates a fundamental misunderstanding.   Put differently, some things surely are settled, and to see uncertainty
everywhere because it arises somewhere is to commit, to use
Hart's phrase, "the fallacy of the disappointed absolutist". For
the positivist, adjudication is generally easy for the skilled, and
uncertainties are the exception.

Positivism achieves its plausibility from the distinction
between easy (usual) and hard (unusual) cases. However, the
distinction is itself relativistic, to use the taboo nomenclature of
the positivist. Asking why a case is clear or easy can only bring
the answer that it is so by consensus (or consensus of the relevant officials in power). Consensus is no more than populated
preference, often in fact convergence of ends without real
underlying agreement, and once challenged leads to relativism. [4]

The hard case argument is, in part, the basis for rights theory,
a view which shares pluralism's explicit use of political and
ethical beliefs and adjudication.   Chapter VI analyzes rights
theory, and shows that it actually breaks apart, as does
positivism, on the hard case argument. A rights theory holds
that adjudication has two separate parts—applying law in easy
cases, creating law in hard—but believes, unlike positivism, that

---

4 See H. L. A. Hart, *The Concept of Law* (1961).

the parts are intimately related. Rights theory, however, founders on the problem of identifying which cases are hard. This is because rights theory uses the core of easy cases to settle hard ones, by means of a political theory which makes consistent the whole. One ultimately unsolvable dilemma for rights theory, though, is the wrongly decided case. As rights theory needs to make consistent an entire corpus, a single wrongfully decided case makes for contradictions, from which any new answer can be implied. Pluralism has no problem here, as it recognizes divergences and conflicts within judicial systems that do not get remedied by the system, but by the individual.

Two other chapters are included. Chapter IV deals with a number of technical, jurisprudential issues. Basically, in order to defend pluralism, it is necessary to show that the general assumptions about the holding of a case, the sources of authority for a decision, and reasoning by analogy are mistaken. The usual picture painted by both positivists and rights theorists is that good analysis will provide clear holdings, holdings which join statutes, constitutions and other recognized authority to determine the basis for further adjudication. The process works through a special kind of reasoning, reasoning by analogy. The purpose of Chapter IV is to show the misunderstandings inherent in this tidy picture; or, more specifically, to show that ambiguities lurk with regard to understanding past decisions, that controversy is endemic to selecting legal authority, and that reasoning by analogy is fallacious. Once this is accomplished, the soundness of the grounds for positivism and rights theory becomes shakier, and pluralism becomes more attractive.

Spending over a third of this book criticizing other theories accomplishes several things. It allows the debate, and by implication, the importance of that debate to be laid out for the reader. It further allows pluralism to be analyzed in detail by contrasting it with other theories. Some of the criticism here of these other theories is, of course, not wholly original. These theories are well established and much discussed. However, the criticism here is meant to be consistent. So many of the attacks on various theories are too broad and all-encompassing. They leave no room for any further or future theory to be valid. Thus, a large part of the discussion of realism is the defense of it from positivist attack, as that attack would also weaken pluralism.

Finally, a word is necessary about purpose. Why expound pluralism? The scholastic answer is that it is right and true and much of the rest of the adjudication literature is wrong and false. There is, however, a broader purpose. As societies tend to be more complex, they become more litigious. Such traditional docket crowders as land ownership, divorce, crime and probate have given way to an explosion of constitutional, administrative, commercial and tort litigation. Issues once outside the courts' domain—abortion, voting, discrimination, labor and employment, hospital or school administration—are now constantly litigated; while new areas of social importance— antitrust, securities, welfare, privacy, regulation of the environment—have never known what life without law is like. Given the growing hegemony of the courts, and the absorption into the judicial system of society's most fundamental and controversial issues, the legitimacy of the judiciary becomes critical. Theories which hold that judges merely apply law or develop it in some canonical manner from prior applications are not only increasingly inaccurate. They encourage contempt for courts for doing what courts must do: decide complex, controversial, and unclear cases.

Court authority is not a panacea, and pluralism is neither prescriptive nor celebratory. In the final chapter of the book, several examples of how different views conflict and cohere within a judicial case are given. Despite starting from very different general political and moral positions, the mediating concept of judicial role acts to reduce differences and allow dispute resolution. While partisans may be thought to have no grounds of agreement, concepts of judicial role and judicial view traditionally (although certainly not necessarily) include neutral judges, consistency between decisions, the right to be heard, appellate review, respect for consideration of other authority (legal sources) and principles of equity. Lon Fuller believed a number of items would need to be included in such a list or something other than law was being conducted. His list—put in the negative includes *ad hoc* decisions, obscure rules, secret rules, contradictory rules, vacillating rules, retroactive legislation, impossible to obey rules, and administrative arbitrariness—cuts across belief or ideology.[5]   Of course, Fuller wanted the list to be more than description. He wished it to encompass necessary conditions for the existence of law. Fuller understood that to say authority is lawful is to imbue it with a greater power, even a perceived moral component. He was thus anxious to guard against tainting adjudication, by allowing (certain) unjust practices to count as law.

Fuller's mistake is easy to make, both by celebrants of law and by those who have witnessed chaos and destruction.[6] Pluralism has a contingently prescriptive element. It suggests (as briefly shown in Chapter VII) that most law generally mediates the worst excesses, encourages a minimal due process, peacefully resolves many conflicts that otherwise would end in violence, and at times achieves an equity and justice hardly possible without it. However, this is ultimately due to the beliefs and attitudes of individual members of society. In as much as chaos, savagery, revenge, capriciousness, and partisanship come into fashion, adjudication can only promise resulting harshness and ruthlessness.

* * * *

A note on method is in order. Jurisprudence would be classified by Kuhn as a primitive study, because the method of proceeding is so controversial and unsettled that each student must begin from scratch.[7] This is, at times, how the field appears. Jurisprudence certainly has no method of its own. The study of legal theory can be approached from the vantage point of law, political science, economics, history, sociology, or philosophy, and a number of schools of philosophy at that. Here, analytic philosophy, in a somewhat modified form, will be used.

---

5 Lon L. Fuller, *The Morality of Law* (rev. ed. 1964). These concepts are discussed on pp. 33-94.

6 This phenomenon occurred in the writings by many German jurists, who reconsidered their positivist leanings in the light of the chaos and destruction of World War II, only to embrace a naive naturalism.

7 See, Thomas Kuhn, *The Structure of Scientific Revolutions* (1962).

It may be wondered why, if the task is description of a social phenomenon, social science rather than somewhat ponderous philosophical theory should not be used. The answer lies in what the problem really is: figuring out conceptually what is going on. Philosophy concerns itself with conceptual clarification, and with providing structures for further analysis. The data itself—decisions of courts and conduct of judges—is too overwhelming even to know sketchily. Generalizations are made and theories constructed based on slim knowledge of a small, not necessarily representative, sample. Llewellyn suggested simply picking up sets of case reports and reading them straight through to get a feel for the myriad diversity and richness of the judicial process.[8] Here, as virtually everywhere, this will not be done.

Instead, a three part scheme will be constructed through the use of philosophical analysis. Discussions will center on judicial reasoning outside or apart from contingent (haphazard) analysis in any particular case. It is necessary to set out the enterprise. The discussion is not about what an actual judge did or does or what he should or should not do (morally, politically, *etc.*). Rather, the focus is on what judges ought to do when they act as judges. The element of prescription involves getting the concept of judging right (just as, what a robber should do, is forcibly take the property of another, in order to fulfill the role of a robber). Counter-examples are difficult, first because it does not necessarily matter what any particular judge did in a particular case; and second, because an essential component in pluralism is the wrongly decided case. Examples generally will be used to amplify and explain, rather than to prove or falsify.

The concept of truth appears throughout.[9] While philosophers generally feel comfortable with the concept, many others

---

8 Karl Llewellyn, *The Common Tradition: Deciding Appeals* (1960). His advice is found, among other places, on p. 6 of his book.

9 Various uses and related ideas to the notion of "truth" will be used here. In its most precise sense, truth can be taken to be a characteristic of the meaning of a proposition. Less precisely, it is merely one predicate that can be applied in the course of the normal use of language. "Water can be salty" is a proposition that may be true. In any case, this is one

are skeptical of its value, particularly as the term "absolute" is seen as its haunting predecessor.[10] "True" here should be taken simply to be a normal, substitutable predicate. Thus, "the grass is green" can be substituted with "the statement the grass is green is true." A problem of skepticism as it arises for both legal realists and legal positivists is that there is no room for truth with regard to at least some judicial assertions. If, on such occasions, something other than true statements are being uttered, then not only would the authority of such assertions be suspect, but the intent commonly noticed behind such assertions would be compromised.

Put differently, philosophers recognize the distinction between the grounds for something being true and the grounds for knowing it to be true. The morning star and the evening star were always Venus, whether or not Copernicus and Galileo had ever lived or the telescope had ever been invented. How we know something, such as the status of Venus, requires some general ability to verify or disconfirm hypotheses.[11] Knowledge

---

instance (at least) where the ordinary use is very close to the specialized or technical use of a term.

Three related notions also should be taken, if any uncertainty arises, to have their ordinary use: "truth value" refers to the concepts such as "true", "false", or "indeterminate" that answer the question as to what truth characteristic a proposition (or statement) has. "Truth conditions" represent the criteria for assigning a truth value to a proposition. In the case of judicial assertions, as we shall see, that criteria may reflect individual beliefs and attitudes, and divergent tastes, pretenses and values. Finally, "truth functional analysis" is the term describing the process of assigning truth values based on ascertaining truth conditions.

10 Some, throughout history, who have doubted any objectivity in the empirical universe have scoffed similarly with regard to any full-blooded use of the predicate "true". Berkeley, certain logical positivists, and presently some anti-realists may be in this group. Any reference in this work should be taken to be at least mildly realist, not dissimilar from the realism without Platonic affections found within Michael Dummett's, *Frege: Philosophy of Language* (1973). See also Dummett's *Truth and Other Enigmas*, Preface (1978).

11 The problem of Venus' status as being contingently both the Evening Star and Morning Star, and it's bearing on truth and meaning, was set out in the classic article of Gottlob Frege, "The Thought: A Logical

has no logical connection with scientific truth, in this sense. Everyone, for example, could get a scientific fact wrong (*e.g.* the fact that the earth rotates around the sun). It is not so easy to see how everyone could be under a misapprehension about whether oral real estate contracts were enforceable in medieval England or whether they are valid in Pennsylvania today. Clearly, the grounds for asserting something to be true is tied, somehow, to their truth, at least with regard to judicial assertions. The language of philosophy, with its focus on the concepts of truth, proof, soundness and assertion, is well equipped (or relatively well equipped) to analyze such facts. The elegance of that language must be tempered by the often pedestrian judicial reasoning suggested by ordinary litigants and performed by mundane judges.

Inquiry", reprinted in translation in *Philosophical Logic* (ed. P.F. Strawson, trans. by A. M. and Marcelle Quinton, 1967).

I

A Structure for Judicial Decision-Making

Law is the wisdom of the old,
The impotent grandfathers shrilly scold;
The grandchildren put out a treble tongue,
Law is the senses of the young.

W.H. Auden

Law is a puzzle. To the ordinary individual, uninitiated in the mysteries and ritual of the legal process, the variety and complexity of law in modern societies can be bewildering. His reaction to any particular legal situation is likely to vary widely, depending on which aspect of law he encounters. A policeman accusing him of theft; a store manager refusing to allow the return of an unsatisfactory purchase; an executor informing him of a piece of land now his; a zoning clerk demanding the removal of a newly and dearly acquired nude statue; a tax collector scrutinizing with disapproval the deduction recommended by his broker; an attorney advising him of a claim brought against him by the milkman crippled by his daughter's rollerskate: each elicits a different reaction. Moreover, it is unlikely that the ordinary observer could readily formulate a set of beliefs or sketch a general and unified conceptual picture of how these different legal bits might fit together, and what he thinks about them as a whole.

Yet, it is even more unlikely that this observer would be without any cohesive set of ideas and opinions at all. His stock of beliefs is likely to reflect his experience and his reflectiveness. If forced to distill his ideas and to formulate a general statement concerning law, and further pushed to focus his attention on the judicial aspect of law—say, by making him a party to a suit—

he would likely discuss the question of the freedom of judges to decide cases. He might settle on this issue simply because it is such a popularly controversial one, or he might see it as a necessary first step in constructing a coherent justification of the various fragmentary, eclectic, and possibly opposing ideas he holds. He might reason that to answer divergent legal questions, it is first necessary to understand under what constraints those professionally called upon to answer these questions labor.

In addressing the issue of judicial constraint, this ordinary individual could embrace either of two popularly held positions (or he might embrace both, although they are contradictory, with the knowledge that he is in a dilemma but unable to see his way out). He might think that judges are highly bound by precedent, statutes, regulations, or just generally, rules, and that in any situation, some specific, ascertainable rule applies. He, as a citizen, and a judge as a judge, each simply follow the rules. Law is complex, and rule ascertainment is not always easy. However, if one had the time, energy, and expertise—if one were, in Ronald Dworkin's term, Herculean—one could discover the rule with some certainty.[1] The role of the judge is to acquire the expertise and expend the necessary time and energy.

The alternate position would also start with an acknowledgement of the existence of a myriad of statements, precedents, regulations, and rules. It would look to their vagueness, their ambiguity, and their incompleteness and would measure those against the need to answer the questions that arise in adjudication. Given these difficulties, the alternate position would say that judges may do pretty much as they please. It might also point out that this is what judges do anyway. Judges must justify their positions, but justifications are easily and sophistically manufactured.

These two positions are in fact widely held, often by the same individual when he initially (pre-theoretically) considers different situations. That such a split is so wide could be passed off

---

1 The term "Herculean" comes from Ronald Dworkin's article "Hard Cases," 88 *Harv. L. Rev.* 1057 (1975), reprinted as Chapter 4 of *Taking Rights Seriously* (1977), discussed generally in this work in Chapter VI.

as a demonstration of the general ignorance and confusion of the legal laity (or at least half of it, if one position is sound). The difficulty, however, is that such a split is reflected in lawyers' briefs and judges' decisions, as well as in learned treatises and jurisprudential discussions. The split has been incorporated in a sophisticated way into a whole judicial literature, and has given rise to schools of advocacy, as well as schools of reconciliation.

Trying to analyze and ultimately to resolve this issue leads to a focus sufficiently abstract to encompass the breadth of the law. Abstraction may be the luxury of the fanciful theorist in a society stable, simple and homogeneous. Perhaps mountain herders do not require a very elaborate theory to understand the proper decisions and criteria for those decisions pronounced by the legal remedy-agent or judge. Modern society however—complex, heterogeneous, changing and law-laden— makes theory necessary rather than luxurious.

The purpose of abstraction or theory, then, must be to allow either the judge hearing a case or appeal, or the interested layman or lawyer addressing the issue facing the judge, to reach a decision. Clearly, however, not just any decision will do. There may be a certain relativism concerning the power or authority of a judge: regardless of integrity, ability or understanding, the fact of the decision remains. But this fact is not enough. Judges employ criteria; they may be themselves judged for their ability to make good or correct or coherent decisions; and, most importantly, society at large behaves in accordance with some expected set of decisional outcomes and criteria which should be used in reaching those decisions.

Understanding which outcomes are correct or what generally is to count as law requires criteria for reaching those outcomes. A three level system is needed to explain judicial reasoning. Three levels are employed because two different kinds of criteria are used to yield or produce answers to questions that can come before the courts. The answers themselves occupy the first level. Criteria that furnish the answers populate the second level. The larger beliefs and attitudes which tell what criteria can be used to reach a legal decision (as opposed to those respecting taste, politics, morality, religion, *etc.*) populate the third level. Here, the members of this third set will generally be called "justifications".

The claim here is not that this tertiary schema is descriptive of how judges or those answering questions addressable to judges actually reason, at least not always. Moreover, this claim is not a prescriptive one telling how such reasoning should work if it is done right. Rather, the three level schema and its attendant theory of judicial pluralism provide a framework for analyzing judicial reasoning. Such reasoning is perceived to be done well or badly, to have reached correct or incorrect conclusions, to have been based on defensible or indefensible reasons, and to be expected or surprising. Society and its members look at judicial decisions and are able to comment on and debate them. An explanation of the ability to do so is in order.

However, before setting forth the propositional schema, several caveats should be given. First, the fact that some proposition can be found on one level does not exclude it from inclusion on another level. The principle of sovereign immunity— "the king can do no wrong"—might be stated as an answer to a tort question to a judge facing the issue of liability to a vassal gored by a royal bull (first order). It might be the criterion used to decide issues of civil liability in its form of a general legal principle or a limitation on a court's jurisdiction (second order). Finally, it might be believed, either because of divine right or as part of a general political theory concerning the separation of powers (third order).[2]

---

2   The principle of sovereign immunity is that no state or government may be sued without its own consent. This doctrine originated with the monarchical, theological, and tyrannical divine right tenet of "the King can do no wrong." Throughout its existence, it has been pressed into service to justify a number of otherwise unjustifiable (and usually unjust) decisions. It has even reached constitutional status in a nation (the U.S.) otherwise not known for favoring royal prerogatives. See, for example, *The Schooner Exchange v. McFaddon*, 7 Cranch 116 (U.S.) (1812); *Keifer & Keifer v. Reconstruction Finance Corp.*, 306 U.S. 381, 59 S. Ct. 516 (1939); *Monaco v. Mississippi*, 292 U.S. 313, 54 S. Ct. 745 (1934). The principle also lives in reciprocal agreements between nations that citizens of one nation cannot sue a second nation without its permission. See, for example, 28 U.S.C. Section 1604.

The same proposition is used in all those levels (or orders), but it is being used in logically different ways. There is no reason to be concerned that such varying placement occurs or that a single proposition might do different kinds of work in the same schema if called upon to do so. Setting out all possible propositions is not the point, any more than it would be in physics. Rather, the propositions—as answers, criteria and justifications—are there (and ascertainable) when needed.

This brings up the second, and related, point. There is no magic in the number three. There could be more or fewer levels. It is a basic truth in mathematical logic that any higher order set can be incorporated into a lower order set. More obviously, the number of levels could multiply as each possible reason becomes a ground for a new level. The breadth of the reasons would then determine the number of levels.

The reason for three is that it reflects the major types of reasons one intuitively employs. Whether, for example, the language of a statute is embodied in a first or second order proposition is largely irrelevant. In general, statutes provide criteria for answering justiciable questions. If one draws the second order more abstractly to include only statutory law rather than individual statutes (*i.e.* all statutes but not a listing including, *e.g.* The Sherman Antitrust Act)[3], that is unimportant. In general, it would be interesting only if statutes are sought to answer questions, and are sought because of certain third order political or social beliefs.

The final caveat concerns the existence of a third level. It might be thought that, as the function of the third or justificatory level is solely to yield the criteria of the second order, its content is trivial. Who could doubt that what have at least since Gray been called "sources of the law"[4]—statutes, past decisions, constitutions, *etc.*—make up the criteria, pure and simple. However, even if that were so (and many controversies about the role of disputed sources such as custom, desuetude,[5] and

---

3 15 U.S.C. Section 1-7.

4 John Chipman Gray, *The Nature and Source of the Law* (2nd ed. 1921).

5 It should be noted that while the formal application of desuetude—which is the disuse or discontinuing application of a statute—is relatively rare,

the role of equity throw such a contention into doubt), the ordering among the criteria would still need to be given.

Judicial Propositions - An Overview

The first, and least abstract, level consists of the set of answers to all existent judicial questions. The answers can be made to be propositional in form. Their variety and content is a function of the questions that can arise in a court: for example, is document K a valid contract, is defendant X guilty of embezzlement, was testator T sane when she bequeathed her wardrobe to a chimpanzee, is a certain piece of evidence hearsay, do the facts stated in the pleadings constitute a sufficient cause of action, what ought to be the proper instructions to the jury? The membership of the set of first order propositions depends upon the first order questions (those upon which the court must rule to resolve the conflict before it) to define what kinds of propositions are necessary. In a trivial sense, this allows that the manner in which the judicial questions are framed—the syntactical, terminological, and judicial styles—partially determines how the propositions will be stated. More importantly, the type and range of questions raised in litigation determines what class of propositions will serve as answers, with the propositional set's range being limited only by the imagination of the litigious mind.

It might be thought that, as every issue appears to be able to reach a court of law, this first order set is extremely crowded. While it is populous, it becomes that crowded only in the uninteresting sense that issues not ordinarily or likely to be the concern of the courts can come before them. While physicists may debate whether light consists of waves or particles, the courts normally are neither concerned nor do they anticipate being concerned with the issue. If the issue comes before them, it would normally pass through unfiltered to the third order proposition that the answer lies with scientists. Such would be the kind of answer given to many imaginary questions that a court could hear.

---

the finding of exceptions and implicit partial or complete overruling of statutes is, if not routine, far from uncommon.

That said, a crucial difference appears if such a scientific issue wears the traditional legal garb. The United States Supreme Court was once asked to determine whether, for purposes of an Act of Congress, tomatoes were fruits or vegetables.[6] While the scientific area of seeds and germination remained untrespassed, the Court did what courts traditionally do: it examined legislative intent.[7] In that first order propositions are interesting here, they need to be filterable by the paradigmatic second order criteria. Seen differently, putting lay propositions into the set of judicial propositions may cause them to be treated quite differently.

The second level contains propositions that justify the set of first order propositions. They serve as criteria for selecting first order propositions or answers. Suppose that some proposition p is a member of level one. Then, for some other proposition q, if q then p, q is a member of the second level. This makes the set of second level members extremely populous. At an intuitive level, it includes the reasons normally associated with legal reasoning. It also includes all members of level one, for a prior answer may serve as a reason to answer a later question in a certain way. (Also, identity contains an implication principle: p implies p for all p). For example, suppose p stands for "The document K is a valid contract." Then p in one case may be a first level proposition, answering the question "Is K a valid contract?" Later in that case (or in another case) we may decide that the defendant's defense in a tort suit for the taking of property (conversion) is good because she had a contractual right to the chattel. That right was based on the fact that the

---

6 The case was *Nix v. Hedden*, 149 U.S. 304, 13 S. Ct. 881, 37 L.Ed 745 (1893). The case is discussed by the legal realist, Thurman Arnold, in *The Symbols of Government* (1935).

7 One excellent, empirical study of the pitfalls of relying on legislative intent—and thus generally easy and sure rules of construction—is that of Richard K. Scotch in his book *From Goodwill to Civil Rights: Transforming Disability Policy* (1985). Scotch shows that any easy appraisal of the location of intent would be misguided in the case of certain legislation dealing with the disabled. The beliefs and attitudes of congressional staffers and administrators caused significant legislation absent much in the way of real intention by any legislator.

document in question constituted a valid contract: in other words, because p. The same proposition is used in a logically different way in the two cases.

The second order includes the reasons normally thought legal. Second order propositions determine answers to judicial problems, and do so by employing as criteria third order sets normally labeled as "legal". For example, an individual might have strong aesthetic principles which form a part of his beliefs and attitudes. She might be repulsed, for example, upon seeing a house painted in non-primary color tones.[8] Yet, she likely would hold that aesthetic principles cannot govern or even much influence her second order judicial propositions. If D burned P's house or if G wished to take by eminent domain P's house, our aesthetic individual would probably believe it inappropriate to protect P less because P painted his house fluorescent chartreuse. In fact, our aesthete may fight politically the construction of a neighbor's house of such a color, but not wish to quarrel with the right legally to erect ugly real estate.

The third order consists of justifications of the second level criteria. These justifications might be moral, political, religious, aesthetic, prudential, or social (or any other general area, such as metaphysical), though they are more commonly some mixture of the above.[9] Because justifications attempt to resolve

---

8 The general right to displease the senses is firmly embedded in such areas as zoning and eminent domain law. However, when the design is displeasing, courts have been known occasionally to be unable to find any loss to a party who is deprived of the ugliness. Such was the result in *Muldoon v. Lynch*, 66 Cal. 536, 6 P. 417 (1885), where liquidated damages were considered an obvious penalty for the delay in constructing a 20-plus ton marble cemetery monument, as that delay could not be the cause of compensable loss.

The issue of aesthetics and the police power is addressed in *Berman v. Parker*, 348 U.S. 26, 75 S. Ct. 98 (1954); of aesthetics and zoning in *People v. Stover*, 12 N.Y.2d 462, 191 N.E.2d 272 (1963) (an ugly clothesline); and *Reid v. Architectural Board of Review*, 119 Ohio App. 67, 192 N.E.2d 74 (1963) (an ugly wall).

9 Prudential justifications or reasons are those done by the individual in his own self-interest. (If done by a second individual to benefit a first individual perceived to be unaware of his own self-interest, the reasons would be paternalistic). Prudential reasons are, to use Derek Parfit's

"why" questions of reasons for action (*i.e.* all are types of rational justification), they tend to infinite regressions or circles. Controversy in the realm of political morality is ubiquitous, and what is conclusive for one person is often merely the starting point for another. Even for a single individual, the question of when explanation should come to an end is a difficult matter, it often being a function of the ponderousness of one's mood. For purposes here, because the third level begins with general reasons of a broader nature, all further levels of justification will be collapsed to the third level.

This tertiary schema needs to be further defined and developed, but a brief example might illustrate the place of each level in an ordinary judicial (legal) controversy. Suppose A, a schoolchild, slips on B's icy sidewalk while on the way to class. A institutes a civil (tort) suit against B for negligence for the failure to remove the ice. A's case may raise a number of questions—evidentiary, procedural and substantive—questions whose proper answers are part of the set of first level propositions. These propositions vary in scope and generality. The same basic propositions may be clothed in a broader or narrower form. A might argue that "Landowners have a general duty of care to keep their premises safe for anyone lawfully upon them" (wide scope) or merely that "Landowners with sidewalks used by children on their way to and from school must keep them free of ice" (narrow scope). Two rather obvious, but extremely important, related points are evident. First, a fact situation can be stated with a varying degree of first level generality limited only by the imagination of the participants in the action. The uniqueness of individual social situations is a trivial social fact

---

distinction, different than those of the egoist, who finds reasons compelling that serve his own immediate self-interest. The prudent individual looks to his long and short term self-interest, but unlike the moralist or altruist, not to the interest of others (other than, of course, in that they add to or enrich his own interests). These concepts are discussed in Thomas Nagel's *The Possibility of Altruism* (1970); Derek Parfit's "Personal Identity", 70 *Phil. Rev.* 3 (1971); and Bernard Williams' *Problems of the Self* (1973).

One analysis of the logical role justifications play in the continuing development of the common law can be found in Levin's "Justification and the Law," 32 *Emory L.J.* 987 (1983).

and an unstartling legal truism. However, social slices rarely need to be compared exactly, and when precise characterization becomes necessary, the triviality disappears. Such characterization is commonplace in the courtroom, and is often what the controversy is all about. Is a bicycle a vehicle for licensing purposes, is a fork a dangerous weapon for criminal-law purposes?[10]

The matter is less one of terminology than of beliefs, as we shall see shortly. What must be stressed now is that determination of the scope of the issue is a crucial matter. The quick response that scope can be determined from other considerations, past cases for example, if not necessarily false, is unhelpful. How past cases should be read presents just the same sort of problem. Does a past case holding D liable for C's injury for tripping on an ice skate on D's property help solve the case of *A v. B*? Is it relevant that ice skates (unlike ice) must be put there by a human agent, that C was on his way to an after-school basketball game, or that D had himself tripped over the skate? Is it relevant that the judge in the first case declared liability in a very sweeping manner? Further, is this first case rightly decided, or is it merely an ill-considered anomaly that ought to be limited to its instant facts if not overruled?

The quick response only moves the problem back a step. The second point is that narrow propositions can be justified by general propositions. B is liable for slippery ice, because B is liable for ice and snow, because B is liable for weather-induced hazards he can alleviate, because B is liable for all hazards he can alleviate, *etc.* Each wider proposition implies and is a criterion of the included narrow proposition. This does not diminish the difference between reason and conclusion. It only suggests that when one is looking to possible first and second level sets of propositions that are actually apt to be helpful, one sees more generality (or wider scope) as one moves to the second level. If A actually sues B, there is not going to be an infinite number of propositions in controversy on the issue of

---

10 Two interesting cases illustrating this phenomenon deal with whether certain games of chance are lotteries. Both were decided by Justice Oliver Wendell Holmes. *Commonwealth v. Wright*, 137 Mass. 250 (1884); *Commonwealth v. Sullivan*, 146 Mass. 142 (1888).

landowners' liability. There may well be preliminary skirmishes before the issue is joined, and propositions may be shuffled between the levels. Certainly, few actual propositions will be discussed. The relation between any related level one and level two propositions can assume many (and logically an infinite number of) intermediate steps. Here, A may argue that B is liable for any injuries on icy public sidewalks of B's which are used by school children on their direct way to school because all landowners owe a general duty of care to invitees to keep their premises safe. Missing from this formulation is any statement equating schoolchildren with invitees or paths through one's property with public sidewalks. These statements, as well as hundreds of others, may or may not come into play in the controversy.

Let us suppose that B admits the presence of a duty, the slipperiness of the ice, his neglect in failing to remove it, and its unfortunate effect on A. Yet B wishes to escape liability by pointing out that A needn't have taken that particular route to the school; that an alternate route through an always cleared public park was available; that B was a known geriatric notorious for being unable to tend his sidewalk; and that A thus assumed the risk inherent in crossing icy paths. B appeals to similar or related past cases, to policy considerations embedded in judicial pronouncements, or perhaps, to the intention implicit in statutes imposing the liability on landowners in the first place. What kind of action is B taking?

Certainly, he is pointing to first order propositions of assumption of risk. He is justifying these propositions by criteria drawn from statutes and past cases. The statute or past case may, because of its authority or its persuasiveness, serve as the second order criterion yielding an answer amenable to B. The contents of statutes and past decisions are quite obviously commonly used as second order criteria, and blend the logically distinct features of being arguments from authority and arguments from reason. B's appeal to policy embedded in statutes or decisions is just a more subtle and indirect use of this criteria. B, like A, asserts first order propositions (*viz.*-"Assumption of risk negates liability due to negligence") by appealing to second order criteria (*e.g.*-"In the case of *C v. D*, C's assumption of the risk was found to bar his claim against D."). While largely in agreement about the membership of the second level, A and B disagree about the relevancy of particular reasons in their case. How is the difference, and thus the case, to be resolved? Assume that A agrees that *C v. D*, as part of the general case law, belongs in the second level. He will likely contest its relevance, perhaps suggesting a case, closer in time, jurisdiction or factual similarity than *C v. D*. He might distinguish *C v. D* on its facts, suggesting that because there is no adequate alternate route here, *C v. D* is unpersuasive.

Finally, A might argue that *C v. D* is irrational and indefensible in its suggestion that those who live in northern climates know how to dress for and move about in winter weather, an assumption factually dubious in the case of young children, and morally outrageous with respect to the very young, the old, the infirm, and the simple. In short, *C v. D* is unfair and should not be followed. This last argument is of a different kind. Normally, *C v. D* is the kind of reason A recognizes as belonging in his second order set. It has the formal requirements for inclusion, being of the right kind of pedigree (a certain type of writing from a certain kind of court rendering a certain kind of opinion) and is factually relevant. A's third order justifications include looking to similar cases. His political theory about how judges should render decisions and his ethical views about deciding like case alike suggest that *C v. D* be followed. However, A also looks to other third order principles (including perhaps the self-serving one of prudence which can be disregarded here if an independent observer or judge is found to agree with A), including ethical ones which suggest fairness or political ones which are concerned with risk allocation and the ability to insure.

Third order justifications do not directly yield first order answers. Some criterion on which to hang the justification is necessary. In finding this criterion—policy, other cases, statutes, equity maxims—the persuasiveness of the argument would also be determined. Excellent third order reasons do not always translate into defensible criteria. Here, a vague equity maxim about fairness may not weigh well against a close precedent from the case law. This is true when second order reasons are weighed, including in those early examples when A and B are arguing the relevancy of *C v. D* or the intent of a landowner liability act. The fact that any of a number of third order justifications would yield the same criteria or that calculating the criteria takes almost no time as the product is transparent should not blind us to the role of the third level even in so-called easy cases. Any case can become like *A v. B* if analysis is thorough.

The set of judicial propositions has been asserted to be distinct and recognizable. Indeed, it is. Individuals quite obviously employ, discuss, ponder and criticize judicial reasoning, making analysis of judicial propositions something more than an empty exercise in metaphysics. However, if judicial propositions are ultimately governed by beliefs, what differentiates the identity of judicial propositions from those of any other belief set? The answer is empirical rather than necessary. Because questions of law are justiciable, *i.e.* able to be heard by courts and judges, the posture of the courts making the decisions determines the answers to the questions. Bound with the hearing of cases is the proper method of resolving them. What is contingent or empirical is simply that when judges decide cases, when they hold forth on the bench or muse in chambers, they are expected to behave as judges. Their judicial role is distinct from the role they otherwise assume.

Moreover, there is no expectation that an individual's concepts of judicial and lay role (or concomitant beliefs) will coincide with his other concepts (or beliefs). In fact, the contrary expectation is probably true. Onerous rules and inane statutes are enforced by judges too fair and too sensible to have advocated their creation.

Society operates with a legal and judicial system run by individuals at odds with other individuals. Beliefs and attitudes vary widely, and with them entire theories of what should be done clash. The explanation for why "law" and the "legal system" are accorded their following and authority lies in large part not with any belief in the infallibility of its judges, but in the belief that these judges behave differently (and in a limited sense, better) as judges. We must then look more closely at the concept of judicial role to understand and assess the validity of the belief.

Judicial Role and Judicial Propositions

Endless learned papers and books discuss what "the law" is, what its contents are, what its sources are, and how individual laws are individuated.   Often the question is approached as though it is important to find the correct *a priori* definition, and then empirically discover what phenomena are thereby captured.[11] No doubt, such a method has its political uses as a way to persuade others of the legitimacy of certain rules or even of a whole political order. To be legal is to take on an elevated status, perhaps (to some) even an intrinsic moral component. It is not only successful guerrillas who are quick to label their commands as laws, even laws of ancient, if neglected, vintage. The most conservative of men sought a Nuremberg tribunal to justify the fair trials of heinous killers by asserting that the prosecutions were not merely just and necessary: they followed some prior, if mislaid, body of positive law.[12] Actions found illegal are often equated with actions that are immoral. The *a priori* approach, then, has its uses. Its difficulty is that competing conceptions of law arise with no way to choose between them. Even upon analysis, there is no way out of relativism.

A better starting point is clearly needed. One ought to look to the role of the judge in formulating judicial statements rather than to categorize legal statements or to search for a proper definition of "law" or "the law". This should be done through an analysis of the structure of judicial reasoning, and through

---

11 For an analysis and criticism of methods that seek to find a definition of law and other major judicial concepts, see H.L.A. Hart, *Definition and Theory in Jurisprudence* (1953).

12 The literature describing the Nuremberg trials, and their supposed justifications, is voluminous and well-known. Also well-known is a narrow debate in jurisprudence, allegedly concerning law and morality, which Nuremberg engendered. The original articles are: G. Radbruch, "Gesetzliches Unrecht Und Ubergesetzliches Recht," 1 *Suddeutsche Juristen-Zeitung*, 105 (1946); H. L. A. Hart, "Positivism and the Separation of Law and Morals", 71 *Harv. L. Rev.* 593 (1958); Lon Fuller, "Positivism and Fidelity to Law - A Reply to Professor Hart," 71 *Harv. L. Rev.* 630 (1958).

an examination of the propositions which make up that reasoning. As a definition, we shall say that some proposition p is a judicial proposition if and only if judges, within a judicial system and while hearing the conflicts that have come before them, either are logically required to hold p to be true or to make use of p to hold some other proposition to be true. The first disjunct refers to the first and second order propositional set, the second disjunct to the second and third order set.

Of course, the reason for worrying about the basis for judicial reasoning is thus a fundamental problem for all those extolling legal virtue or defending legal power: how to separate legal command from mere political preference. Critics of any particular legal decision routinely claim foul, declaring that the law is no more than pretext for politics. Legal skill is thought to reside in those who clearly differentiate between the two, and judicial conservatism meant to apply to judges able to park their political agenda outside the courtroom, and decide cases according to the logic of statutes, prior decisions, *etc.* Scholars, both historians and anthropologists, study societies for signs that politics has departed from the law, and a mature legal order has become based in some objective, consensual, determinable, and discrete body of dogma or source for dogma.

The desire to differentiate law and politics permeates the judicial system in countless and crucial ways. The debates hovering around "the rule of law" and "governments of laws not of men" concentrate on the requirement of a minimal content of due process and the legal system that excludes the political vagaries of arbitrary individuals and partisan debate. Wandering from this context is thought to be straying from law into politics. The debate regarding whether judges make or enforce law (create v. find, chart v. apply, enact v. imply), between the competing virtues of judicial activism and judicial passivity, are debates about the entry of politics into the legal system.

It is one of the theses of this book that such a debate is fundamentally misguided. No final distinction between law and politics is worth making, not because judicial decisions are mere fraudulent dressing for naked political power, but because the requirements of constructing a legal order involve an irreducible political element.

Part of the problem, surely, is that one concept (law) is being defined by association with another (politics), when that defining concept is itself problematic. Politics in the context of the jurisprudential debate covers tremendous ground. In the broadest sense of being concerned with the workings of the state or the science of government, politics includes law by definition. In the narrowest sense of partisan interest for narrow constituencies, with the goal of attaining some tangible and parochial short-term end, law (or at least the judicial system) is hardly political. Basically, politics tends to imply partisanship while law is defended as universal and objective. Because neither description is accurate, and in that both issues and judges carry political baggage, the debate appears impossible of resolution.

That, however, is not the criticism set out here. Rather, because the basis for judicial decisions ultimately includes political preferences, law and politics can not be wholly divorced. Further, because it is the preference and not the correctly worked out view that matters, there is a jarring note of subjectivity and individuality in judicial reasoning. This is only the beginning of an explanation. Judges customarily do not employ their preferences directly: they take on views of judicial conduct which demand they behave as judges, and not as they otherwise would. Politics enters when determining and defining how judges should act: for example, basic notions of retribution versus mercy, executive versus legislative authority, deference to precedent, corporate intent, judicial ability, fairness, constitutional exegesis, jurisdiction, to name only a few, involve basic political questions. More fundamentally, what constitutes the proper role of a judge in a society is itself a political question.

The issue of politics is really an abbreviation for a myriad of other parallel issues. Religion, ethics, custom, social goals, convention, manners, economics, even science, all bear on judicial reasoning through the ultimate criteria thought relevant and true for judges. Saying that one's religious or political beliefs shape the outcome of judicial decisions is misleading, unless we recognize the indirectness, remoteness, and generality of the shaping. A politically and economically conservative judge might believe that a regressive federal corporate tax is bad judgment, bad economics, and bad government. However, none of that would, in the normal course of rendering a decision, bear on a criminal conviction of a corporate tax evader or on a question of construing legislative intent in ascertaining a particular tax rate.

If all judicial issues have an indirect political (using this as a shorthand for other types of programs, beliefs and attitudes) component, sometimes the indirect and direct aspects mirror one another. Whether, in an apportionment case like *Baker v. Carr*, the court should become involved in putting a legislative house in order is a political question. It involves separation of powers, the right to vote, and the bounds of pure democracy. Assuming a system that separates power and universalizes the franchise, the issue of a rotten borough legislature unable to reapportion itself effectively is one which is not only political, it can easily become justiciable. Whether the court should hear such a case is certainly (in one sense) a political issue, and eventually, like other political issues, may remotely shape an outcome. That shaping occurs through the concept of the judicial role. The concept of judicial role is a narrow one and concerns how judges ought to do their jobs of deciding cases. Judges' opinions while off the bench, or their random thoughts while presiding and deliberating, are of little importance. The dynamics of the judicial role are shaped by the nature of the conflicts brought before judges. A further distinction should be made between judges and judicial role. An examination of a set of judges, even while sitting and presiding, will only evoke a generalization about their behavior, whether that behavior concerns decorum, fashion, race, or decision-making. No practice, however regular, itself implies an obligation upon others to follow. Moreover, a majority may be mistaken. Judicial role is an abstraction, and one, though empirical in some aspects, with a normative component. An individual is fulfilling a role if he meets certain standards, and these standards can exist in our minds whether all, many, several or no individuals comply with them.

It does not matter whether any particular judge is involved in the decision. This is a game, or more exactly, a convention, which anyone can play, and play with equal adeptness. Figuring out answers to judicial questions can be done outside the courtroom, just as calculating chess moves or the reaction of chemical mixtures may be done in the shower. Judicial reasoning is a theoretical exercise and the ability to execute one's ideas is logically distinct and irrelevant to their validity.

The focus, then, is on what one would do as a judge: more precisely, the term "judge" indicates not only judges in their judicial role, but judges more commonly in their conflict-resolution sub-role. Judges fulfill a myriad of other tasks besides directly resolving conflicts: they negotiate, they regulate the bar, they preside at weddings, they issue *ex parte* writs and orders, they guide and instruct juries, they may swear in government officials and other judges. It is their conflict-resolution role that is of concern here.

The definition uses the term "true", demanding only those propositions necessary to be held true. The term "true" is rarely found in judicial opinions, especially appellate judicial opinions, which claim to handle matters of law rather than matters of fact. Putative facts are paraded before judge and jury and must be found to be true or false. Such matters—as, for example, whether a tort defendant was intoxicated or speeding while behind the wheel, whether an interested witness told the truth, or whether a contractor substantially performed the contract—are the only issues in countless legal actions. Conflict resolution necessitates knowing or trying to know what occurred, and that is often, perhaps usually, disputed.[13] But after the facts are settled, the range of questions usually labeled "legal", and, without controversy, "normative", remain. These questions, the almost sole concern of higher courts, are rarely

---

13 This occurrence has occasioned one experienced judge to question the use of past decisions to resolve instant cases. Jerome Frank states that "in most cases in the trial courts the parties do dispute about the facts, and the testimony concerning the facts is oral and conflicting. In any such case, what does it mean to say that the facts of a case are substantially similar to those of an earlier case? It means, at most, merely that the trial court regards the facts of the two cases as about the same." *Law and the Modern Mind* xvi (Sixth Ed. 1963). The plausibility of such a position will be examined in Chapter III.

framed as matters of truth.[14] The very phrasing of the courts appears antithetical to anything so unyielding as truth. The talk is often enough of analogies and competing precedents, of choices and of majority versus minority rules, of differing statutory interpretations, or whether a certain rule or principle should apply, or can be made to apply.

But if the term "true" is alien, the concept is indispensable. It gives sense and meaning to judicial statements just as it does to all statements, indeed all language. If two witnesses are a requirement for the creation of a valid will, we can say either: "Two witnesses are required to validate a will" (or p), that "'Two witnesses are required to validate a will' is true" (or p is true), or that "It is not true that two witnesses are sufficient to validate a will" (or -p is true). If the dispute before the court concerns a doubly witnessed will, then the issue is whether or not p is true. Certainly the truth or falsity of p is the paradigmatic problem of the courts, even when it is not discussed in such stark terms.

Finally, the use of the concepts of judicial role and truth allows us to judge judicial performance from outside. If there is a truth value (if the statement or proposition can be said to be true or false)[15] to the statements, and the statements are the result of the judicial role being performed, then when a particular judge speaks, the truth or falsity of his statements may be evaluated. There are two immediate qualifications to this. First, it applies only to those statements which are susceptible to the simple truth conversion used above. If it is found that some or

---

14 Typical of the distaste of higher or reviewing courts for matters thought factual and ascertainable of truth is the attitude embodied in Federal Rule of Civil Procedure 51. There, it is made clear that only when the truth screams out will the court get involved. (*e.g.* -"Findings of fact shall not be set aside unless clearly erroneous").

15 By truth value, reference is being made to the concept used in the philosophical logic literature. Simply put, statements or propositions might have the property of truth, just as grass (if well-kept) might have the property of greenness or Shakespeare's works' brilliance. Certainly, not all questions are susceptible of a true or false answer, nor are all statements. Those which are can be described by a two valued (either true or false) logic. The classic work on propositions and two valued logic is Ludwig Wittgenstein's *Tractatus Logico-Philosophicus* (first English ed. 1922).

all of the pronouncements from the bench take the form "It's my personal feeling that two witnesses are necessary to validate a will", or worse, "today, I declare that two witnesses are necessary to validate a will, although in the past that has not always been my opinion, nor is it consistently that of my colleagues", then the truth functional analysis would have little application. This would hold if some more likely and less preposterous subjective standard were found to be empirically accurate. "True" would still be a relevant predicate in these cases, it would just be trivial. The statement "p is true" would entail only that a certain judge said it was true. A standard is subjective if its truth depends solely on . an individual's preferences, falsity occurring only if the individual was lying about those preferences.

The fact that feelings are injected into judicial discourse does not, of itself, disqualify such discourse from truth-functional analysis. At a terminological level, "I feel" may mean, upon scrutiny, "I believe". Such terms may reflect style rather than theoretical intent. However, the fact that such terms are employed for any reason does not make them valid or right. It is not what any particular judge (or judicial reasoner) does as what she should do that is important. If she is squeamish about belief or universality (here meaning with Kant, that any one in a particular situation would be treated the same—time, place, and trivial individual factors all being excluded), she would have to be shown that she is already committed to the vitality of those concepts by using legal language.[16] Straying from the discourse of propositions which are truth functional may serve as grounds for criticisms. One can imagine justifications, perhaps more at home in a society outside the acquaintance of western lawyers, where feelings, bias, prejudice and arbitrariness have an explicit place. This empirical possibility would undoubtedly weaken the authority of law, and is so far outside any legal system (western or non-western) known, that it can be considered a disturbing, if irrelevant, consideration.

---

16 Immanuel Kant's famous reformulation of the Golden Rule in terms of the concept of the categorical imperative or universalization is found in his *Foundations of the Metaphysics of Morals* (1785). This concept has been updated and expanded in R. M. Hare, *Freedom and Reason* (1963).

The second and related qualification refers to any use of the concept of judicial role. In using the concept, an appeal is being made to a normative role of judges, although normative in the weak sense. "Normativity" is a concept which suggests how judges should act (as opposed to "empirical", a description of how they do act). The weak sense of the concept suggests that there are recognized standards of conduct and performance, but does not promote the belief that a single and comprehensive standard should measure all judicial acts at all times (this is the strong sense). The weak sense (at minimum) is necessary to give generality to truth values of judicial answers. A specific judge may declare p, q, r, s, t and (u or v), but if her standards are unique to her, the case outcome would not only not be objective, it might well not be repeatable. In part, ordinary talk of someone being a "good," "bad," "incompetent," "competent," or "capable" judge often can be taken as referring to a weak normative sense of judging. The speaker might be unable to conceive of, let alone articulate, what judicial behavior ought to be in all cases at all times, but does believe that a certain judge fulfills (or falls short of) certain ideals in some cases.

With some understanding of judicial role behind us, we can proceed to a discussion of judicial propositions. A first order proposition might be "Two witnesses are required to validate a will." These first order propositions populate legal textbooks and are commonly thought of as the rules of law. They govern behavior of those bound by the legal order. Perhaps a more neutral description would be to say that they serve notice of norms generally perceived to be enforced generally by most courts.

First order propositions can be defined as the set of propositions which answer questions a judge encounters. These propositions vary in generality as do the issues. "Are wills valid when witnessed by only two persons?" is more general than "Is this will valid when it has features x, y, and z?" Such issues demand different types of answers, and propositions embodying those answers will vary accordingly. The fact that first order propositions are responsive to a divergent set of issues does not mean that they need to be contingent and haphazard. Issues can be anticipated and theories formulated to meet them. Consistency in a wide sense can be sought. However, this does not need to happen.

Where are these first order propositions located? They are not found, simply, in such locations as judicial cases, statutes, administrative decisions or constitutions. To think that they are is to make a subtle category mistake. Such documents are records. They serve to document various political proceedings. They may contain first order judicial propositions, but so may a newspaper editorial or a children's comic book. Moreover, such documents are at best often vague and incomplete, at worst contradictory.

These documents may embody statements that coincide with what judges hold, they may suggest what judges should hold, they may often be a reference for a judge in making his decision. But this set of written prescriptions and explanations is not at all the same as mental beliefs. To say that both (a case containing p and articulating a belief that p) are normative statements collapses physical and mental states. Nor does it help to say that both offer a certain kind of authority: so do a poisonous spider and an army general. One may pay heed to both of them while recognizing their basic differences.

First order propositions, then, are based upon an individual's (second order) criteria for selection of answers, criteria that are embodied in a complicated set of propositions. While propositions may be irrationally formulated or randomly selected, both the internal (decisional) evidence of their consistency and the external empirical evidence of a vast literature created by judges explaining and defending their decisions suggest that a rational decision process is the general rule. [17]

Because the set of judicial propositions is dynamic and empirical—dynamic because the set changes as beliefs and opinions change; empirical because it is the relevant community's actual beliefs and opinions that are important—the judge's actual

---

17 See, *e.g.* Benjamin Cardozo, *The Nature of the Judicial Process* (1921); Patrick Devlin, *The Enforcement of Morals* (1965); William O. Douglas, *The Court Years, 1939-1975.* An unusual addition to the often mundane and celebratory literature is Richard Posner's *The Federal Courts: Crisis and Reform* (1985). These four works were written by sitting judges.

decision becomes relevant to understanding first order propositions. Put another way, each decision for a judge has an empirical and a normative aspect. The set of first order propositions can be used to judge the correctness of the normative conclusion the judge reaches. The empirical aspect becomes a datum for future decisions.

This picture, of an answer to a decision capable of being judged according to some set of propositions and not merely a prediction of a judge's intentions, might be called the objective as opposed to the psychological picture of judicial decision making. Two remaining features should be sketched in before the usefulness of the picture or model can be tested: first order propositions must be tied to higher order propositions; and the method or analogue for extracting specific answers from the various propositional sets must be discussed.

One lingering problem must, however, be examined first: proposition individuation. Putting aside the problem of controversial propositions (*e.g.*-"Oral wills are never valid" in a jurisdiction where statutes are silent, past cases divided, academic writings split,[18] and educated lay and professional opinion polarized), two difficulties arise. First, there is a problem of extension: which propositions should be included? Certainly, action-guiding rather than fact-stating propositions are the important ones. Thus "a knowingly false statement intentionally given, under oath in a courtroom during a proceeding is punishable as perjury" (or p) certainly would qualify, while the factual report that "X lied before this court" (or q), even if reported during a judicial decision, would certainly not. What about the statement that two witnesses are required to validate a will? It is in a general form, while the statement about X is specific, but this difference is unimportant. An uninstantiated "Some men have lied before this court" is still a fact-stating,

---

18 Ordinarily in civil law jurisdictions and occasionally in common law jurisdictions, the writings and academics become legal sources. Currently, in the United States, the *Restatements* have appeared to be the authoritative successors of Glanvill, Bracton, Littleton, Coke, Holt and Blackstone. An excellent discussion of the problems of making the *Restatements* criteria for answering judicial questions can be found in Henry Hart and Albert Sachs, *The Legal Process* 748-771 (1958).

if unhelpful, proposition.[19] A witness' statement such as q is
without an explicit direction for action or a sanction.

Yet there is clearly a difference. To understand the meaning
of the statement "Two witnesses are needed to make a will", or
r, another action-guiding statement must be understood as
forming a prior condition. This implicit prior condition would
have to be of the sort: "Only wills with two witnesses should be
valid (*i.e.* - enforced)". It is possible to see how this could be
otherwise—how fewer or greater numbers of witnesses could be
needed—but it has been decided, for obvious or latent reasons,
that two be required. This reasoning need not be embodied by
anyone now (as with the case of Roman Law) or anyone ever (as
with a proposed code drawn by a cynical, perhaps solonic,
author and not yet adopted).[20] The contrast is with a factual
statement such as "Six men are required to lift a car" or "Two
persons are (traditionally) needed to create an offspring." Such
statements resemble the "witness" statement r, in reporting a
fact and guiding action if one needs information on either how
to lift a car or start a family. The prior normative condition is
absent. It is important to see that the reasons for thinking a
statement action-guiding in this way need not be reasonable,
rational, or relevant. The actual English common law rule
which emerged from the middle ages required three witnesses
to a will, and that number may well have been as much based on
the sanctity and magic of the number three as on any respect
for the veracity of three signators when joined. Put differently:

---

19 The concept of "instantiation" refers only to filling in general terms with
a specific instance. Stating "Jim signed the contract" when before it was
said "someone signed the contract" is an example of instantiation. The
concept is generally related to the larger concept of quantification. The
concept is discussed throughout Willard Van Orman Quine's *Word and
Object* (1960).

20 The early seventh century B.C. Athenian statesman, Solon, authored a
wide-ranging set of legal and economic reforms to replace the existing
Draconian constitution. Reportedly, Solon could have made a more
moral and just set of laws, but did not do so because the citizenry was
not sufficiently moral and just to obey and take advantage of such a
code. Solon thus made a more mundane code for a more mortal populace.

poor, sloppy, ill-considered, malignant norms are just as much norms as magnificent ones.

The second difficulty for first order propositions is one of division: how are they to be divided up? There is a cogent literature and concomitant controversy about legal propositions and their individuation.[21] Whatever the merit of the positions in this area, it can with some integrity be set aside on the ground that "legal" does not mean "judicial". The purpose of the debate over legal individuation is to separate individual propositions and thus analyze and explain legal systems. Our purpose is not so grand. While "legal" may also be used here, it is always in the sense of statements cognizable (and often regularly found) in judicial propositions. Yet there are related difficulties. Are judicial propositions to be general or specific; are they to be listed as a countably infinite series or more manageably in the form of rules and their exceptions; is some sort of all-possible-situations-accounted-for completeness to be expected? Put differently, just how populated are the judicial propositional sets?

The answer to these questions lies with the empirical nature of judicial decision-making. Individuals, not analogues or formulae, answer judicial questions. These individuals, in formulating their answers, will give personal answers—even individuals with the same answer will express their reasoning (and reason their expressions) differently. Propositions are thus made personal and distinct by personal creativity, perspicacity, prejudice, and ignorance. Some judges, or those putting themselves in the place of judges, quite clearly use different premises from other judges.

Moreover, as individuals, they are apt to use different kinds of premises. They may mix general with specific statements; they may concatenate a series of detailed prescriptions in one place while in another form a general rule and give (or fail to give or even to imply that there are any) exceptions. What this

---

21 Joseph Raz's book *The Concept of a Legal System* (1970) presents perhaps the clearest exposition of the view that individuating legal norms contributes to a better understanding of legal systems. Anthony M. Honore's "Real Laws" in *Law, Morality and Society: Essays in Honour of H. L. A. Hart* (eds. P. M. S. Hacker and J. Raz 1977) contests Raz's position.

means is this: if individual behavior is part of the standard for determining proposition individuation and individuals employ generally conflicting and personally divergent ways of individuation, then a priority system of propositions would be too personal to be relevant. There is a further logical ground for thinking that exact individuation is an unnecessary exercise. Two series of propositions may have an equivalent content, but a different ordering. In that competing sets are merely divided up differently, compounded, no normative difference would necessarily follow.

We turn now to higher order propositions. The structure of propositions is held together by justifications. A lower order proposition is justified by the next higher order proposition. Justifications can be trivial, self-evident, or sequentially endless, so it is necessary to characterize the type of justification we are interested in. Although the term "criteria" is used for second order propositions, this "criteria" operates as justification, if here by a different name. However, in all cases, the question is what justifies the proposition below. Implication is, of course, a form (a logical one) of justification.

When judges are asked to justify a ruling, (as they often feel constrained to do within the text of their opinions), they are apt to cite widely divergent criteria. A brief perusal of any volume of court reports shows judicial reliance on statutes and past cases, international or local custom, the writings of authors learned and otherwise on topics legal and otherwise, general rules and principles, moral conundrums, public policy, well-known fact, common sense, and most commonly, reasons supposedly self-evident (immediately or derivately). Much rarer is any direct reference to third order justifications. Such reference is usually reserved for those instances either when the pedigree of the second order criteria is suspect (as with desuetude or a precedent which may have been overruled), when the question being argued has clear political or moral ramifications,[22] or where the judge is given to philosophical musings or

---

22 One should not confuse, as Herbert Weschler did, moral precepts which have a place in a judicial view and those which do not. See, Herbert Weschler, "Toward Neutral Principles of Constitutional Law", 72 *Harv. L. Rev.* 73 (1959) and *Principles, Politics and Fundamental Law* (1961).

introspection.[23] The common lack of such discussion does not mean that reference to second order criteria ends the matter of judicial reasoning.

None of this is adequately reflected in the literature on adjudication or judicial reasoning, which divides easily into one of two accounts. Sociologists, political scientists and historians look to the development of case law and see the workings of psychological, social, political, and economic forces shaping it. This attitude ranges from irreverent to resigned, depending on the degree to which they see the stamp of individuals in the course of history (*i.e.* - the degree to which they see a social or economic determinism operating on historical events).[24] More legally professionally oriented writers, by contrast, try to fit cases into logical normative models, often with the idea of showing the failure or triumph of doctrinal development when measured against some moral or political standard. [25]

Both types of account will at times analyze specific cases. Often the analysis will focus on discrepancies between announced reasons for these holdings. A particular case will

---

23 An interesting example of this, with disconcerting language for those who see narrow criteria as determining legal propositions, is *Commonwealth v. Donoghue*, 250 Ky. 343, 63 S.W.2d 3 (1933). See also the well-known case of *Repouille v. U.S.*, 165 F.2d 152 (2nd Cir. 1947).

24 Examples of such arguments include Howard Zinn, "The Conspiracy of Law" in *The Rule of Law* 15 (ed. Robert Paul Wolff, 1971), and many of the essays in both that work and *Law Against The People* (ed. Robert Lefcourt 1971). A much better work would be E. P. Thompson's *Whigs and Hunters: The Origin of the Black Act* (1975).

A number of lawyers have also entered into this field of social determinism, with varying degrees of enthusiasm. Two quite different well-known examples include Morton Horwitz's *The Transformation of American Law 1780-1860* (1977) and Richard A. Posner's *Economic Analysis of Law* (2d ed. 1977).

25 This type of analysis dominates constitutional law. See, for example, any of the works of Alexander Bickel: *The Least Dangerous Branch* (1962); *The Morality of Consent* (1975); *The Supreme Court and the Idea of Progress* (1978). This type of reasoning, although not Bickel in particular, is poorly criticized in Judith N. Shklar's *Legalism* (1964).

appear to say: "If p then q, p, thus q."[26] The concern is often with the initial premise, p. What is actually being averred is that a broad principle is being made determinative of a narrow principle. Judges must decide specific cases, not lay down general rules or solve abstract problems.[27] The narrow principle, or p, is merely an abstraction of a result of the case. Suppose in a negligence action it is important to judge whether the plaintiff was at the time of the alleged tort an invitee on the defendant's land. Suppose the plaintiff entered the property to make a telephone call.[28] The narrow question could be: is a public telephone user a business invitee for the purpose of property

---

26   This discussion is to be kept separate from the kind of factual reasoning of weak implications via instantiation of the sort: a penal statute proscribes the sales of liquor to a minor, X sold liquor to a minor, X violated the penal code.

27   Of course, in deciding cases, judges may in addition do what they want in terms of declaring theory or enunciating principles. The requirement to decide cases has a weak and a strong sense. The weak sense comes close to being an analytic truth of the semantics of the term "judge". To judge is normally taken to mean that one is called upon to resolve a dispute or a case. Failing to rule at all is a failure to judge. However, missing the point of a case is just merely judging badly, but still judging.

The strong sense involves the necessity only to resolve actual disputes, and not to discourse on law, rules, and justice generally. This sense, the ordinary practice of many courts, is given constitutional dimensions in the United States Constitution. See Article III, Section 2; *Aetna Life Ins. Co. v. Haworth*, 300 U.S. 227, 57 S. Ct. 461, 81 L.Ed. 617 (1937). Although this is not the law everywhere—see, E.C.S. Wade, "Consultation of the Judiciary by the Executive", 46 *Law Q. Rev.* 169 (1930) and George Neff Stevens, "Advisory Opinions - Present Status and an Evaluation", 34 *Wash. L. Rev.* 1 (1959)—it is the ordinary rule and a general limitation, such matters as declaratory judgments notwithstanding.

The weak sense is the one being used here.

28   This question of an injured, uninvited, telephone user suing the landowner was raised and settled in favor of the injured telephone-using plaintiff in *Ward v. Avery*, 113 Conn. 394, 155 A. 502 (1931); *Haley v. Deer*, 135 Neb. 459, 282 N.W. 389 (1938); *Coston v. Skyland Hotel, Inc.*, 231 N.C. 546, 57 S.E.2d 793 (1950).

tort law (trespass to land)?[29] An affirmative (or negative) result creates a narrow principle or rule. This could be stated to be: "All telephone callers are protected from landowner negligence(q)." The broader principle, p, would be that all invitees are protected from landowner negligence.

The difficulty in the actual case will not be over p, which may be generally accepted, or that the facts supporting q occurred, if the phone call is not in doubt. The practical difficulty for the court is whether acceptance of p commits us to acceptance of q. The logical difficulty for the writers and critics is to explain how one ever moves from p to q or p to –q. This problem is often overlooked by the social scientists because of their desire to see pretext disguised as reason when decisions are inelegant or ambiguous. Almost by disciplinary definition, social not logical causes yield results. The logical difficulties are also often disregarded by legal writers who allow too much logical leeway in their desire to find models and systems.[30] The look is backward, with the history of doctrine establishing the validity of superimposed models.[31]

---

29 It is unimportant in this entire discussion that the business invitee rule is everywhere in retreat. See William Prosser, *Handbook of the Law of Torts* 385-399 (4th ed. 1971). It was once alive, could be so again, and in any case, presents interesting situations for discussion.

30 This difficulty is famously discussed by Benjamin Cardozo in *The Nature of the Judicial Process* (1921), but while he raises the problem eloquently, he does not give a clue as to how it might be analyzed. He admits many different kinds of "forces" on judicial decision-making, and calls on them (legal writers) to recognize these forces so as better to use them. The law is a thing, to be set along side history, tradition, popular morality, politics, *etc.* in reaching subsequent decisions. What analogue one is to use in reaching these decisions—even if construction of such an analogue is possible, workable, or desirable—is left open without comment.

31 This is the approach of Edward Levi in *An Introduction to Legal Reasoning* (1948). Levi looks at three doctrinal developments—the "inherently dangerous" doctrine in tort, the judicial treatment of the MANN ACT (the white slavery act), and the wandering ways of the Commerce Clause of the United States Constitution—from hindsight—and superimposes a certain determinist inevitability in the development. Levi is discussed more thoroughly in Chapter III.

The above case illustrates the place of second order propositions. Second order propositions can be defined as the set of propositions which justify or yield first order propositions and are in turn justified by other second order propositions or third order propositions. Suppose our plaintiff above, (P), had entered the lobby of defendant D's building to use the telephone. As he was about to enter the booth, a chandelier which D had attached to the ceiling with chewing gum came down on P, causing him severe injury. P might seek to recover damages. If asked why D ought to pay, P, if he were versed in court decisions, might appeal to the rule that invitees are generally owed reasonable care. If asked why that is so, he might answer that innocent people ought to be protected from foreseeable danger placed there by those with a duty to maintain their property. Each of these responses is a justification and serves as a reason, good or bad, for the previous statement.

We said above that second order propositions justify first order propositions. To justify is not necessarily to convince. Weak implication illustrates this: if P claimed that r ("Telephone users are invitees") because s ("Both telephone users and restroom users are invitees"), P would have justified r through logical implication, while undoubtedly failing to convince the previously unconvinced of the truth of r. However, small steps often lead to surprising results, and are necessary for establishing the validity of a reasoning chain.

The occurrence of implication in a chain of propositions ought to make us suspicious again of any attempt to individuate reasons for the purpose of counting them all or using a particular chain as the exclusive exemplar of correct reasoning. One can, as always, add an infinite number of logically equivalent or weaker statements. Further, second order propositions seem particularly susceptible of divergent characterization. What may seem an adequate justification for one person, to one person, or in one circumstance may seem to fail in a later or different context. The reasons, rooted as they are in varying individuals' interests, intelligence, backgrounds, and situations, hardly need delineation. The occurrence of many second order reasons in a chain may point to the complexity of the ties which order the propositions, but it may equally well speak of individual style or the rhetorical need to convince a particular audience. [32]

Third order propositions justify second order propositions or other third order propositions. They are the final level in our model, and thus, all theoretically higher order levels are collapsed into the third order. Earlier in the chapter, it was stated that the difference between the first and second levels and the third level has to do with pedigree. The lower levels contain certain propositions found in legal forms. Their occurrence there may be a matter of controversy or ambiguity; the form itself may be of disputed validity; the proposition may conflict with some other proposition found in a legal form. But, true or not, the claim of pedigree often gives these propositions a *prima facie* authority. There may be other reasons for respecting the contents of such propositions than merely their attachment to legal forms. For example, a rule against murder or against child abuse may be thought to carry ethical, social, political and prudential force as well as the force of certain legal forms. (A more detailed discussion of legal forms can be found in Chapter IV).

Common legal forms include statutes, edicts, constitutions, past court decisions, codes, ordinances, equity principles, executive orders, leading authors' works, certain kinds of recognized customs, international agreements and treaties. Any list must be more suggestive than definitive. Criteria are necessary to decide which statutes, edicts, *etc.* count (*e.g.*—which might not be considered to be foreign, superceded, have fallen into desuetude, or in some other way not be presently valid) and perhaps more basically, which things count as statutes, edicts, *etc.* (*e.g.*—what administrative proclamations have force, which customs are binding, what is the status of a statute overturned by a years-later reversed court decision, or a court decision reversed by a statute which is subsequently repealed).

The intuitive notion that it is easy to recognize what has membership in the set of legal forms, and only difficult to specify the grounds for membership, is clearly called into question

---

32 The connections between law, justice and rhetoric are discussed at length in C. Perelman and L. Olbrechts-Tyteca, *The New Rhetoric: A Treatise on Argumentation* (English ed. 1969).

during times of serious political and social unrest.[33] However, it is the general use of legal forms which give them their authority. New York judges look to enactments of the New York legislature, but not to the pronouncements of Gaius or Solon, and thus it is to the New York statutes that one turns to locate a New York legal form. The relationship is casual, empirical, and contingent. If judges were not expected to look to local statutes but to astrological charts, then astrological charts, regardless of their irrationality and their apparent irrelevance, rather than local statutes passed by those theoretically having political authority, would be the relevant legal form in New York.

The utility of a tertiary schema lies in its ability to exhibit the distinct types of justification apparent in higher order propositions.[34] When justification centers on the issue of pedigree, it is second order. However, not all members of the second order can be traced to legal forms. Rather, the issue is what ought to be the criteria for selecting second order propositions. For any particular first order proposition, many different types of justifications are possible. Suppose the first order question asks whether or not self-defense excuses intentional killing. One might state that it does so excuse because saving one's own life is an inalienable individual right; because such a policy diminishes the pool of potential prisoners, hospital patients, and convalescing workers; or because self-defense is a necessary process in assuring the survival of the fittest, a process which allows for a constantly improving level of civilization. These justifications might be respectively characterized as deontological, economic, and consequentialist or socio-biological. Each of these justifications is impeachable on grounds of rationality and value. None

---

33 This theme is taken up in Chapter VII. However, the idea of searching for criteria in times of revolutionary change is discussed in J. M. Eekelaar, "Principles of Revolutionary Legality" and John M. Finnis, "Revolutions and Continuity of Law", both found in *Oxford Essays in Jurisprudence*, second series (ed. A. W. B. Simpson 1973).

34 One problem with the two level schema which divides between "sources of law" and "law" advocated by Gray and Frank is that the differences between all justifications are collapsed. See John Chipman Gray, *The Nature and Sources of the Law* (2nd ed. 1921), and Jerome Frank, *Law and the Modern Mind* (1930).

appeals to the idea of an empirical authority that bears respect, or to a reason worth following because it is generally considered to be worth following.

A very different type of justification is being employed when self-defense is justified as an excuse because a certain statute or series of past decisions suggests that it ought to be an excuse.[35] An empirical component—the force of a legal form—becomes a consideration. If the relevant statute is repealed, overturned, falls into desuetude, or is found to be improperly enacted, then the second order justification based on that statute is similarly impeachable. However, the set of propositions found in legal forms and in the second order propositional set is not coextensive. First order questions arise for which no first order proposition, justifiable by reference to legal forms, exists. The justifications for these questions are not immediately found within the third level (though they are mediately so, of course). Broad categories with labels such as "policy" or "principles of law" are commonly used to supplement the set of legal forms. Second order propositions are not characterized by their pedigree, but they are circumscribed by the subset of formal second order propositions. The initial issue in justifying first order propositions is always: is there some formal authority for asserting such-and-such a first order proposition?

Third order propositions are neither limited by considerations of pedigree, nor circumscribed by such considerations. Propositions are drawn from wherever necessary to justify sufficiently the lower order propositions.[36] Certain kinds of posi-

---

35   That even the most basic moral principles can be omitted from the set of judicial propositions is exemplified by the denial of the privilege of self-defense in early English law. Until the case of *Chapleyn of Greye's Inn v.–*, Y.B. 2 Hen. IV 8, pl. 40 (1400), it has been said that "the man who commits homicide by misadventure or in self-defense deserves but needs a pardon." Frederick Pollock and Frederic William Maitland, 2 *The History of English Law* 479 (2nd ed. 1898).

36   There is the inclination to think only of moral reasons doing battle with legal reasons for control of our actions and beliefs. Other conflicts arise however. The United States Supreme Court, after lengthy discussion, held that tomatoes are vegetables rather than fruit. *Nix v. Hedden*, 149 U.S. 304, 13 S. Ct. 881, 37 L.Ed 745 (1893). As fruit is botanically speaking the seed of a plant or that part which contains the seed, the Court's

tions trivialize the third level, and in order to continue making use of our tertiary schema, it is necessary to understand why these positions are inadequate.

This position might be called legal isolationism. Legal isolationism asserts that reference to legal forms is usually sufficient to provide first order propositions, that manipulation of legal forms in order to extract a second order proposition is a straightforward matter, and that those few cases not within the purview of legal forms are tightly circumscribed by the legal forms. The isolationist wishes to deny that political, moral, prudential, or social considerations play an important, independent part in the propositional sets. The reason that the third order is trivialized is that reference to legal forms alone is sufficient for disposition of most cases. The results engendered by the isolationist may allow for results which are ethically reprehensible or politically debilitating, but criticism on these grounds would be considered logically irrelevant.

There are difficulties with the isolationist position. When there is a constitutional conflict within a society, lower order propositional selection is a difficult matter. Which legal forms are valid may be in doubt.[37] Moreover, the manner of determining non-formal second order propositions is left vague. Circumscribing an answer is not the same as determining it. If the third level is a rich set from which to select justifying propositions, then the fact that circumscribing alone occurs is not fatal. Where the third level is impoverished, though, one is left to individual preferences to select non-formal propositions, an essentially subjective method.

There is a deeper difficulty in the isolationist's position. The isolationist believes that the task of sifting through legal forms may be cumbersome, but it is not, on the whole, conceptually

---

holding makes for revolutionary biology. A similar botanical principle contrasting a legal one occurred in that Court's earlier refusal to label either beans or walnuts as types of seeds, oblivious to what occurs if either is planted. See *Robertson v. Salomon*, 130 U.S. 412, 414, 9 S. Ct. 559, 32 L.Ed. 995 (1889).

37 The *prima facie* authority residing in legal forms is not unlike that residing in Raz's exclusionary reasons, although the reasoning structure here differs on the need for further justification from that suggested in Raz's analysis. See Joseph Raz, *Practical Reasons and Norms* 35-106 (1975).

difficult. These legal forms, moreover, may be examined without resort to any potentially controversial set of political, social, or ethical beliefs. For example, a statute requiring two witnesses' signatures to validate a will is in no further need of interpretation. Its meaning ought to be the same regardless of one's beliefs. To suggest that even such an unambiguous statute as this requires a political justification misperceives the very authority inherent in legal forms. There is a certain justificatory finality in legal forms that makes further reasoning unnecessary. The meaning of a form may present difficulties of syntax and semantics, but resort to larger sets of beliefs is unnecessary.

The isolationist fails to do credit to the complexity of the judicial method. A certain answer appears obvious often because third order beliefs are used, not because they are unnecessary. An example from aesthetics might be helpful. If one asked a seventeenth century Dutchman such as Johannes Vermeer why his seas and sky in "View of Delft" have a greenish hue to them, he might reply that the answer is obvious. That is just the color they needed to be. He might reply further that if Ruisdael or Rembrandt were consulted, they would say the same thing. Yet we could imagine a Van Eyck, a Titian, a Renoir, or a Dali completing the picture differently. The very idea of a light bulb being the sun in Picasso's "Guernica" epitomizes the variation imaginable. Of course, Dali's completion of Delft's sea and sky would yield a different picture. Vermeer might say of Dali's suggestions as to what colors should be used to shade the sketch that, for a surrealistic picture, Dali might be right. Vermeer would claim, however, that for his (Vermeer's) own realistic pictures, Dali's opinion is irrelevant.

But if Vermeer were pressed to use arguments rather than labels to defend his position, and he was told further that Dali, Titian, or Renoir had suggestions at odds with his own on how to complete his pictures in a style authentically his, Vermeer would need to appeal to some generalized set of beliefs concerning art. Vermeer may not be able to enunciate the central ideas of these beliefs or to explain all or even very many of their implications. He and his Dutch contemporaries need not have realized that they employed a highly conventionalized and arbitrary set of techniques and artifices in translating the empirical world to the coded shapes, forms, perspectives and hues they did. Their view of art and artist may well have been due very largely to the peculiarities of a society prosperous, Protestant, bourgeois, maritime, optimistic, and admiring of Italian culture. Within their own world, Dutch artists took many problems as having obvious solutions, and would have failed to see that arguments might be necessary to justify their particular conception of art. However, that their own beliefs of art were often implicit does not make them any the less higher order beliefs.

This somewhat remote illustration suggests that what appears obvious need not be universally so regarded or without need for justifying argument. A further set of propositions is needed. In art, such a propositional set might explain the relation of copy to original or beholder of an object to the creator of that object; or it may deal with more technical matters of light, form, image, and material. In adjudication, the proposition that "Two witnesses are necessary to validate a will" appears obviously true because one's set of third order propositions gives some analogue for sifting precedents, reading statutes, and otherwise reaching a solution. The obviousness of the result is irrelevant. Judicial belief sets—whether partial, incomplete, finished, or refined—involve a third level and third order propositions. This is especially telling against the timid isolationist, one who recognizes that some cases, at least those commonly tagged as requiring judicial discretion, allow for third order propositions. For him, some method must exist to sort between discretion and discretionless cases. The method or analogue would decide, perhaps, whether past precedents are sufficient for resolving the instant case, and what test tells us that. This calls for an enriched set of higher than second order propositions.

Judicial Views

In this final section, we shall examine how one might employ the three level propositional structure. We might summarize briefly the discussion up to this point. A judge is required by her institutional role to provide answers to the questions which come before her. These first order questions require an answer, provided here in the form of the first order propositions. In seeking to provide a first order proposition, one is required to justify the assertion of that proposition. Certain justifications can be found by looking to legal forms: that is, other propositions marked by their pedigree can be found to justify these first order propositions. Other justifications do not possess such a pedigree, nor do justifications of those pedigreed propositions which they themselves justify. These unpedigreed propositions form the third order set, and are drawn from the set of political, ethical, and prudential (and other) beliefs and attitudes. How the third order set is constituted is a function of an individual's understanding of what the judicial role involves.

Taken together, the three tiered propositional set can be called a judicial view. The purpose of the view is to provide answers to specific questions, but it ought not to be thought that judges actually use views to arrive at their conclusions, (though many judges do engage in a course of reasoning very similar to the method described here). Rather, a view is necessary for assessing whether or not a judge's decision is correct.

The construction of any particular view turns on the contents of the third order propositional set. We mentioned earlier that the sources of the third order propositions might well include political theory, ethics, and principles of prudence. However, an individual does not borrow propositions as she finds them. That is, the set of third order propositions are chosen not for their truth but for their relevance. One's concept of what the judicial function is within a society dictates what sources one selects in allowing that function to be fulfilled.

Because the components of the judicial views are chosen, in part, from value-laden areas such as politics and ethics, it might appear that personal preferences alone determine third order propositions. If this were true, something akin to a judicial ideology rather than a judicial view would occur. An ideology, like a view, is a system of related concepts about some facet of human culture.[38] It, too, has attitudinal as well as belief

---

38 The term ideology has a complex modern history. It was put into widespread use by Karl Marx as the propagandistic opposite of history or true history. Ideology was to Marx a false conception or set of concep-

components, and allows one to reach decisions about problems previously unconfronted. However, while an ideology may serve as a source for third order propositions, those propositions are chosen and used differently when they are so transferred. The difference in choice is apparent in the not uncommon judicial sentiment that "I would rather I did not have to reach this result. It goes against many of my beliefs, values, and opinions to do so. I think that little good will come of it. Nevertheless, I reluctantly will go ahead and hold . . ." The judge may be unhappy with what she sees as being the only available alternatives, or she may plainly disagree with the wisdom of the course of action that others, whom she takes to be authority, have pursued. Propositions are picked out from ideological and other sources because of the demands of role.[39]

---

tions of social and economic history, rooted in the unconscious biases of bourgeois thinkers. See Karl Marx and Frederick Engels, *The German Ideology* (first written 1844; complete English work, 1965). It came to take on a broader meaning as a Marxist concept, denoting the general difficulty of historians to entertain thought and ideas alien to their own times and status. See letter of Frederick Engels to F. Mehrig of 14 July 1893, found in Karl Marx and Frederick Engels *Selected Works* 699 (International Publishers, 1968). Later, disillusioned leftists used it to refer to socialist rather than non-socialist writings, and added a derisory tag to it of being rigid and heavy-handed. See Arthur Schlesinger, *The Vital Center* (1949). It subsequently degenerated to a pejorative comment on one's opponents connoting the dogmatic position, unscientific, and very often communistic, thus coming full circle from the scientific attribution which originally distinguished Marx's claim from other value-laden and myopic positions.

Ideology has been accorded a place in modern legal writings by the Critical Legal Studies Movement. Contributions to the Movement are less than clear or unified. Several relevant claims may be attributed to the Movement. There are the descriptive claims that ideology implies first, second, or third order propositions, and the prescriptive claims that these implications are proper. Two works serving as an introduction to critical legal studies are Roberto Mangabiera Unger's lengthy article "The Critical Legal Studies Movement," 96 *Harv. L. Rev.* 561 (1983) and the articles collected in *The Politics of Law: A Progressive Critique* (ed. D. Kairys 1982).

39 Role differentiated behavior among the bench invites the obvious comparison with role differentiated behavior within the bar. Such behavior has produced an entire literature, mainly under the guise of

Moreover, when they are picked out, they may not have the same meaning they did previously. This can be because they have been chopped up: taking them out of a consistent, well-ordered set and placing them in a quite different set may change their denotation.

Of course, seeing role as prior to propositions makes the definition of judicial role more difficult. It is insufficient, even incorrect, to say that it is the role of the judge to apply the correct proposition in the form of an answer to every issue that is adjudicated. Role determines how the propositional set is constituted, and thus any statement that one performs one's role by using the correct propositions fails to understand that it is the selection of propositions to be used that must come before their application is possible.

It might be helpful to conclude with an example which shows how judicial views are dependent on role for third order membership. Let us consider *Riggs v. Palmer*,[40] the case which held that an impatient beneficiary to a will who had murdered the will's testator would not be permitted to take the fruits of

---

"professional responsibility", as well as legally-binding rules of conduct. See, for example, Lon Fuller and John Randall, "Professional Responsibility: Report of the Joint Conference", 44 *A.B.A.J.* 1159 (1958); *Model Rules of Professional Conduct* (1983).

Such behavior has not been without its critics. Typical in its vitriol, although almost unmatched in its elegance, is the comment of Macauley on Francis Bacon, who reportedly would not

> inquire . . . whether it be right that a man should, with a wig on his head, and a band round his neck, do for a guinea what, without those appendages, he would think it wicked and infamous to do for an empire; whether it be right that, not merely believing but knowing a statement to be true, he should do all that can be done by sophistry, by rhetoric, by solemn asseveration, by indignant exclamation, by gesture, by play of features, by terrifying one honest witness, by perplexing another, to cause a jury to think that statement false.

Thomas Macaulay, 6 *The Works of Lord Macaulay* 135, 163 (ed. H. Trevelyan 1900). In that Macaulay's rhetoric embodies certain telling observations, it stains judges as well as lawyers.

40 115 N.Y. 506, 22 N.E. 188 (1889). This case is discussed and defended in Benjamin Cardozo, *The Nature of the Judicial Process*, Chapter I (1921).

the expedited inheritance. The usual rule in probate cases was to honor the explicit terms of any will where there was no indication of any fraud, documentary irregularity, or undue influence. This rule, however, was held not be determinative of the instant case because of the principle that no one shall be permitted "to take advantage of his own wrong, or to found any claim upon his own iniquity, or to acquire property by his crime."

I do not want to examine here the merits of *Riggs* or the relative importance of rules versus principles.[41] Rather, I wish to show how the imposition of what we will call the "fairness principle" might be considered improper.

The fairness principle says that, in the courtroom, no man shall benefit by his own wrong. It is a principle which might be found in at least three places: one might find it in a number of moral theories, whether consequentialist or deontic; one might find it in past cases in the form of equity; or it might be found within the cases merely in the form of ordinary holdings, as with more mundane judicial standards.[42] The court in *Riggs* does not give its source for the principle. Let us suppose, however, that one disagrees with the use of the fairness principle. The disagreement lies not with the content of the principle, which is blandly unexceptionable, or even with the need for such a principle in adjudication, for fairness in all its aspects seems a commendable goal for a judicial system. The disagreement lies in the feeling that one or the other of the putative sources of the fairness principle is either somehow illegitimate or out of bounds for judicial consideration, or that the source has been misused by the *Riggs* court. A number of scenarios are possible, and we shall look at two.

The first scenario would involve the attribution of the use of the fairness principle to the realm of equity jurisdiction. Equity is usually considered a system of principles which aims to

---

41 This problem is not directly addressed in this work, although rule-based and principle-based theories are discussed in Chapters V and VI respectively.

42 There are some who believe that it is not there to be found in court holdings, at least not in explicit or transparent manner. See Arthur L. Goodhart, *Essays in Jurisprudence and Common Law* 7 (1931).

remedy defects in the case law by allowing for considerations of fairness, justness, and right dealing.[43] Its jurisdiction is generally limited within a judicial system (although its appearance, according to some observers, reaches to all judicial systems[44]). When one looks to the past incidents of equity jurisdiction, one notices that the jurisdiction has spread into new areas, but within well-demarcated boundaries.[45] One way of justifying *Riggs'* employment of the fairness principle would be to see it as part of the role of the judge to make use of equity (where it is relevant) whenever it is not specifically proscribed by past court decisions. A contrary position would see equity as a limited tool, liable to easy abuse, and a fundamental infringement of the general powers of the legislature to lay down the bases of judicial standards. The first position sees the application of equity as an inherent component of the role of a judge. The second position sees this application as taking third place to the more important considerations of limited judicial power and deference to established past rules. The extension of equity generally, and the application of the fairness principle specifically, are functions of what role one believes the judge ought to adhere to in deciding individual cases.

---

43 One compelling definition of equity was given by an English Chancellor, Cardinal Morton, in 1489: "every law should be in accordance with the law of God; and I know well that an executor who fraudulently misapplies the goods and does not make restitution will be damned in Hell, and to remedy this is in accordance with conscience, as I understand it." Y. B. 4 Hen. VIII, Hil. no. 8; cited in Theodore F. T. Plucknett, *A Concise History of the Common Law* 685-686 (5th ed. 1956). That Morton and other chancellors were themselves often less then equitable is notoriously documented in their running of the Court of Star Chamber. See, *e.g.*, J. A. Guy, *The Cardinal's Court* (1977); G. R. Elton, *The Tudor Constitution* (1960); *Select Pleas in the Court of Star Chamber* (Selden Society, Vol. 16, 25).

44 Such a position is taken by C. K. Allen in *Law in the Making* 383-425 (7th ed. 1964).

45 For a tracing of the development of the growth of equity in English common law, see Theodore F. T. Plucknett, *A Concise History of the Common Law* 675-707 (5th ed. 1956); S. F. C. Milsom, *Historical Foundations of the Common Law* 82-96 (2nd ed. 1981).

A second scenario would involve the attribution of the use of the fairness principle not to any organized set of equitable maxims and principles, but directly to an ethical theory which included such a principle. Justice generally is a concern of the courts, and *Riggs* seems to be a case where the matter of justice is squarely in issue. An advocate of the *Riggs* decision might suggest that it is the prerogative of the judge, an aspect of his role as a judge, to suspend the normal application of judicial standards when doing so would result in a grave injustice. A contrary opinion would hold that it is beyond the legitimate ken of the judge to employ principles of fairness and justice apart from those which are embedded in legal forms, at least in those cases where a rule clearly applies (as the rule which calls for respect for the written testamentary intentions of a sane testator not under undue influence clearly does).

In both scenarios, the proper scope of the judicial role is a factor in determining what is the source of judicial propositions. Rarely, however, are sources rejected or accepted in such an all-or-nothing fashion. One uses a concept of role to determine which sources are legitimate for obtaining judicial propositions, and such a concept will pick out, among other things, certain legal forms as well as third order sources.[46] Such a concept, if it is more sophisticated, will allow for greater specificity in the selection of propositions. The difficulty in circumscribing satisfactorily the bounds of equity can illustrate why it is that such specificity is required, and gives a clue as to how such specificity might be obtained.

The fairness principle also illustrates how one's own personal preferences and values are not simply incorporated unadulterated into the third order set. One may agree with the fairness principle and yet see its application as being outside the scope of proper judicial behavior. One might be either a consequentialist or a follower of Robert Nozick[47] and yet see the judicial

---

46 One's concept of role is just a matter of individually held beliefs. The perception of role is a conventionally held conception, not subject to truth functional analysis. This point is discussed at length in the next chapter.

47 Robert Nozick, *Anarchy, State and Utopia* (1974).

role as one that uses the ethical source of a deontological theory only. A consequentialist might justify this as being more practical, as a constant weighing of principles for membership might be beyond the ability of most sitting judges; while a Nozickean might see this method as one which limits as much as possible governmental interference with the individual. Judicial role is a concept partly empirical. Nozick and consequentialists may notice that, in a given society, it is to deontic principles that judges do in fact look, and thus incorporate into their own (Nozick and the consequentialists) concept of role the provision which a judge, if not a moralist, ought to apply deontic principles. Both Nozick and a consequentialist could thus take the position of supporting deontic sources for the third order set despite the apparent conflict with their own respective ethical positions.

Different conceptions of role result in different propositional sets. The truth functional status of these sets have yet to be discussed. It is to this issue that we shall now turn.

II

Foundations of Judicial
Decision-Making

Law, says the priest with a priestly look,
Expounding to an unpriestly people,
Law is the words in my priestly book,
Law is my pulpit and my steeple.

W.H. Auden

We began the last chapter by suggesting an individual might be uncertain as to whether judges are bound to make certain decisions—reach a particular result in the case before them—or whether they have a choice, commonly called discretion, in their actions. That question can now be reformulated. For some possible answer the judge might reach, where such an answer is embodied in some proposition p, is p either true or false? After the last chapter, the reformulated question can be divided into two separate questions. Is p either true or false for lower order propositions? Is p either true or false for third order propositions? The first question is to be answered yes and the second no, but in order to sustain this assertion, something more must be learned about third order propositions. The first part of this chapter details the status and makeup of third order propositions. The second part shows how their construction circumscribes lower order propositions. The third part sets out briefly, but explicitly, what will be developed in later chapters: the theory of judicial pluralism.

The Status of Judicial Propositions

Judicial views are constructions. They are assembled by taking an object from one place and a second object from another place and joining them. The obvious resemblance is to building a house. Conceptual constructions, like material ones, are in part slaves of function—whether the function is to solve cases or to shelter people—but in part open to the individual imagination. One constructs according to knowledge, taste, resources, prudence, and values. Constructions tend to be culturally specific. We can see this when we compare varieties of castles in the fifteenth century Loire valley, wigwams in sixteenth century America, or steel and glass condominiums in twentieth century Holland. A cross-cultural relocation of any of these structures would be more than a curious anomaly: it would require an explanation which would be socially discontinuous, perhaps relating to building a museum or being conquered by an advanced civilization.

Diversity among judicial systems is not always as great and within judicial systems is usually minimal. Views held by legal observers of the New York State judicial system as to judicial standards are less varied than views held by New York architects and builders as to what constitutes a correct set of procedures and designs for constructing a building or development. The similarity among the views of legal obervers is manifested in several ways. First, when actual cases or distinct issues raised in those cases are presented, there is often ready agreement on the outcome.[1] That is, if a court needs to decide whether a particular document is a (valid) contract (p) or whether an oral land agreement is a valid contract (q), in most cases judges and scholars will agree as to what the right answer is. Ready agreement would be apparent that p and q (each is true), and that "-p and -q" (neither is true). Put differently, few could disagree about excluding most documents from the set of valid contracts (laundry lists, magazine articles, romantic novels, historical monographs) or would disagree on inclusion of most documents which constitute the set of valid contracts (standard sales agreements, employment pacts, bank loan papers).

---

1 Discretion, itself a complicated concept, here is an oversimplification for the type of choice involved. This problem is discussed in more detail in Chapter VI.

Second, similar sets of reasons and concepts are used to explain and defend decisions. In the case of concepts, resort is often made to some common concept, such as *res judicata*, tender or estoppel, which is assumed to be certain and generally understood in the same way.[2] The concept's familiarity and popularity may give the impression of easy certainty. Reasons (or second order propositions) often fall prey to this same impression, particularly when they are widely used. This tendency is heightened by the many judicial concepts and reasons which are employed to disguise real disagreement. "Reasonable man", "free speech", "proximate cause", "informed consent", "public nuisance", "fiduciary duty", "no one shall benefit by his own wrong", "contracts made under duress shall be voidable" and "no person shall be denied due process of law" are all terms and statements subject to widespread use by individuals who agree on little else but the terms' utility and the statements' validity.

Third, there is a reification of law which has yielded a strong notion of legal concreteness. The tendency—so vilified by

---

2 In the field of employment law, for example, decisions were based on the seeming agreement as to central concepts of contract. Employees were hired at will, because the analysis of an oral exchange of promises dictated that contracts without a duration clause could be ended by either party without liability. See Samuel Williston, 1 *Williston on Contracts* Section 39 (rev. ed. 1938). Such conceptual agreement has masked political and social disagreement, however, as to which contractual concepts apply. The traditional cases, reflecting a *laissez-faire*, development, capitalistic ethic, all cited as their authority H. G. Wood's formulation, written in the tellingly titled treatise, *Master & Servant*. Wood states that "with us the rule is inflexible, that a general or indefinite hiring is prima facie a hiring at will, and if the servant seeks to make out a yearly hiring, the burden is upon him to establish it by proof." *Master & Servant* at 272 (1877). If the same cases are viewed as unilateral contracts, involving a promise for an on-going performance, then the lack of a duration clause may be irrelevant. See, for example, the reasoning in *Toussaint v. Blue Cross & Blue Shield of Michigan*, 292 N.W.2d 880 (Mich. 1980); *Drzewiecki v. H & R Block*, Inc., 24 Cal. App.3d 695, 101 Cal. Rptr. 169 (1972). In this area, concepts once understood to be used in the same way were discovered, when political power and social awareness shifted, to admit of a variety of meaning.

common language philosophers—of making real any common sentential object ("there is x" makes x real) is a natural one.

Our rationality is rooted in the familiar set of objects of the empirical world around us, and we use this concrete world as metaphor for more abstract ones. Agreement about the properties of tables and chairs comes easily because statements attaching existence predicates to tables and chairs are so easily verifiable. While verification does not operate in the same manner in the case of judicial statements, it is nevertheless easy to view the judicial arena as not unlike the empirical arena. The consequences of judicial statements are empirical and important.

Such statements are commonly the result of knowledge and investigation. If judicial statements do not take their sense from any simple method of verification, neither, a philosopher might argue, do empirical statements.[3] What is central to both is the concrete aspect that is imprinted in any intuitive or pretheoretic notion of such statements. Individuals are arrested, assets are impounded, accounts escheat, wages are garnished, witnesses are subpoenaed, sworn and harried, property is given, taken and confiscated: these are more tangible actions to most people than those which result from more ethereal statements in the form of ethical imperatives, religious injunctions, or mathematical proofs.

Reasons for the belief that a consensus of judicial views exists are easy to understand. Ultimately, though, these reasons are inadequate. To see why, a distinction must be drawn between "consensus" and "convergence" of judicial views. A consensus of beliefs involves a general agreement between individuals about first and second level propositions. In order to have a consensus, there must exist a shared body of beliefs. Complete coincidence of held belief, sentiment, and judicial conceptions is not required, but a solidarity, a collective opinion, a shared set (or substrate) of values and method must be present.

---

3 The difficulties of simple verificationism are well known. Those who tried, the logical positivists, never reached a satisfactory formulation of the verification principle, even by their own admission. See, for example, A. J. Ayer, *Logic, Truth and Language* (1936); *The Foundations of Empirical Knowledge* (1940).

"Convergence" is a weaker concept. Mere agreement on outcome will suffice. Some reasons will be shared, but important ones will not be. More to the point, different conceptions and a different weighting of reasons occurs. Where convergence is in force, no agreement is inherently guaranteed. There is no reason or necessity for agreement. Agreement can occur, and can be statistically significant—*i.e.* there may be a high correlation coefficient—because of factors other than a shared set of third order propositions.[4] Concurring opinions are perhaps the clearest example of this.

Convergence is too often confused for consensus. Consensus involves agreement as to both reasons and conclusions, convergence agreement only on conclusions. The agreement as to ends but not means to those ends is no more coincidental than (and in fact mirrors) the general agreement within society about the aims of the commonweal and the disagreement about how best to achieve those ends. Convergence is a concept well known to paleontology and evolutionary biology. There, it suggests the development of independent but parallel characteristics among species because of similar habitat, environment or functional necessity; development which is, at times, confused with causally linked evolution. For example, it is presently an open question as to whether birds are descended from certain species of dinosaurs rather than from other reptiles or protoreptiles. One can compare skeletons of modern birds, perhaps emus, with members of dinosaur families such as coelurosaurs, and see similar upright posture, diet selection, bone structure, locomotion, limb and claw development, dental structure, and the ability to climb and jump from trees, and

---

4 Justice Cardozo, a long and close observer, speaks of this convergence of views when he relates how individuals view cases, even conduct themselves "with no rules except those of custom and conscience to regulate their conduct. The feeling is that nine times out of ten, if not more often, the conduct of right-minded men could not have been different if the rule embodied in the decision had been announced by statute in advance." Benjamin N. Cardozo, *The Nature of the Judicial Process* 142-143 (1921). Such a statement is revealing, for it implicitly suggests that third order propositions could account for decisions as easily as first order. Whether the concept of "right-mindedness" could do the work suggested is much more problematic.

believe that the latter animals descended from the former. However, it might conversely be the case that in order for reptiles of a certain size to survive, in particular to feed on low trees and bushes while being able either to escape from or defend against certain kinds of predators, while being able to provide some protection for their nuturing young, all of the above features, at least in a somewhat simplified way, might be necessary. The similarity itself no more proves causal relationship than any conclusion figured backwards would imply cause. The convergence of ends might be a result of identical underlying conditions, or it might just be that similar conditions or parallel development have pushed to the same end. Even flying might be convergent, as with the archaeopteryx and birds, as the parallel ability and need to climb trees and alight from them along with the need to cool extended limbs, might allow independent wing development.

On the other hand, where there is a consensus, individuals not only reach the same results, they tend to do so for the same reasons or, at least, they tend to agree on which particular reasons count and for how much they count. The mistake in paleontology would be to assume common ends (shared characteristics) imply causal linkage (evolution). The mistake in law would be to see agreement on the outcome of particular cases as implying a general consensus of judicial views. Convergence is a concept suggesting outcomes can be reached different ways and for different reasons. An illustration may be useful.

Suppose plaintiff P is suing defendant D in tort for assault and battery. D defends. The facts are straightforward. After a minor automobile accident—where P and D scrape bumpers in a large parking lot—P and D trade angry words. P, dissatisfied by a mere verbal exchange, and noticing a vendor of baseball bats 50 yards away, proceeds to purchase a bat to use against D. P tells D of this. D decides to face P and his bat, although he could easily escape in his automobile. P is smaller than D and appears likely to hurt D, but not put his life in danger. D is a karate expert, however, and during the course of defending himself, severely injures P. P decides to sue.

D's claim of self-defense comes to this. Even though a reasonably safe way of escape was open, not to have stood one's ground would have been an affront to one's dignity and sense of honor. Under judicial view v, D's argument is accepted. Honor, dignity, and pride are important third order values and figure in the construction of all (rational) views. Certain other, contrary values—such as pacifism and the sanctity of the human body—figure, but much less importantly.[5] Under judicial view w, D also wins. View w reasons that holding one's ground discourages the initial use of force. A publicized holding of the courts that "one who stands his ground is afforded a certain degree of judicial protection" might deter initial displays of violence. A large reduction in initial assaults would have greater weight in a balancing calculus than the small amount of extra violence occasioned by legitimizing self-defense here.

Holders of views v and w might agree on the first order proposition: "a person attacked may stand his ground against an assailant, even when a reasonable and safe means of escape exists." They may even agree on the same second order proposition. This might be statable via a reference to affirming precedent. It might also be done through agreement on second order propositions which are held either for different reasons or because individuals have different conceptions when they employ the same concept. The first could occur if the second order reason is "holding one's ground is a deterrent to assault," or p.

An advocate of view v might endorse p because she believes that holding one's ground serves as a deterrent to assault. An advocate of view w, on the other hand, might endorse p because he believes that public realization that self-defense is a good legal defense would act as a deterrent to assault. The conceptual ambiguity (the second) can occur if the second order proposition states "retreat is an affront to one's dignity". The term "dignity" can be taken as a direct aim or virtue worth having and protecting (view v) or it can be a part of a conse-

---

5 This is probably the prevailing opinion in American jurisdictions, especially in the American rural South and the West, where a competent, in-place police force is often a relatively recent event, and personal dispute settlement is a way of life. See *Brown v. United States*, 256 U.S. 335, 415 S. Ct. 501, 65 L.Ed. 961 (1921); *State v. Hiatt*, 187 Wash. 226, 60 P.2d 71 (1936).

quentialist schema, where it is a useful end worth pursuing in certain societies at certain times, but expendable when the situation demands (view w).

Among the other possibilities for resolving and arguing this case is a utilitarian position that D is liable, or view x. x is very close to w, sharing many values and conceptions, but it would diverge in the instant case because of a different way of seeing the general empirical circumstances. A holder of view x (as well as w, for that matter) might believe that in a civilized world—or an almost civilized world which aspires to civilization—the defense of personal honor does not justify the wounding or killing of another individual when safe retreat is open. [6]

Views v and w are convergent. Views w and x are consensual. These latter two share reasons. When their (w and x's) results agree, they can be said to have reached the same results, whereas v and w reached in the example coincidental results. Nothing stronger than convergence can be implied from consistent (shorter-term) coincidence of results. [7]

Given this distinction between consensus and convergence, we see how it is possible for third order propositions to vary widely. In fact, because judicial views are constructed as matters of individual choice, there is no fact-of-the-matter about the contents of these propositions and no right answer as to whether one or the other of them is properly included within the third order set. In terms of a meta-language, there is an indeterminate truth value for the statement p (where p stands for a propositional member of the third order judicial set). An appropriate label for this argument might be "judicial plural-

---

6   This is a favored position of many legal academics and some American jurisdictions.   See John Beale, "Retreat from Murderous Assault", 16 *Harv. L. Rev.* 567 (1903); *Restatement of the Law of Torts* Section 65 (1934); *State v. Cox*, 138 Me. 151, 23 A.2d 634 (1941); *Ford v. State*, 222 Ark. 16, 257 S.W.2d 30 (1953).

7   This argument is a rather more defensible illustration of the grand Humean slogan that constant conjunction does not imply causation. Taken at face value, one wonders what, for a Humean, does imply or could imply causation. See David Hume, *An Inquiry Concerning Human Understanding* (1748).

ism", for it suggests that there exists a number of co-equal third order views.

Judicial pluralism, as developed here, contends that no definitive test exists for what is the proper judicial view. Views are constructed from an individual's beliefs and attitudes through the use of his conception of judicial role. As individual preferences form a basis for the criteria for constructing a view, no objective standard relevant for judging the correctness of that criteria exists. However, views are conventionally constructed, as the criteria used may be more or less appropriate *vis-a-vis* the general expectations and practices of a given society. Moreover, the language of judicial discourse contains shared public concepts and embedded societal values which limit the scope of view construction. Social components—including education, family background, information networks, mores, folkways, workplace and neighborhood groupings, ties of organized religion, association networks, and class structure—shape individual views, and suggest how the relevant conventions will be constructed and whether they are likely to change. Failure to respect a social component as an indicator of a convention's formation might suggest irregularity, or even, in extreme cases, irrationality. If one's view is inappropriately constructed—employing deviant criteria—it nevertheless cannot be criticized on those grounds as incorrect. The fact that a view is just a matter of belief sets suggests that its status is conventional, and a conventional status, although subject to criticism on moral, political, or logical grounds, is not subject to truth functional analysis.[8]

In saying that judicial views are conventional and that the convention is rooted in individual choice, it must also be

---

8 Wittgenstein's maxim from the *Tractatus* that the limits of our language are the limits of our thought represents a strong theory of conceptual dependence on linguistic structure. Such a theory suggests that the way we think and reason is in large part a function of the language we use and our understanding of and ability to use it. Thus, widely deviant (or wild) interpretations of concepts or aberrant reasoning are likely to be an indication of either a failure to use language properly or the presence of a different language. See Ludwig Wittgenstein, *Tractatus Logico-Philosophicus* (1921, first English ed. 1922).

stressed that the choice is one which appeals to a public scheme. Judicial propositions are declarative of present judicial questions. An essential part of the judge's role is to settle disputes rationally. The dispute settlement—like the actions giving rise to the dispute—is a public matter. The community takes at least enough notice of the dispute to employ a judge to hear it. The judge, in turn, is expected to use some recognizable, available, knowable criteria for judgment. This is not a suggestion that laws must be in every way public in order to be law. Lon Fuller, in *The Morality of Law*, seems to suggest this when he says that the attempt to create and maintain a system of legal rules miscarries if there is "a failure to publicize, or at least to make available to the affected party, the rules he is expected to observe."[9]

The existence of public first order propositions is at times doubted in at least two common settings:[10] first, when, because of changing moral or political attitudes, potential parties to a case are subject to potentially harsher measures than they could have expected; second, and very much related, when there exists a number of views regarding a topic, and the approach any particular court will settle upon, or even temporarily employ, is in doubt. A good illustration of both occurred in

---

9 Lon Fuller, *The Morality of Law* 39 (rev. ed. 1969). Fuller appears at times to require a total failure (p. 39), while at others only a partial failure (pp. 152-186). A total failure—where no rules are ever known—seems empirically impossible. It is a serious defect in Fuller's theory that he does not make clear that failure proceeds along a continuum and that one is not faced with either no law or law, but the presence of a greater or lesser number of legal features. Fuller does not give the reader the theoretical equipment necessary to assess the (ubiquitous) possible intermediate cases. Moreover, there are undoubtedly intermediate cases, as is evident by the enormous and growing body of unreported case law, law at times available for all practical purposes only to judges who use it as controlling.

10 The suggestion that third order propositions are neither true nor false applies, of course, only to those propositions when they are in the third order set. Put in another context, they may well be susceptible of being true.

Henningsen v. Bloomfield Motors, Inc.,[11] a case which broadened the scope of strict liability in the products liability sales area by eliminating the barrier of express disclaimers in written contracts. In *Henningsen*, the injured wife of a consumer, who bought a car through an independent dealer, was able to sue the car's manufacturer for losses caused by manufacturing and design defects despite an express disclaimer in the contract governing the sale, which drastically limited liability. The defendant car manufacturer argued quite persuasively that, based on the holding of past judicial decisions, it did not imagine that it would be held remotely and strictly liable when it sold the faulty automobile. However, it might have noticed that there had been a several hundred year evolution toward greater liability which culminated in the instant case; that certain propositions of contract law and equity suggested that remote disclaimers, not seriously the object of real bargaining, should be (and had been) ill-treated by the courts; and that certain commentators had long believed liability would be invoked in such cases.[12] *Henningsen* epitomizes a whole category of cases which represents not only a major shift, but a shift long argued for and long in coming. The manufacturer may not have predicted the *Henningsen* case, but the backdrop of tort, contract and equity which motivated this kind of decision was known, even well known. When we spoke of a public set of criteria, we referred to a theoretically knowable set, one knowable at least in hindsight. The knowability goes toward the rationality of a view, not toward the selection as certain of any particular view.

That a view is conventional may be true, but it remains necessary to consider more fully just what being a convention entails. A useful starting point is the well accepted picture of a convention painted by David Lewis in his book *Convention: A Philosoph-*

---

11   32 N.J. 358, 161 A.2d 69 (1960). This case and its consequences are analyzed in Friedrich Kessler, "Products Liability", 76 *Yale L. J.* 887, 889 (1967).

12   Edward Levi, in *An Introduction to Legal Reasoning* (1949), discusses this evolution, pp. 6-19.

ical Study.[13] It is Lewis' explicit aim to analyze conventions with the hope of achieving a better understanding of specific problems in language, problems concerning analyticity, entailment, synonymy, and in general, the semantics of natural languages. He admits that language is only one conventional activity among many others,[14] but the examination of the semantics of natural languages is virtually his sole focus. Lewis' approach is typical for its focus and its perspicacity: the best treatments of convention are by those preoccupied with the vagaries and importance of language. Thus, in that Lewis' theory is here discussed primarily for its possible non-linguistic applications rather than its major focus, this attack is not against a strawman, but a giant in the only thriving populace. Moreover, as the theory Lewis advances is meant to be general, the fact that criticism wanders afield from his intended area is hardly unfair.

Lewis defines a convention as follows:

"A regularity R in the behavior of members of a population P when they are agents in a recurrent situation S is a *Convention* if and only if it is true that, and it is common knowledge in P that, in almost any instance of S among members of P,

(1) almost everyone conforms to R;

(2) almost everyone expects almost everyone else to conform to R;

(3) almost everyone has approximately the same preferences regarding all possible combinations of actions;

(4) almost everyone prefers that any one more conform to R, on condition that almost everyone conform to R;

(5) almost everyone would prefer that any one more conform to R', on condition that almost everyone conform to R', where R' is some possible regularity in the behavior of members of P in S, such that almost no one in almost

---

13 Published in 1969.

14 *Id.* at 3.

any instance of S among members of P could conform both to R′ and to R." [15]

Lewis' definition does not require agreement, although it allows that agreement is one of several possible methods for initiating a convention. [16] He sees a convention as a regularity in behavior which holds as though there did exist an agreement on how to behave or act. The regularity is maintained because of a preference among members of the population that there be conformity to the regularity.

Lewis' definition presents a number of difficulties:

1. The first difficulty is with understanding what is meant by population. Lewis himself never discusses just what is meant by the term, but from the examples he gives, "population" refers either to broad geographically proximate groups, or to groups which share a specific interest. He speaks of the set of individuals who are residents of towns, of countries, and of groups of countries. [17] He also includes examples of people who are fellow campers or canoeists and share certain immediate interests in safety and efficiency, of two men who need to see each other and must necessarily coordinate scheduling, and of a group of logicians needing to work out a common symbology. What is shared by this otherwise eclectic set of convention-makers is a certainty of criteria for inclusion within the group. There may be some vagueness about where to draw lines—Lewis' use of Welshmen is a good example of this, where Englishmen living in Wales, former Welshmen not now living in Wales, and mixed-parentage offspring with a Welsh ancestor all present borderline cases—but there is an identifiable core group with an ascertainable existence apart from association with the convention. For Lewis, members of a population belong both to some set with non-convention existence conditions for

---

15 *Id.* on p. 78. Lewis offers an equivalent quantified definition on pp. 78-79.

16 He discusses several others at pp. 85-88 of *Convention*.

17 See *Convention* at 43, 60 (town residents); 44, 49 (country residents); and 44 (country groupings).

membership and to a set of convention employers. If this were not true, his first condition of the definition "almost everyone conforms to R" would be absurd. Some members do not employ the convention and these people are identifiable.

There exists the small initial difficulty that in two person conventions, there is no room for everyone to conform. This objection is rendered trivial if Lewis decides to change the definition to "almost everyone or everyone." It would still leave, however, the difficulty of how one identifies a population apart from the convention if it has a membership of two. This appears to be an insolvable problem for very small populations and for populations which employ actually agreed upon conventions. If a group of one hundred card players attending a bridge tournament with several thousand participants specifically agrees to use a series of hand signals to indicate their bids, thereby lessening the possibility of giving illegal information through unintentional but recognizable voice inflections, how is one able to speak of a population identifiable apart from the convention-makers?

The reason that there is a problem with not knowing of a population apart from its convention-using behavior is that: if almost everyone or everyone is to conform (condition 1) and expects their fellow members of the population to conform (condition 2), it is necessary to know who everyone is. Where there is no actual agreement, one cannot know by seeing who signed the pact. Where there is actual agreement, it is easy to ascertain who the convention-makers are, but Lewis fails to specify how to determine the set of potential convention-users. He thus fails to offer criteria to tell when a practice rises to the level of a convention. Without these criteria, Lewis' definition suggests no more than people know that others perform/ behave/believe as their contemporaries at times do. This definition is thus too weak to allow us to individuate the concept of convention, or in other words, to separate conventions from other social regularities. Moreover, it does not allow a distinction between individuals getting the convention wrong and individuals choosing not to use (or to ignore) the convention. There is no room for a theory of mistake.

2. Lewis' third condition—"almost everyone has approximately the same preferences regarding all possible combinations of actions"—is unnecessarily restrictive. One does not need to believe in the rules to play the game. A good illustration would be the behavior of non-fascist judges who remained on the bench during the years Germany was ruled by the National Socialist Party. Suppose the population is the German bench (and possibly bar) and the regularity is the enforcement of Nazi rules in situations when these judges are sitting and such rules are applicable. The existence of a convention would be denied under Lewis' criteria if these judges are acting under coercion, and preferring to see their fellow judges (and Germans generally) disobey the Nazi regime. These judges' behavior is outwardly indistinguishable from that of Nazi judges, who endorse the rules they enforce. Given the fear so widespread during that time, perhaps there could be no way to discover the anti-fascist judges' true feelings. Under Lewis' third condition, two conventions are in force. A society could be envisioned in which thousands of conventions exist—based on the various degrees of alienation which judges feel toward a totalitarian political system.[18] The difficulty would only be the empirical one of figuring out just how many.

3. Lewis' difficulties with the third condition are compounded when one looks closely at his fourth condition: "almost everyone prefers that any one more conform to R, on condition that almost everyone conform to R." In that those anti-fascist judges secretly and silently cheered non-conformity by their judicial brethren, they were not employing any convention when deciding cases. Lest Lewis be allowed simply to respond that they were just not engaging in conventional behavior, and thus they were rightly excluded, a parallel example in language—an area he wants always to include as the paradigm case of conventional behavior—comes to mind. Suppose a group of young Welshmen are raised speaking only English. They are politically nationalistic and desire the complete and

---

18 Though totalitarian, this society could have certain attractive qualities—perhaps increased safety, a profitable economy, a low unemployment rate—which would allow for this spectrum of feeling to be held by the various judges.

eternal separation of their beloved Wales from imperial England. As part of their political program, they are promoting the resurgence of Welsh as a spoken language and intend, when they have the time, to learn to speak it themselves. They applaud those who do speak Welsh and experience self-loathing and loathing of their English-speaking peers for speaking English. In point of fact, though, the non-Welsh-speaking Welshmen are not speaking pure English, but a hybrid English-Celt language. Suppose this group (population) became a majority in Wales. These people would fall afoul of condition 4 and their language would not be conventional. While they may not care about English-Celt being spoken in, say, Southern Wales, (which they consider hopelessly Anglicized), they do not wish it spoken everywhere. They thus do not wish everyone to conform to regularity R. Besides contradicting Lewis' explicit statement to the contrary,[19] this illustration highlights that cases of reluctant agreement ought not to be excluded.

4.   Lewis' condition 2—"almost everyone expects almost everyone else to conform to R"—is also too restrictive. This condition asserts that within the relevant population, there is a general expectation of mutual compliance with the convention. Lewis formulated the condition in such a way as to allow for a "few abnormal agents" but not to tolerate "a convention to which most people want there to be exceptions, however few the exceptions they want."[20] These two worries, however, miss the real concern. A convention might exist which is in competition with another or several other conventions. Non-conformity is then not a matter of a few abnormal agents, but a large set of individuals promoting a competing view. Again, the concern is not with some population members wanting exceptions to their own convention, but with the convention of other individuals.

This idea of competing conventions is a difficulty for Lewis under either interpretation of what the proper domain of a population should be. If population is determined independently of convention usage, then there is no way of making

---

19   This is stated, among other places, in *Convention* at 203.

20   Both quotations are from *Convention* at 77.

sense of competing conventions. If in the case of language, for example, there is deviant usage, there would be no way of distinguishing dialect from idiolect. If population is tied to convention, then deviant usage would be symptomatic of a different activity. Competing dialects would constitute different languages.

Lewis' point of expecting conformity from others is empirically difficult to imagine. We have come to expect dialects in language, variations in many types of games, and certainly disagreement in judicial decision making. If one takes the convention of table manners—the proper way to eat, correct use of cutlery, restrictions on table discussions, the method of passing platters, appropriate dress, the subject matter of table talk—one might find a large set of people who would agree as to what good table manners ought to be. Few, however, would be surprised if many in that group failed to conform their behavior to this stated belief.[21]

These criticisms of Lewis' definition provide the basis for a better drawn idea of convention. The fundamental difference between Lewis' view and the one being suggested here lies in the area of conformity to convention. The view here is that often conventions compete. This would require a condition (one which might be latent in Lewis' definition) that individuals consider their own convention superior. They may do so for strongly held political, aesthetic, or ethical reasons; or for weakly held reasons of convenience or inertia. The latter would hold if there were some question about a minor rule change in a recreational game (a dispute, say, as to whether to use collegiate (NCAA) or professional (NBA) rules of dribbling and defense during playground basketball games), where factors such as past practice, greater familiarity with one method, or ease of putting one rule rather than the other into practice would be decisive.

We could thus reformulate Lewis' definition. This might be seen as stating that:

---

21 A convention would not necessarily be established under condition 5 if there existed any substantial split of opinion on the language issue within Wales.

A regularity R in the behavior of members of a population P when they are agents in a recurrent situation S is a Convention if and only if it is true that, and it is common knowledge in P that, in almost any instance of S among members of P,

(1) a significant group within P conforms to R;

(2) almost all members of P will conform to some regularity, and one or more groups will claim that the regularity they practice is superior. (Disagreement is thus possible about contenders for the designation of the best R);

(3) personal preferences in R are mediate: they are executed through R, such that if R did not exist, their practices might be different;

(4) a significant group prefers that any one more conform to R, either
   a) on condition that almost everyone conforms or ought to conform to R, or
   b) because that group has reason to conform to the preferences of another group that follows conjunct "a";

(5) a significant group would prefer that any one more conform to R', on condition that almost everyone conform to R', where R' is some possible regularity in the behavior of members of P in S, such that almost any instance of S among members of P could conform both to R' and to R.

Given this definition, let us turn to the convention of judicial reasoning to illustrate the description of conventions. It is evident that both judges and individuals addressing judicial problems hold different views about judicial questions.[22] They possess different values, beliefs, and backgrounds. These differences shape individual conceptions of the judicial role.

When put in situations where they are required to judge, they employ a convention based on this conception or role. They are aware of competing conventions which provide different

---

22 See Chapter VII for a lengthy empirical demonstration.

solutions to the common questions. When one tries to answer the questions a judge faces, one employs a convention. It is not necessary to know in advance how many individuals adhere to any given convention or even who is a member of which. Attorneys notoriously look for judges whom they feel are sympathetic to their view and, just as notoriously, are often mistaken in their estimate.

Moreover, as convention conformity is only randomly related to population percentage, a judicial convention can be unique to a single individual. The lack of need for total conformity allows for the logical possibility of what in fact occurs: a continuum of similar conventions, overlapping (sharing regularity) in their approach to certain situations. This involves no terminological difficulties because Lewis' second condition of the widespread expectation of general conformity is dropped, and his fourth condition of widespread preference is expanded. Judges do not expect universal agreement within the bench, but are accustomed to different schools of thought, each with their own approaches to and means of interpreting judicial questions.[23] Moreover, the very generality of certain basic terms of judicial discourse—including "sane", "reasonable", "due process", "negligent", and "knew or should have known"—serves to allow competing conventions to coexist within a society.

Lewis' definition focuses on behavior. He finds that conventions are instantiated by regularity of action. His is not a behaviorist model though, for he requires investigation of such mental processes as expectations and hypothetical preferences. We shall need to make the belief component slightly more explicit.

The regularity in judicial decision making is manifestly evident. Regular use of certain authorities (statutes and cases), regular court procedure, and regular patterns of notice of the empirical world (narrowly called "judicial notice" but more broadly using basic precepts of common language, reason and common sense in resolving cases) are commonplace. Judicial

---

23 Lewis does allow for degrees of convention (*Convention* at 76-80), but for him dissent undermines the existence of a convention. Here, it merely undermines the popularity of a convention.

regularities, however, are a matter of reason and justification. A judicial convention is constructed from shared preferences backed by shared attitudes and beliefs relevant to those regularities.[24] Because a set of attitudes and beliefs about a matter as broad as the set of judicial propositions is unlikely to be the same for any two persons, it might be thought questionable as to whether a judicial convention is really a convention. Even if some disparity between different individuals' patterns is allowed, is the degree of disparity too great to overcome? Does explicitly introducing beliefs destroy the idea of a convention?

Fortunately, this is a terminological difficulty only. It does not matter whether or not a judicial convention is in this restrictive sense truly a convention. What is important is that it otherwise behaves as a convention. Judges are not expected to impose directly their own preferences, but are assumed to have applied propositions drawn from the conventionalized construction of a judicial view. Moreover, the judicial view is dependent in part upon one's understanding of how judges have, in the past, operated. Thus, one who shares few particular preferences with most of a population subject to a particular judicial system will nevertheless be constrained to adapt his judicial view, *vis-a-vis* that system, to the preferences of that society. Empirical regularities of themselves count in constructing a judicial view. This allows us, for example, to construct a view of Roman Law during the time of Gaius, although one may

---

24   The meaning of the terms "beliefs" and "attitudes" should be taken to be the ones common in philosophy of mind, and borrowed more directly from Roger Scruton. Paraphrasing only slightly from Scruton, we can say that if the statement s expresses a belief, then the rules governing the use of the expressions must refer to the truth conditions of this belief. Their being answerable to truth conditions, and identified by reference to these conditions, is what distinguishes beliefs from all other mental states. It follows that, if statements of the form s express beliefs, then there will be criteria for their truth. On the other hand, if statements of this form express attitudes, there will be no such criteria; such statements will answer only to necessary conditions, conditions governing the kind of thing to which they are applied. Scruton's usage is the one adopted here. See Roger Scruton, "Attitudes, Beliefs, and Reasons" in *Morality and Moral Reasoning* 25, 54-55 (ed. John Casey 1971).

share few Roman values, and fewer Roman political or social beliefs.

It is crucial to remember that employed beliefs and attitudes are derivative: they depend on a conception of role. The difference between the derivative and the direct can be seen when a judge reaches a result in a case which is inconsistent with the way he would have resolved the difficulty if he were not a judge. For example, the Massachusetts legislature enacted a firearm possession act which required without exception the imposition of a one year prison term on anyone found carrying an unlicensed firearm within the commonwealth. Judge K, appalled by this piece of legislation, believes that at least in the case of persons without a previous conviction, the penalty is at minimum twelve-fold too stiff. She subsequently sits on a criminal court and finds herself required to sentence defendants found guilty of illegal possession of firearms. K believes it is the role of the judge to provide the sentence the legislature requires in criminal cases. Her derivative belief conflicts with her direct ethical and political beliefs.

The fact that K's derivative belief and direct belief do not immediately square does not imply any ultimate inconsistency. If K believes that a duty to conform to a legislative act is more important than personal beliefs about criminal sentencing, she can square the apparent conflict. But it should not automatically be assumed that K has in fact squared the conflict just by the fact of having made a ruling. This assumption might arise because the fact that K did make a decision is seen as indicative of some rational weighing of the competing choices. This weighing involves the evaluation of all relevant judicial propositions and an ordering of those propositions according to importance. This assumption is faulty. There is no logical guarantee that one's choices are consistent with one another. Choice inconsistency is not necessarily a matter of irrationality, where one makes decisions manifestly at odds with other decisions. It is more likely to be a matter of a failure to work out a completely consistent plan in advance. Given the range of possible questions which a court might be called upon to address, it would be unreasonable to expect very many individuals to have a thorough and complete set of answers to them all.

As answers are then provided on either an *ad hoc* or partial set (of answers) basis, inconsistencies can be expected.

The example of Judge K raises the final problem to be discussed in this section: the status of the third order view. We said that the view is constructed, and constructed according to convention. The third order propositions assembled are valid according to the convention, not absolutely. That is, the propositional set is dependent on role, not on general considerations (as seen with Judge K). But are conventions themselves somehow true or false, or logically right or wrong?

From the very name of the theory propounded here—pluralism—it is apparent that those questions must be answered no. Pluralism states that there are a number of different views and in that they are not self-contradictory, they are all equal with respect to any question of truth or validity. Third order propositions do not necessarily have a truth value in a two valued logic,[25] and may have an indeterminate truth value in a three valued logic.

Conventions are commonly taken to be arbitrary: that is, their features are not necessary ones. There is a possible argument that judicial conventions, or more exactly the set of third order propositions of any particular convention, are susceptible of being objectively true or false. The argument is this. The judicial decision making role is a precise one. Not just any description of it will do. A proper characterization of the role is available based on a proper understanding of political morality and a knowledge of the political workings of the society. A variation of this idea would tie judicial role-characterization to what the prevailing opinion among some relevant group—government officials, the bench, the bench and bar,

---

25 Depending on one's approach to the problem of the excluded-middle, there may have to be a "false" value for third order propositions in certain logical systems. This would present difficulties with negation which are beyond the scope of this work. One possible line of analysis for handling three order judicial logic would be to put it in a modal logic (possible-worlds) form, such as the one developed by David Lewis in *Counterfactuals* (1973). For a thorough discussion of the parameters and limitations of a two valued logic, see Crispin Wright, *Wittgenstein on the Foundations of Mathematics* (1980).

educated individuals, all citizens of the society—is. These two positions might be called the objective moral position and the popular moral position.

There are a number of difficulties with the objective moral position. It assumes at the outset that there is an objective moral realm, a position recently under severe attack.[26] It assumes further that there is an objective public morality, a morality that is capable of judging, in particular, governmental acts and the public acts of individuals. Public morality is a more complicated matter than personal morality,[27] and one where the widespread controversies undermine confidence that commonly accepted tenets of the type found in private morality will be found. But even if an objective morality is conceded, such a position confuses idealistic conceptions of role with ones actually held. If some measure existed by which to judge role, and an entire society—because of ignorance, malevolence, or plain contrariness—decides on a different measure, then if it is to be considered as being wrong, there will be a convention which is followed by no individuals and a non-convention which reflects a widespread regularity in behavior, with shared beliefs and mutual (successful) expectations in a discrete population. This flatly contradicts the meaning of a convention.

The popular moral position aims to avoid this dilemma by basing the measure of what a role should be on prevailing opinion. However, choosing the correct group for the standard of judgment is a difficult matter. The example of language is

---

26 A skeptical or relativist position is put forward in J. L. Mackie, *Ethics: Inventing Right and Wrong* 15-49 (1977); Gilbert Harman, "Moral Relativism Defended", 84 *Philosophical Review* 19 (1975); Bernard Williams, *Problems of the Self* 166-204 (1973); and in Simon Blackburn, "Moral Realism" in *Morality and Moral Reasoning* 101 (ed. John Casey 1971). These works and others make clear that ethical objectivity is not a self-evident position, but one open to severe doubt, at the least.

27 My reasons for this follow Stuart Hampshire's. They include greater consequences of action, the need to understand a greater number of interests, and the necessary use of force and even violence in certain recurring situations. See Hampshire, "Morality and Pessimism" and "Public and Private Morality" in *Public and Private Morality* (ed. Stuart Hampshire 1978).

instructive here. Controversy is commonplace on the issue of whether general usage or educated usage should determine which words are acceptable to a good language user. Lexicographers need to make a decision, and are often faced with a choice between using obsolete criteria and using mediocre criteria.[28] The dispute is reducible to a debate between seeing ordinary language usage as central and seeing good language usage as central, but the dispute is reducible no further. The same kind of dilemma exists in settling what group should determine the proper conception of role. No method seems available for final settlement of the controversy.

There is a further difficulty for the advocate of the popular moral position. There is no reason why any normative consequences should flow from the fact of majority opinion. Merely because most people believe in a certain role for judges, it does not follow that they are right or should be followed. This type of move would be from "is" to "ought" and within the naturalistic fallacy, even if the backdrop of convention were not involved. Moreover, as convention is rooted in regularity, the availability of conflicting conventions based on competing regularities among different sub-populations renders any claim of exclusivity independently invalid.

If any particular set of third order propositions is not susceptible to a test of correctness, are judicial views unable to be crit-

---

28 For example, the leading American unabridged dictionary attempted to update its contents so as to stay abreast of current American language usage. One response from a legal organization exemplifies the wide disparity in standards in the area, as it was willing to advocate continued use of the obviously inadequate, older dictionary instead of the new edition with its faults:

> "The editors are unable to recommend that the Third Edition *Merriam-Webster New International Dictionary* replace the Second Edition as a general authority for definition and italicization. The New Edition fails to distinguish those foreign words which would be italicized in English writing, and is in general insufficiently prescriptive. Continued reliance on the Second Edition is recommended."

A Uniform System of Citation ii (eds. *Harvard Law Review, Columbia Law Journal,* eleventh ed. 1967).

icized? Is each individual's judicial view just a fact about the world, and entitled to equal respect with all other views? The answer is clearly no. Views may be criticized as irrational, immoral, impolitic, cumbersome, unworkable, imprudent, too complicated, too ethereal, contradictory, inelegant, and even irrelevant. Certain apparent areas—logic, ethics, politics, aesthetics, sociology—serve as ways to judge judicial views. One reason that the practice exists of allowing minority or dissenting opinions to be published with the majority opinion is a recognition that even though these opinions have no standing (that is, no standing in American jurisdictions, a limited standing in English jurisdictions) as legal authority, they reflect an alternate view which may be ethically, logically, politically, aesthetically, or sociologically superior. Such superiority is not a function of majority approval, and this fact is widely recognized.

There is a final point which we shall return to later.[29] It might be thought that because third order propositions reflect beliefs, and are commonly stated as assertions, the speakers of these statements believe them to be right. Incorporated into the judicial convention is this "someone-must-be-right" component. The adversary system where a single answer must be and is reached reflects this component, as does ordinary language talk of legal facts-of-the-matter. This includes, for example, seeing contracts as either valid or invalid, evidence as either being admissable or inadmissable, commercial paper as negotiable or not, and real covenants as either having been created or not.

While the language in these types of statements is somewhat misleading—as the propositional form that yields statements is common to very different types of assertions—there is an underlying point. Individuals engage in argument about third order propositions, and the argument often focuses on which of two contradictory propositional sets is right. However, such an argument, in fact, mistakes a desire for conformity with a belief in correctness. If X holds a certain view, he may well be eager to have others endorse that view. He may want others to

---

29 See Chapter VI.

conform their views to his. When they do not, he will criticize these individuals and attempt to undermine their position, with reasons where possible. The attempt he makes is in part polemical. He succeeds not by some proof that his view is right. He succeeds when others agree, when they conform to his position. The advocacy system in courtrooms is best seen this way. Attorneys seek to convince, and when they convince they stop, whether or not there are additional points which might theoretically be relevant, and certainly whether or not the best reasons have been put forward. Attorneys do not act as scientists or scholars. They do not seek all evidence which would bear on a problem and present it, even if it is contrary to their cause. This desire for conformity rather than truth runs throughout the whole fabric of judicial reasoning. Whatever the psychological process, where a need for approval arises which must be cured through the endorsement of one's idea by others, it provides enough passion to allow for third order argument.

The Logic of Judicial Propositions

We began this chapter by stating that although third order propositions are devoid of truth value, such is not the case for first and second order propositions. They can be tagged as being "true" or "false", and are so in lieu of the commitments made on the third order. This is easily seen. Third order propositions need to have as much validity as any set of postulates. Their status, however, does not affect theorems or lower order propositions which flow (follow) from them.

A sharp distinction needs to be drawn between lower order propositional validity within a view and the relative validity between two or more competing views. There may be an incongruence of sets of propositions between two or more conventions with no way to settle which set is right. Within a convention, however, the result is determinable and no inconsistency is necessary. This process is analogous to systems based on different sets of postulates in mathematics. For example, if one uses the Lobachevskian postulate in place of Euclid's fifth postulate in constructing a geometry—that is, rejecting the postulate that one and only one line parallel to a given line can be drawn through a fixed point external to the line, and allowing more than one parallel line through the fixed point—one can develop a system as self-consistent as the Greek's. A theorem in the Russian system, however, is no more true outside the postulated geometry than one in the Greek system.

Views were first introduced to explain how actual individuals formulate answers to judicial questions. An ambiguity has seemingly arisen, for "view" is not only used here as reflecting an empirical reality, but as a logical construct for yielding answers to all possible questions. Judges (and others) have views, while views denote a reasoning structure for solving problems.

The reason that these two aspects of "view" do not seem coterminous is because the views judges actually have tend to be incomplete, fragmented, vague, and even contradictory constructs. As such, they appear inadequate for generating a self-consistent, let alone complete, set of lower order propositions. But if we take a closer look at the nature of the inadequacies of actual views, we shall see that inelegant as they are, they commit their holder to consequences which they may not foresee or even be able to articulate.

Actual views suffer three kinds of infirmity. The first is that of incompleteness. Those considering judicial problems, often judges and lawyers, are not required to be general social or legal theorists. They do not need to possess answers to every possible question before being allowed to respond to limited and immediate questions. They are instead called upon to do just the opposite: give responses to the ongoing series of questions which they face. When a question arises not previously considered—a common occurrence in modern societies where increasing social complexity makes for an endless stream of new judicial problems—it is often without any immediate answer, or seemingly without a method of determining an answer. One situation where answers are thought to run out is the so-called *sui generis* case. The *sui generis* case, one intuitively thought to present a new or unique question, occurs when resort to third order propositions does not readily yield a first order answer.

(Readiness here is a sliding concept, making the *sui generis* case one of degree.)

Incompleteness is routinely ascribed in those situations when a novel claim for relief is presented: the first instance of a suit to remedy a wrong not previously remedied in the courts. For example, in *Wilkinson v. Downton*,[30] the victim of a perverse practical joke sued the joker for intentional infliction of severe and extreme emotional distress. The practical joker told a woman that her husband had been severely injured in an accident which left him with two shattered legs. She was to come to the accident scene with two pillows to bring him home. The shock of this false report caused the woman serious and permanent physical consequences and temporarily altered her reasoning. The only relevant prior cases appeared to be assault cases, which allowed for recovery for emotional distress where the distress was incidental to physical contact or the apprehension of physical contact. If, absent the physical contact, there was no precedent for recovery, neither were there any cases involving such extremely egregious behavior. The existence of such behavior had itself been considered a basis to impose liability in certain public carrier cases,[31] although it had never been extended to ordinary cases. *Wilkinson* thus presented a problem for those whose view allowed assault-type recovery, but denied ordinary insult and indignity recovery. They had not formulated concepts sufficiently rich and complete to include the *Wilkinson* case. Their view was incomplete. In the actual decision, it is evident by the court's tone and shocked reaction that this type of situation was one not previously contemplated or foreseen, and was beyond the court's existing judicial view. In allowing recovery by the aggrieved wife, the court self-consciously worked to complete an incomplete view.

If the *sui generis* case exemplifies the problem of incompleteness, it is not coincidental with it. Views are constructed

---

30 2 Q.B.D. 57 (1897).

31 This occurred first in a contract cause of action with *Chamberlain v. Chandler*, 3 Mason 242, 5 Fed. Cas. No. 2575 (C.C. Mass. 1823); and then in tort with *Cole v. Atlanta and W.P.R. Co.*, 102 Ga. 474, 31 S.E. 107 (1897) and *Boody v. Goddard*, 57 Me. 602 (1868).

from a number of areas. These areas are themselves difficult and complex. Thus, although the areas are the building blocks of judicial views, they are unlikely to be the product of consistent and developed thought. Judicial views have a doubly inchoate quality: neither the views nor the basis for those views should be expected to be entirely cohesive, coherent, consistent and complete.

Thus, even in ordinary cases, one facing a first order judicial question may find that the third order set runs out. He may find that he makes decisions without being able very adequately to justify or defend them (they are intuitive rather than reasoned). Legal fictions or technicalities may be employed to bolster a position. This occurred with many courts in the early emotional distress cases, finding contract liability where there was no contract,[32] and technical assault,[33] battery,[34] or false imprisonment[35] through a convoluted reasoning process not ordinarily used, or ever used with great confidence.

A judge's difficulty sometimes involves a conflict between competing third order propositions. Individuals often hold conflicting beliefs. This is sometimes manifested in strictly conflicting propositions, such as where part of the view yields p and another part -p. This can be due to belief uncertainty, cognitive dissonance, or inadequate consideration of the consequences of one's commitments. When cases are retrospectively "confined or limited to the facts" there is an explicit recognition of this. For example, in *Grain Dealers National Fire Insurance Co. v. Union Co.*,[36] one court stated that:

---

32 See *Texas and Pac. R. Co. v. Jones*, 39 S.W. 124 (Tex. Civ. App. 1897); *Moody v. Kenny*, 153 La. 1007, 97 So. 21 (1923) (involved a yet-to-be-registered hotel guest where recovery was based on a contract not yet agreed to and without consideration passing).

33 See *Atlanta Hub Co. v. Jones*, 47 Ga. App. 778, 171 S.E. 470 (1933); *Kurpgeweit v. Kirby*, 88 Neb. 72, 129 N.W. 177 (1910); *Leach v. Leach*, 11 Tex. Civ. App. 699, 33 S.W. 703 (1895).

34 See *De May v. Roberts*, 46 Mich. 160, 9 N.W. 146 (1881).

35 See *Salisbury v. Paulson*, 51 Utah 552, 172 P. 315 (1918).

36 159 Ohio St. 124, 111 N.E.2d 256, 261 (1953).

> Some of the members of this court are of the opinion that if the exact facts of the *Pickering* case should again come before the court the judgment therein shall be re-examined, but we are of the opinion that that judgment must be confined to those facts.

Were it not for the need to reconcile one's judicial views, such a statement would be no more than an unjustified, illogical, irrational, and embarassing confession.

More often, contradiction is avoided by alteration of one's view. Third order principles are formulated so incompletely or vaguely that by the time the contradiction is apparent—made so, for instance, by a difficult case—it can be avoided by lightly changing the view without seeming to do so. Take, for example, *Riggs v. Palmer*,[37] the case of the impatient legatee who murdered his testator in order to gain his legacy more quickly, mentioned in the previous chapter. Suppose that prior to hearing the case to strip him of the legacy, or even being apprised of the facts of the particular situation, an individual or judge believed both that "a will is binding when it disposes of an estate of a testator in conformity with law" (p), and that "no man should profit from his own inequities or take advantage of his own criminal wrong" (q). Here, p and q lead to contrary results if taken as broadly as stated, at least in a *Riggs v. Palmer* situation. Yet the actual court in *Riggs* did what individuals constantly do: it redefined either p or q or both so that "p.q" becomes true. But in all other ways p and q are unchanged. (This could be accomplished, for example, by letting p=s, where s is some set $\langle s_i \rangle$ with members s_0, s_1, $s_2...s_i$. Then if "s.q" is false, a new set $\langle s_i' \rangle$ is constructed with members s_0, $s_2...s_i$ which excludes $s_1.s_i'=p'$, and the *Riggs* court endorses p' instead of p). The original p and q did conflict, but it is likely that there was no one who realized they conflicted.

The third empirical view inadequacy is also evidenced by *Riggs*. It is vagueness. A principle is vague if there are cases in which it is in theory indeterminate whether the principle applies. Of course, such philosophers as W.V.O. Quine have

---

37   115 N.Y. 506, 22 N.E. 188 (1889).

argued that there is an indeterminancy in all language, [38] but the vagueness here is of the type reducible (if not, according to a Quinean, eliminatable) by simply further specifying which cases fall under the principle.[39] This is just what the court did in

---

38 Argued for by Willard Van Orman Quine in *Word and Object* (1960).

39 Joseph Raz in *The Authority of Law: Essays on Law and Morality* 52-57 (1979) speaks of an indeterminacy which cannot be closed in judicial statements. As I understand it, this indeterminacy occurs either because of the vagueness of terms (the Quinean reason) or because of what he calls closure rules—rules which settle cases which fall into the gap between the reach of neighboring rules—are inapplicable. If one agrees with the theory of meaning which argues that a certain amount of vagueness in language is inevitable and irreducible, then Raz and Quine are right, but only in a trivial way. The terms can be given truth conditions for proper usage which come as close as we would want.

The second reason for indeterminacy is due to an incompleteness of second order propositions. While this is a theoretically possible occurrence, it is not a likely empirical one. It requires a third level which neglects the problem, that is without relevant overdetermination, and that lacks a decision-rendering proposition (see below). Raz's example examines a statute requiring "ship-owners to Φ." Subsequent to the enactment, a new vessel is built that is not clearly a ship. Raz says of this vessel that "it is neither true nor false that the legislator intended the obligation to apply to the owners of such vessels" (p. 72n). Raz is using an extremely restricted notion of "intention" here. Legislators *qua* legislators cannot be said to have intentions in the same way as they do outside their role. As legislators, they are part of a corporate unit. When they act, it is unreasonable to assume that the same component of foreseeability commonplace in ordinary intentionality ought to apply. When I say "x should Φ" it is fair to assume that I have some idea of what x is. If a new kind of x should be encountered, then it is certainly proper to say that I had no intention concerning whether this new x should Φ. But that is hardly the case with a group of legislators. They can be expected to know that new cases will arise, and that these new cases will have to be settled. To say, as Raz does, that there is a necessary indeterminacy if a new fact situation (outside the purview of the statutory language) arises, is to limit intention by foreseeability. This does not allow that a legislator might intend for reasonable adjudication of disputes under the statute through judicial interpretation and extension of the statutory language. Raz thus claims that indeterminacy occurs when a legislative intention is to limit intention with foreseeability, and not to allow for intending for reasonable settlement through the judiciary later.

Riggs, where p and q were originally vague, but, after the case, made less so. The tendency to think hard about the specific case in hand while hedging one's bets on future cases—because the facts of the future are unconsidered and potentially difficult—is encouraged in judicial systems. It is also a tendency which is well-handled by employing vague third order propositions. It might be argued that *Riggs* did not change the deciding court's view, that *Riggs* merely forced the court to reason toward an answer inherent in the prior view. This misunderstands what vagueness implies. If an object's vagueness is removed through specification of the cases under that object, then the object's meaning has changed. It thus cannot be said that the *Riggs* Court merely applied p and q and worked out the consequences. In working out the consequences, the court altered p and q.

If actually held views are faulty when judged by a standard of logical completeness, consistency, and precision, how can it be claimed that the set of third order propositions yields a unique and consistent set of answers to lower order questions? The logical answer is that these are limitations on a view's scope, but they do not affect the fact of truth value being ascribable to lower order propositions. Where a view is too vague or incomplete, it fails to provide answers.

The degree to which a view provides answers can be called its determination level. If a third order proposition yields a lower order proposition, it can be said to determine that proposition. Similarly, if a set of third order propositions yields a set of lower order propositions, it determines that set. Underdetermination occurs when the third order propositions are not suffi-

---

But even if Raz is correct that intention can fail this easily, indeterminacy would occur only if the third level proposition underdetermined the second order issue. Here, the proposition underdetermined the second order issue. The third level would have to allow a restricted use of intention, and no other way to settle the case of whether the new vessel should Φ. Raz might argue that *vis-a-vis* one's third order subset of propositions on intentionality, there might be indeterminacy, even if one's whole view would settle the matter. But this is not to argue for any necessary vagueness in the view, only necessary vagueness in terms, as discussed above. A more thorough look at several of Raz's assumptions on judicial reasoning is attempted in Chapter V.

cient to give definition to some set of lower order propositions. Overdetermination occurs when different third order propositions each are sufficient to yield a single lower order proposition.[40] An illustration here would be useful.

Let us suppose that P agreed to loan D a small sum of money in local currency in return for a much larger sum to be paid back later in a foreign currency. D agreed to the bargain because she was in desperate need of local funds to assist her escape to freedom in a foreign country.[41] D fails to repay and P brings suit. If the only first order question raised by the case is whether or not D should be forced to repay the loan, it would be easy to imagine a judicial view which overdetermined the outcome of *P v. D*. If on-point precedents had occurred, one third order proposition might state that such precedents should determine relevant cases (*viz.- P v. D*). If equity considerations were found in third level propositions, they too might suggest that one who makes a promise ought to keep it. Again, if considerations such as protecting and encouraging commercial transactions, ensuring the freedom of individuals to bargain, and limiting judicial interference in regard to the fairness of the terms of otherwise unexceptionable contracts all were represented in third order propositions, then *P v. D* would be determinable from five different higher order propositions. It would, in short, be overdetermined.

P v. D as given is a simple case, and overdetermination, being in part a function of the complexity of first order questions, is unsurprising. Suppose, however, that D introduced the defense of usury. She claimed that the amount to be repaid was so much larger than the amount borrowed, when either currency was converted, that the contract ought not to be enforced as made. Suppose also that usury is a recognized defense to certain contract claims, and that each of the third order propo-

---

40 The idea of determination is borrowed from philosophy of language. The senses of most words are both under and overdetermined with certain consequences for a theory of meaning. See Michael Dummett, *Frege: Philosophy of Language* 585-627 (1973).

41 The facts, although not the issues, are essentially those of *Batsakis v. Demotsis*, 226 S.W.2d 673 (Tex. Civ. App. 1949).

sitions stated—those concerning precedent, equity, commercial enterprise, bargaining freedom, and judicial interference—was limited in its application to non-usurious situations. Usury was a concept, though, which in the past had been held to apply only to same currency transactions. If no other third order propositions would be relevant, then the answer to *P v. D* is underdetermined. That is, the third order propositions, while circumscribing the limits of the first order answer, are insufficient to shape it fully.

Finally, if the five original third order propositions are not specifically held to apply only to non-usurious situations, then we may have an example of overdetermination resulting in inconsistency. Until *P v. D*, such a set of propositions might have been thought to be consistent as stated. However, conflict can be imagined if propositions ensuring respect for precedent, and promotion of commercial transactions and contractual enterprise, are seen to be at odds with propositions guaranteeing judicial equity and the promotion of fair contractual dealing. In finding that one's view is faulty because of overdetermination, one would, if desiring to maintain a rational and consistent view, be required to alter the third order propositional set.

Those uninitiated or ignorant in judicial reasoning are likely to have an impoverished judicial view. Virtually every lower order answer will be underdetermined. Enriched judicial views are laden with overdetermination. A view is enriched to the degree that the propositions in it are fertile with consequences. The judicial systems of modern, western societies, with their abundant judicial tradition and their sophisticated social and moral theories, tend to generate enriched judicial views among their populace.

One can view legal history as a movement from underdetermination to overdetermination.[42]   Initially, judicial role is

---

42 The process stops, or is at least sidetracked, when there occurs serious socially or politically rooted disruption to the legal order. Given the deep-seated cultural and social bonds which tie communities and states, judicial views are rather slower to change than political institutions. For this reason, what may to contemporary observers look like a major upheaval in a judicial system due to a political revolution is often judged a minor diversion in retrospect. Both the American and the English Civil

uncertain, and the criteria for formulating lower order propositions are extremely vague. As a tradition of dispute resolution
develops, a concomitant increasing sophistication takes place in
incorporating social and ethical ideas into one's judicial view.
The move toward overdetermination can easily be wrongly
interpreted as merely a movement toward determination,
toward the closing of choices for selection in the third order set.
But subsets of third order propositions change independently
and unevenly. English Tudor common law saw increasing
sophistication in trust and property law at a time when tort,
procedure, and contract remained primitive. Under Lord
Mansfield, contract law, commercial paper and restitution were
areas which in a few years moved from being impoverished to
being enriched.

Part of an enriched view is a decision-rendering proposition.
The legal laity in sophisticated legal systems, and any individual
in primitive systems, might possibly exclude a decision-
rendering proposition (DRP) from their view. The former may
defer to the bench and bar while the latter to some deity, fate,
or private dispute resolution. Not having a DRP means a view
can allow questions to go unresolved. Any particular DRP may
have a greater or lesser scope over the domain of conflicts.

We can now tie view as empirically held by individuals to view
as logical construct. An individual's view is usually found to be
either under or overdetermined.[43] If it is underdetermined, it
will fail to accomplish what the construct will do. But this is the
case only in elementary systems or among the legal laity. An
overdetermined view will allow for a self-consistent set of lower
order propositions, and if it contains a DRP, a complete set.
But in formulating these lower order propositions it will
change. It will not be the same view. It will become more like

---

Wars, with their dramatic consequences for governmental institutions
and political process, failed to make a similar imprint on judicial institutions or judicial views.

43 One can develop, of course, a precisely and exactly determined view.
This logical possibility is a remote empirical one. The system of
Dworkin's Herculean judge perhaps would qualify, but it is likely that
even he is employing overdetermined principles to reason his way to a
result. See Ronald Dworkin, *Taking Rights Seriously*, Chapter IV (1977).

the view it should be, if we assume a normative principle which demands full logical consistency to be introduced. This "should" comes to this. A third order set of propositions yields an analogue for reaching lower order propositions. When that analogue is a result of overdetermination, then application of the analogue will give a new view and thus a new analogue. Schematically, this means $View_{overdetermined} \rightarrow$ Analogue $\rightarrow$ $View_o \rightarrow Analogue_o$.

An example allows us to see just how this process works. Let us begin by looking at the case of *R. v. Dwyer*.[44] In that case, the Motor Trade Association (MTA) was empowered to put on a stop list those automobile vendors who sold cars at other than a fixed price. One vendor, Read, not a member of the association, had discounted on price and was told by an officer of the MTA, Dwyer, either to contribute £250 to an indemnity fund of the MTA or face publication as a price violator. Read refused; the MTA published his name; and Dwyer was charged under the Larceny Act with essentially committing blackmail.[45] He was convicted and lost on appeal.

There are a number of interesting points of statutory interpretation and precedent concerning the case, but it is not these which are important here.[46] The case can be seen as one where ordinary notions about contract and crime conflict. The contract notion is this. Parties ought to be able to bargain freely. Where a *quid pro quo* is offered, it should be left to the offeree to accept or reject it. If what the offeror is offering is a thing he has a right to do or have, it is all the more certain that

---

44   2 K.B. 258 (1926).

45   THE LARCENY ACT. 1916, contains the following relevant provision:

> "29. Every person who—(1) utters, knowing the contents thereof, any letter or writing demanding of any person who menaces, and without any reasonable or probable cause, any property or valuable thing; . . . shall be guilty of felony, and on conviction thereof liable to penal servitude for life."

46   They are discussed in an admirable technical manner by A. L. Goodhart in "Blackmail and Consideration in Contracts", 44 *Law Q. Rev.* 436 (1928), reprinted in A. L. Goodhart, *Essays in Jurisprudence and the Common Law* 175 (1931).

the thing furnishes good consideration.[47] The criminal notion is this: where parties do not stand in any personal relationship, one party should not be able to threaten the other with some odious act for the purpose of extracting money. Threats to reveal publicly some act of the offeree, in order to shame, ridicule, or cause his arrest, are to be discouraged.

Let us go one step beyond the facts of *R. v. Dwyer.* Assume that Read agreed to make the payment and Dwyer left his name off the publication list. Read then refused to pay and Dwyer sued for breach of contract.

A judge may approach this case (in at least) three different ways. In the terminology of the common law courts, one might see the problem as one of criminal law, contract law, or procedure. If one approaches *Dwyer v. Read* from a criminal-law perspective, one would be using certain third order propositions involving protection of individuals from threat and coercion. These propositions would be related to a wider set of propositions which express beliefs and attitudes about public safety, the role of the police, intentionality and motive, and justifications for anti-social acts. This subset of the judicial view relevant to criminal matters involves a complex maze of psychological, social, political and moral concepts. If an individual had no ready answer to *Dwyer v. Read*, this subset could provide an answer.

The first approach would label the agreement criminal and thus unenforceable, giving the answer p as the holding of the case.[48]

A second, contract approach would involve areas of consideration, consent, duress, and unconscionability. The third order view embodies beliefs about marketplace economics, transactional freedom, and the place of contract in a modern society. The contract subset within the third order could give an answer to *Dwyer v. Read* of q. A third approach, based on procedural

---

47 This position was stated by Lord Justice Scrutton in *Hardie and Lane v. Chilton* 2 K.B. 306, 319 (1928) during a discussion where he criticized *R. v. Dwyer.*

48 The view could also lead to -p, depending on the third order propositions.

beliefs, would act in the same way. The main question could be
the effect of *R. v. Dwyer* on *Dwyer v. Read*. Issues of the relevancy and admissibility of the criminal finding in *R. v. Dwyer* on
the civil suit would arise. Again, a finding of r could follow
from the third order procedural type beliefs about procedural
fairness, institutional morality and credibility, and even matters
of double jeopardy for the same act. Also to be considered
would be beliefs about equity and the practice of allowing
parties who share the blame for their own injury, those the
equity court considers having "dirty hands", to ask for the aid of
the court.[49]

Each of these three subsets of the third order set—labeled
here the criminal, the contractual, and the procedural[50]—is sufficient to resolve *Dwyer v. Read*. The proposition which answers
the question as to whether Read entered into a valid contract
with Dwyer is overdetermined. If $p = q = r$, then this overdetermination has no effect on the view. If $p \neq q$ and $q \neq r$ and $p
\neq r$, then the compatibility that there may have been earlier,
ends, (or to use Dummett's phrase, falls apart[51]). When "$p = q
= r$" is not true, then in order to solve the case, a new view must
come about. Such an occurrence is common when view subsets
have the sweep of the type seen above. When discussion of a
contractual matter involves beliefs regarding the concepts of
freedom, safety, and fairness—concepts at once broad and
difficult—overdetermination should not be surprising. Each
subset yields its own analogue or method for settling questions
which fall under its scope. When overdetermination is present
and analogues yield different results, the subsets must cut back
on that scope to avoid contradiction.

It might be objected that this is an improper description, that
if $q = -p$, then one cannot hold p and q at the same time. One

---

49 We may assume a full merger of law and equity in contract suits at the
time of the case.

50 It is not essential or even necessarily practical to divide the third set
according to legal subject headings. Discrete groupings of actual view
subsets are likely to be organized on a much smaller scale, and certainly
in a vaguer manner.

51 Michael Dummett, *Frege: Philosophy of Language* 624 (1973).

discovers that the breadth of one's sub-views through the testing procedure inherent in solving cases is often unforeseen.[52] When it is discovered that $q = r$, *Dwyer v. Read* does not change an individual's view: it merely helps him discover what his view truly (correctly) is.

This objection is misconceived. Suppose a third order set at time T_1. Two futures are possible after T_1. *Dwyer v. Read* might occur at T_2 or some case might arise where the contract sub-view is in conflict with, say, a property sub-view. If this second case arises after T_1, but before T_2, the results of *Dwyer v. Read* could well be different. The resolution of the prior case will cause adjustment due to overdetermination. Vagueness will be alleviated and an analogue will result. The determination of this case will create sub-views different from those which would have existed at T_2 if the intermediate case had not preceded *Read*. Individuals' actual views are not written down for ready use. They are mental entities, and a variation in the temporal case scenario will cause a difference in views.

The picture presented here is not meant to play fast-and-loose with the concept of identity. It merely attempts to show how the third order set at T_1 becomes the third order set at T_2. It has two interesting consequences. First, it does answer the question as to whether lower order propositions can be considered true or false. They can be so considered. Their truth value is a function of third order propositions. However, because the third order set is susceptible to constant evolution, any enumeration of the set of lower order statements at some given time is not of much interest. The second consequence is that it shows one way that judicial views change over time. The intuitive picture that familiar concepts continue to yield new results has been shown to be more-or-less accurate when analyzed through the construction of judicial views.

Judicial Pluralism

Thus far, a number of arguments have been made for discussing judicial reasoning through the use of a conventional-

---

52 Varieties of this position are discussed and criticized in Chapter VI.

ized, tertiary, internally consistent, truth functional, propositional schema. The schema is determined by a conception of judicial role, and employed through the method of justification. Before refining the pluralistic picture further by comparing it to competing theories, it might be useful here to state at one point, and with a minimum of justifying argument, what exactly judicial pluralism entails.

In societies with judicial systems, judges are called upon to address the issues that litigants put before them. These raise initial or first order, judicial questions which require concomitant answers. The answers given by any particular judge in any particular case will have a certain authority, one ordinarily defined by the constitutional law of the state. However, apart from this direct authority, the particular judges' pronouncements may themselves be judged to be true or false, rational or irrational, relevant or misguided. That is, apart from what the particular judge chooses to state, the question to be answered can be discussed in terms of what the correct answer should be by specifying in general the truth conditions for judicial assertion. Such a discussion can be used either to predict or to criticize actual judicial outcomes, and more typically, to allow individuals to understand the standards of the legal system, so as to guide their own behavior, assess that of others, and participate and shape the local political system.

The theory of judicial pluralism attempts to specify truth conditions by analyzing the grounds judges assert or should assert for their answers.[53] Pluralism constructs a three level schema, where the answers to the questions faced by judges constitute the first level, the grounds or criteria for those

---

53 The term "assertion" rather than "statement" or "sentence" is used here in an attempt to avoid certain difficulties and controversies in the philosophy of language concerning logical commitments entailed by the use of "statement" or "sentence". The issues are complex and nothing said here rests on the validity or ultimate vindication of any side of the controversy. One preface to these issues can be found serially in Michael Dummett, "What is a Theory of Meaning, I and II" found in *Mind and Language* (ed. Samuel Guttenplan 1975) and *Truth and Meaning: Essays in Semantics* (eds. Gareth Evans and John McDowell, 1976).

answers constitute the second level, and the grounds or justifications for the second level constitute the third level.

There is no magic in the number "3". Judicial reasoning
could easily be explained by resort to more than three levels,
and with some difficulty, to two or even one level. Because it
reflects ordinary, pre-theoretic (intuitive) conceptions of judicial
reasoning, three levels represent the least complicated,
complete explanation. Judges are expected to use certain criteria to answer properly the issues before them, and resort to
social, political, ethical and other beliefs to determine criteria
use and selection.

If the form of particular judicial issues and the reasoning
path of particular individuals are arbitrary and distinctive, the
particular questions asked admit of degrees of generality and
ambiguity. Moreover, the number of facts taken to determine
an answer to those questions varies with the way the questions
were formed and the beliefs and reasoning of the individual
reasoner. That said, the tertiary schema is meant to be sufficiently complex and rich to allow answers to a large number of
questions. The levels suggest types of justifications, not that
three propositions are needed to give a complete explanation
for each potential issue. A consequence of the individualistic
nature of judicial reasoning chains is that the same proposition
may occur on different levels or may occur twice on the same
level, but serve a logically different function.

Not only the intuitive possibility of the three level schema,
but its entire logic and contents, is an empirical matter. Neither
a law nor the legal system in any given society needs to be as it
is. Moreover, between societies, the degree of similarity is also
an empirical and contingent matter.

If the contents of judicial statements are contingent, their
logic has an essential normative element. Normative language
takes different forms: rules, principles, policies, or standards.
While, for example, the enterprise of tagging particular normative statements in actual legal systems as rules rather than principles may be fruitful in understanding how that system operates, only the general category of undifferentiated standards is
suggested here. In fact, the scope and weight of the standards
may not be merely a matter of correct characterization, but

rather one of employing different higher order propositions in a particular judicial view.

Suppose that rules apply in an all-or-nothing fashion and principles have weight, but admit of exceptions. Then, characterizing a particular standard employed in judicial reasoning—as in the case of any maxim of equity such as that requiring legal purity ("clean hands") before obtaining injunctive relief—depends upon whether such standards inure in second order (precedential or otherwise) propositions or directly in third order propositions in their initial use and changes in their subsequent uses. For example, *Rylands v. Fletcher*[54] was the first case to discuss the proposition that land owners who put their land to "unnatural" uses should be held strictly liable for the consequences of such uses.[55]   Whether the "unnatural use" standard originated in a general political belief about land, in a natural law theory about natural use, in the prior trespass and nuisance cases in a way previously not articulated, or in a policy maxim about land use in an industrializing society, will not only determine the law of the case, but will also suggest the type of standard employed.   Type selection is then a matter of judicial view.   One judicial proclamation which illustrates the varying approaches to agreed upon lower order judicial propositions is Lord Dennings' statement:

> What is the argument on the other side? Only this, that no case has been found in which it has been done before. That argument does not appeal to me in the least. If we never do anything which has not been

---

54 [1868] 3 H.L. 330. Below, the case was reported as *Fletcher v. Rylands* in [1865] 3 H. & C. 774, 159 Eng. Rep. 737 (1865), reversed as *Fletcher v. Rylands* in [1866] 1 Ex. 265.

55 The famous case of *Rylands v. Fletcher* involved a dispute between two tenants of land, one who used it to mine, the other to mill. The miller built a reservoir (with the aid of independent engineers) which, through no fault of his own, caused the mine to flood. The question for the courts was who, between two innocent land users, should bear the loss. As the case wound its way through the courts, the justifications both argued as and found persuasive changed. See, for example, the array of arguments advanced by both bar and bench in *Fletcher v. Rylands and Horrocks*, [1865] 3 H. & C. 774.

done before, we shall never get anywhere. The law will stand still whilst the rest of the world goes on: and that will be bad for both.[56]

The three levels of propositions are held together by justification. Each higher level justifies the lower level. Justification differs from implication in its method of impeachment. Not only does an attack on justification entail a wide range of logic, ethics, empirical observation, and political beliefs and attitudes: the entailment is necessarily less tight and more controversial than in the case of implication.

Construction of judicial views is a matter of convention. The conventionality works in a number of ways. That three tiers explain judicial reasoning in actual judicial systems and the assignment of particular propositions to each level are matters of convention. More fundamentally, though, the conventionality of judicial reasoning operates through the conventional nature of judicial role. Judges are expected to reason in a certain way, to employ certain sources, to use certain of their beliefs and attitudes, in short, to step out of their normal reasoning posture and reason as judges. At the semantic level, the meanings of judicially related terminology take their sense from the concept of judicial role. The common judicial discourse the few judges, and many concerned with judicial

---

56 *Packer v. Packer*, [1953] 2 All. E.R. 127. *Packer* involved a suit for custody and maintenance of a child of the divorced parents. The child was born before the marriage of the parties, while the father was married to someone else. Because children born as a result of adultery were not allowed the usual legitimization, even if their natural parents eventually were married, this child was never legitimized. Section 26(1) of the MATRIMONIAL CAUSES ACT OF 1950, virtually identical to its 1857 predecessor, allowed provision for "the children of the marriage of whose parents" had been divorced. Earlier decisions had held that illegitimate offspring were excluded from such provision. Lord Denning found the precedent unpersuasive in light of the overwhelming unfairness of the result, and the fact that such a result hardly seems dictated by the statute. However, the court divided evenly, and the denial of benefits by the trial court was affirmed.

Certainly, the conflicting opinions of Denning and Morris, L. J. reflect an agreement on the use of legal forms, but evince a sharp divergence as to conceptions of judicial role and concomitant propositional sets.

pronouncements, employ assures that judges assume a particular posture in their reasonings.

Falling outside the tolerable societal limits as to role would indicate not merely deviation from accepted judicial standards, it would indicate a failure to understand the very meaning of judicial reasoning. At the political level, judges are allowed to act in a system which assumes legitimacy from the fact that judges do not merely impose their preference on litigants.[57] In that these preferences are allowed, it is only through the supervening filter of the judicial view.

The culmination for judicial views is the set of third order propositions. These propositions are constructed from certain beliefs and attitudes. The existence of attitudes in a set is sufficient to make the third order irreducibly non-truth functional. That is, if attitudes are taken to include mental states which can only be expressed in assertions whose use is not governed or governable by rules answerable to truth conditions, then there is no factual, discoverable criteria for their truth. However, the selection of certain beliefs, even if governed by rules circumscribed by truth conditions and thus assigned a truth value, is a matter nevertheless rooted in varying conceptions of judicial role. A part of accepting any particular conception includes allowing that certain preferences are selected.

Once the third order propositions are selected, the lower order propositions can admit of truth or falsity. A justification analogue can be constructed from the third order which will indicate whether any particular lower order propositions are or are not correct. Determinate truth values then attach to the lower propositional sets. Constructing the analogue is prob-

---

57 The legitimacy is reflected in such maxims as declaring that a particular state is made up of the rule of law, not men. The rule of law is easily touted as an ideal, but virtually impossible to describe or analyze as a concept. It appears to mean, when it has any meaning at all, that legal rules are less arbitrary than personal judgments. The basis of this belief is rooted in the contingent fact that the judicial process generally is fairer, more ethical, and more deliberative than many other areas of human action. Empirically, the belief would be harmless; as a political and moral goal, it usually implies a conceptual (logical) confusion.

lematic when over or underdetermination impedes any one-to-one propositional correspondence between levels.

If judicial views are not in any simple way susceptible to being judged true or false (or, as a kind of general theory, not susceptible of having some measurable verisimilitude), there are other measures of judicial views. Views may be tested for their coherence, understandability, reasonableness, workability, consistency, popularity, political efficacy, or morality. The importance of any of these measures may be a matter of dispute as, for example, the fact that a judicial view is almost impenetrable in its complexity might be considered irrelevant to a view's defender who argues that the density reflects the dense reality of court actions.

Presented at such a level of generality, there may be the question as to why bother articulating a vague, far reaching, but ultimately less-than-useful-in-making-everyday-decisions theory. Related to that is the question as to whether judicial pluralism should be taken to be a normative theory, a descriptive theory, both, or neither. The answer to the second question is that it is both; and that is related to the fact that judicial reasoning is extremely broad and complicated, a defense of the concern of the first question.

There is a temptation which lures otherwise ascetic students of judicial reasoning, a temptation without general attraction to philosphers of other disciplines, for example, philosophers of science. The basis for truth in judicial statements lies in convention, rather than the less manipulatable, less personal, less anthropomorphic basis for ordinary, empirical or scientific statements. Thus, there is a temptation not merely to describe, but to tinker. British or French law is perhaps acceptable as practiced, but could greatly benefit from a few improvements. When the system is employed and explained, the tempted filter the imperfections and strengthen the best already present.

When measured on the scale of utility, the tinkerer is a great success. Not only is the system analyzed, but guidance is given as to how to do better in the future. A judge can look at, say, Dworkin's rights, Kelsen's norms, or Finnis's goods and use them as criteria not only for going forward with future decisions, but for enunciating what in fact have been the true propositions in the past. No harm is done as long as—and this is the temptation—the system described is not viewed through the prescriptive tint of the writer's own theory.

One justification for putting forward judicial pluralism is that it describes judicial reasoning apart from any platform. Moreover, the claim is that this has not been done successfully before, in part because of temptation. The system described is a prescriptive one, and tying it together involves prescriptive reasoning (or more pretentiously, deontic logic). Whether pluralism is to be considered, given that fact, "prescriptive" or "descriptive" becomes a matter of mere terminology. In whatever way one labels it, explicating judicial reasoning has a great number of benefits: it explains how legal systems accommodate diverse views, it enumerates the criteria used in judicial decisions, it shows how criticism of the correctness of judicial decisions is possible, and it demystifies judicial process, while debunking less complex, but popular views.

Pluralism perhaps could be made clearer through a brief look at an old English decision: *Foone v. Blount*.[58] *Foone* involves litigation of a will which left money to individuals who practiced the Roman Catholic religion. The money was not to be taken directly from the estate of the decedent, but was to be raised by the sale, upon death, of certain real estate. Unfortunately, for those (pecuniary legatees) in line to benefit from the sale, the will was probated in an 18th Century England still wary of Catholics. Statutes had earlier been enacted which had "taken off from the Roman Catholics that weight and influence which naturally connected with landed property, beyond what personal estate can give."[59] They were excluded from benefits other than those connected with their own living: that is, nothing of marketable value, or profit, by sale or lease, was allowed.

Winifred Warham died in 1751, leaving Foone as one of her Catholic beneficiaries. However, because Foone's legacy was the result of a profit from real estate, the Chancellor (who ruled on probate matters) was reluctant to award the funds. After

---

58 [1776] II Cowper (K.B.) 464.

59 This, and the following quotations, are taken from *Id.* at 466.

some indecision, he referred the matter to the Court of King's Bench and Lord Mansfield, where it was heard in 1776. The issue was whether the proceeds from the sale of real estate by an executor were covered under the statutes.

In holding that Foone could finally receive the proceeds, Mansfield wrote that the set of statutes against "Papists" "were thought, when they passed, necessary to the safety of the state. Upon no other ground can they be defended." Mansfield, then, indirectly attacked the soundness of the statutes, and stated that "they are not to be carried by inference, beyond what the political reasons, which gave rise to them require." He then argued that because Foone had no right to possession of the land, the statutes were not violated, ignoring the clear language prohibiting "any other interest or profits whatever of lands".

It is easy to construct the first and second levels of reasoning. The first order question was: should Foone or any Catholic be entitled to proceeds from a probate sale of real estate? The second order criteria used involves, at the very least, the Act of Parliament and the required rules for construing such acts, and perhaps other, applicable common law decisions, principles or policy.

It is also easy to see, either from reading the case or from knowing much about his general views, that Mansfield found this kind of discrimination extremely distasteful. While he could have ruled in favor of Foone on political or moral grounds, and used either directly as third order justifications, it is clear from other decisions that Mansfield would have considered such reasoning other than judicial. He wrote that "the legislature only can vary or alter the law." His view of judicial role mediated his political and moral beliefs. A judge (for Mansfield) has limited authority when the legislature has spoken. However, where the reasons for the legislation have disappeared, inferences otherwise bearing and binding are without force. A judge can thus scrutinize legislation and limit its application if the purpose for enacting it has weakened.

The variety of positions judges with similar political or moral beliefs could take in such a situation is enormous. It could be argued that natural law or due process (both widespread ideas in the 18th Century) allow the judge simply to avoid the legislation; that the legislature only intended such an onerous statute to last as long as the danger existed and then fall into disuse; that religious tolerance elsewhere in the law would allow the curtailing of never proper and now embarrassing relics of a less tolerant era.

Each of these positions involves a different conception of the proper role of a judge.　In the situation here, each would imply the same conclusion as did Mansfield.　However, in more straightforward real estate cases, where technical distinctions of title and the capacity of executors are not involved, these other conceptions could lead to different results.　In the case of, for example, the simple inheritance of a great landed estate, Mansfield would strike down the bequest:　those with convergent political (or moral, religious, or other relevant third order views) might not.

Judicial pluralism, the term used here to introduce the tertiary, conventional, reasoning structure, contrasts with the three other existent theories of judicial reasoning: legal realism, legal positivism, and Dworkin's rights theory.　That it shares significant features with each is hardly surprising.　The same empirical situation has been analyzed by many shrewd observers within these existing theories.　Much of their analysis is both cogent and useful.　In order to understand how these theories differ and where each goes wrong, they must be individually addressed.

III

Skepticism and Adjudication

Others say, Law is our Fate;
Others say, Law is our State;
Others say, others say
Law is no more
Law has gone away.

W.H. Auden

The previous two chapters have discussed the status of judicial propositions, particularly third order propositions. It was argued that they were constructed conventionally and, although susceptible to criticism drawn from such areas as logic, ethics, and politics, are not able to be labeled as true or false. This position owes something to a larger skeptical position, one arguing against the existence of an entire range of legal objects. This skeptical position has been advanced with different degrees of extremity by a school of legal philosophers called the "legal realists". Pluralism is skeptical about a certain kind of objectivity in judicial reasoning—the objective truth of third order propositions—and is, to that extent, at the moderate end of the legal realism spectrum.

This chapter will examine other positions on the spectrum. An analysis of the defects of these positions will serve to justify the pluralist position. That, however, is not the main purpose. Skepticism and anti-skepticism are continuing temptations in legal philosophy, as they are in philosophy generally. The readily apparent becomes doubtful with analysis, while rejecting skepticism wholesale glosses over the inconsistencies in a pretheoretic or intuitive view. If Hume and later Kant felt elation at the concept of mitigated skepticism,[1] it was perhaps because it acknowledged the rational belief that all was not well with common sense. Here, understanding where skepticism is right and where it is misguided is essential to analyzing judicial reasoning.

It should be mentioned that few skeptical positions were articulated in terms anything like the ones used here. This was in large part because the realists borrowed their terminology from social psychologists rather than philosophers, and thus addressed issues of truth and ontological status only indirectly. It might also be useful to say a word about actual legal realists and their present obscurity.

The legal realists were first American and later Scandinavian jurists and academics who found unsatisfactory the artificial and formalistic legal analysis they perceived as prevalent in Europe and America. They believed that philosophy of law should be conducted in the same way as cases in law: starting with the specific, and moving toward the general with the intention of returning to the specific. The legal realists saw this approach as a sharp contrast to the neo-Kantian approach which began with categories, in an attempt to fit law into the larger category of morality on an *a priori* basis.[2] They viewed the analytic school of John Austin and the British empiricists as being preoccupied with classification, to the detriment of actual decisions and legal

---

1   David Hume's views on causality, inference and skepticism are found in *A Treatise of Human Nature* (1734) and *An Inquiry Concerning Human Understanding* (1748). Immanuel Kant's esteem and enthusiasm are well-known, and found, among other places, in *Prolegomena to Any Future Metaphysics* 6-7 (ed. Lewis Beck 1950) and *The Critique of Pure Reason* 55, 606-612 (ed. Norman Kemp Smith 1968). Whether Hume and Kant actually agreed to much more than that a thorough-going skepticism is misguided and that experience is some guide to understanding belief is far from clear.

2   It is less important whether this is true than the fact that at the time it was perceived to be true. One neo-Kantian who was so characterized was N. M. Korkunov for his *General Theory of Law*. Roscoe Pound, himself not a legal realist, shared many of their views and prejudices. His account of the aridity of these schools is typical. See his *Law and Morals* (1923) generally and pp. 89-124 for a picture of neo-Kantian and related schools.

process. John Chipman Gray said the analytic study "may easily result in a barren scholasticism" and that the sin of the analytic school was that once terms were defined and classified, the classification became irrevocably final." [3]

The early legal realists—Oliver Wendell Holmes, John Chipman Gray, Karl Llewellyn—scorned independent, conceptual analysis. They desired always to construct theory directly from empirical study. Logic and system-building alone mislead. Holmes said as much in what became the slogan of the legal realists:

> It is something to show that the consistency of a system requires a particular result, but it is not all. The life of the law has not been logic: it has been experience. The felt necessities of the time, the prevalent moral and political theories, intuitions of public policy, avowed or unconscious, even the prejudices which judges share with their fellow-men, have had a good deal more to do than the syllogism in determining the rules by which men should be governed. [4]

If the legal realists turned from logic to experience as the object of their study, they moved from philosophy to social science as their method of study. Roscoe Pound called for a "sociological jurisprudence"[5] and later realists such as Thurman Arnold in *The Symbols of Government*[6] and Morris Cohen in *Law and the Social Order*[7] attempted to use social scientific tools to analyze actual legal systems. This move carried with it a sense that prediction was the goal of the jurist. The sociologist, after all, attempted to predict. As decisional results were being examined, it was those that were to be predicted. The legal realists found that rules alone could not predict with certainty, and thus they felt some confirmation of their abandonment of

---

3 Both comments are from John Chipman Gray, *The Nature and Sources of the Law* 2, 3 (2nd ed. 1921).

4 Oliver Wendell Holmes, *The Common Law* 5 (ed. Mark De Wolfe Howe 1963).

5 Pound's term is widespread throughout his works. One example of his approach is found in his *An Introduction to the Philosophy of Law* (1922).

6 Published in 1935.

7 Published in 1933.

analytic jurisprudence. This discovery led one of them to say that:

> Rules are important so far as they help you to predict what judges will do. That is all their importance except as pretty playthings. [8]

These legal realists, in rejecting what they thought to be bad philosophy, moved to a social scientific method which purported to use virtually no philosophy. Theirs was a program, a way of proceeding. This program contained minimal theoretical commitments, including a belief that no law existed apart from what the judges declared there to be. This originally seemed to mean no more than actual laws are those that are enforced, not quite a truism[9]. It can be interpreted as saying much more: no law exists, despite rules or statutes to the contrary, until a judge makes his decision. The ambiguity in this position is reflected in Holmes' statement that "The duty to keep a contract at common law means a prediction that you must pay damages if you do not keep it—and nothing else."[10] Holmes' statement allows for no explanation of what a contractual duty may mean to a judge. The duty must seem sufficiently binding for a judge to enforce it. Moreover, in those cases where the validity of a contract is in doubt—for reasons of duress, fraud, public policy, illegality, formal irregularities, failure of mutuality or consideration—even the contracting parties may need to gauge whether the contract ought to be enforced as a precondition to understanding whether or not it is likely to be. For Holmes' statement to be true, a judge would have to be a passive agent of some ethereal determinism which would then allow predictions to come true without the consideration of

---

8   Karl Llewellyn, *The Bramble Bush* 14 (3rd ed. 1960).

9   The truism fails both because many laws by their nature are unlikely candidates for enforcement in the courts (for example, a law which mandates the existence of an administrative agency or the renaming of a public square) and because individuals can miscalculate the enforcement of laws, thus obeying despite the fact that obedience ultimately is unnecessary.

10 From O. W. Holmes, "The Path of the Law", 10 *Harv. L. Rev.* 457 (1897); reprinted in *Collected Legal Papers* 167, 175 (1920).

human agents. One might see how statements concerning future weather conditions would qualify as such determined predictions, for weather results do not require human intentions or considerations. Legal predictions do not, however, behave similarly. In any case, the legal realist's abhorrence of philosophy allowed him to be saddled with certain philosophical positions attributed to him by others, positions he was often unwilling or unable to shake.[11] The realist position, that the rule stated in the case was not necessarily the rule that caused the judge to decide the case, was seen to be a rule skepticism rather than a simple psychological observation.[12]

If the realists did not generally abhor or question rules, they did assume at least one skeptical stance about rules: that legal validity was a function of judicial decisions. Thus, where a statute or rule existed, individuals could follow it, but it had no legal validity until passed on by a court. A distinction can be made here between consequences and validity. A putative law may cause individuals to change their behavior, it may even

---

11 A good example of a legal realist unhappy with the philosophical criticism he encountered but without any idea of how to meet that criticism was Karl Llewellyn. In the third edition of *The Bramble Bush*, he claims critics have showed him "to disbelieve in rules, to deny them and their existence and desirability, to approve and exalt brute force and arbitrary power and unfettered tyranny, to disbelieve in ideals and particularly in justice. This was painful to me." (p. 10). However painful, he was unable in the foreword or the text to put his position aright. He can only manage to state that his views do not constitute a philosophy.

12 Ronald Dworkin's characterization, typical in its overstatement of the claim of the legal realists, is instructive. "This is an error, the realists argued, because judges actually decide cases according to their own political and moral tastes, and then choose an appropriate legal rule as a rationalization." Ronald Dworkin, *Taking Rights Seriously* 3 (1977). It is misleading in two ways. Realists thought judges decided cases according to some criteria, but that criteria might be more rational and complicated than taste. "Taste" implies arbitrariness and subjectivity, a position no realist ever endorsed. Second, the method they endorsed was observation. Realists tried to look at cases and see why they were decided the way they were. They made no claim as to whether all judges rationalized their decisions. This was the kind of statement they despised. Some judges rationalized; some judges decided the cases for the reasons they said. A social scientist simply looks at cases and tries to see what process occurred.

cause a policeman to arrest them, but it would not be a valid law until the judges approved it. The skepticism concerns any claim of equal status between putative law and the law of the judicial decision. The immediate difficulty with this position—beyond the question as to whether precedent falls into the category of putative law (as Jerome Frank thought it should)[13] or good law (as Gray believed)[14]—is that the criteria the judge ought to use to reach his decision appear to be relativized. It is simply a matter of unbridled choice.

This position was attacked, and an altered legal realism was born. This new realism, called Scandinavian realism after the region of its greatest number of adherents, allowed for a second level of prediction. One can predict the criteria judges use, as well as the results. This involves a certain hybrid of the psychological and the logical. Alf Ross states the position as: "'A=D is valid law' is a prediction to the effect that D under certain conditions will be taken as the basis for decisions in future, legal disputes."[15] One consequence of this position is that the criteria a judge uses to decide can be discovered by predicting the criteria a judge in the same position would use in deciding a case. There is thus a normative standard for a judge deciding a case: it arises in employing a prediction of what a judge ought to do.

This remedy robs legal realism of much of its original point. No longer will law be explained in terms of judges' results: an irreducible normative element is introduced. Yet, the basis of this normative element is obscure. It leaves open the issue of an objective standard by which to measure judicial behavior, and it fails to provide any criteria for a judge to use in adjudication. The position is unsatisfactory both to those who see law as primarily a social phenomenon and to those who wish to know the logical structure inhering in legal statements. The legal

---

13 See Jerome Frank, *Law and the Modern Mind* 35-52, 183-199 (sixth ed. 1949).

14 See John Chipman Gray, *The Nature and Sources of the Law* 96-104 (2nd ed. 1921), where he invokes the traditional distinction between settled and unsettled case law.

15 Alf Ross, *On Law and Justice* 75 (1958).

realists spoke, appropriately enough, in general legal terms, but they were primarily concerned with judicial reasoning. The legal realists differed among themselves, of course, and their positions can be reconstructed as skepticism of four kinds: first, second, and third order skepticism and emotivism. Each of these kinds, if true, would be fatal to the pluralist thesis and the entire reasoning schema presented here.

First Order Skepticism

Realists might be skeptical about first order judicial propositions.[16] They may believe, that is, that there are no correct answers to the questions faced by judges. This is the most general sort of skepticism. It includes a spectrum which at one end denies that there is even a discrete set of issues properly ascribable to an individual case and, at the other end, the position that rules may exist, but their application is a pretense. First order skeptics point out that cases are often complicated, and they are by definition controversial. The judge is in a position to define the issues and to shape, if not manipulate, their content.

This position includes the legal realists who called themselves fact-skeptics. Their position was put forward forthrightly by Jerome Frank:

> No matter how precise or definite may be the formal legal rules, say these fact skeptics, no matter what the discoverable uniformities behind these formal rules, nevertheless, it is impossible, and will always be impossible, because of the elusiveness of the facts on which decisions turn, to predict future decisions in most (not all) law-suits not yet tried.

---

16 There is a certain irony in labeling as a realist anyone who is arguing for a skeptical position. In modern philosophical lingo, skepticism is part of a related group of positions called anti-realism. In fact, the legal realists are all steadfastly anti-Platonist, in that they believe the abstract truths of law are not there ready for discovery, but are constructed by individuals. For a further characterization of these often misleading tags, see Michael Dummett, "Truth", 59 *Proceedings of the Aristotelian Society* 141 (1958), reprinted in *Philosophical Logic* 49 (ed. Peter Strawson, 1967); and John McDowell "Truth Conditions, Bivalence and Verificationism" in *Truth and Meaning: Essays in Semantics* (eds. Gareth Evans and John McDowell, 1976).

The fact skeptics, thinking that therefore the pursuit of greatly increased legal certainty is, for the most part, futile—and that its pursuit, indeed may well work injustice—aim rather at increased judicial justice. [17]

The first order skeptic believes that the way judicial questions are put is a matter of individual judgment. Because of the uncertainty of first level propositions, any pyramiding that includes higher order statements is futile, for it is a structure rooted on a shifting base. There are two claims to the first order skeptic's position and they are both incorrect.

The first claim is that somehow the facts are inherently unclear in a case. The strong version of this claim would say that facts are always unclear, and that one can never know for certain any precise piece of information about the outside world. This position is akin to a general philosophical skepticism, and is liable to all the criticisms of it brought forth since Berkeley. Refutation takes the form of: how can we say that x is false if there does not exist some y which is true, by which we can measure the falsity of x? The existence of y defeats skepticism.[18] The merits of this debate aside, the strong version is not the one actually advanced by any legal realists, who are fundamentally empirical in their approach. The weak version, though, is. It says that facts are often, even usually, unclear in court cases and one must make stabs in the dark at truth. Witnesses exaggerate, lie, or forget, documents are fragmentary or forged, verification procedures are faulty, lawyers often mislead or are themselves misled, and a great deal of relevant evidence is unavailable. Notorious examples of factual mistakes in the courtroom are so commonplace as to call into doubt their notoriety. The result of this unclarity of facts is that the findings of courts can have little correspondence to the actual

---

17 Jerome Frank, *Courts on Trial: Myth and Reality in American Justice* 74 (1949).

18 This type of argument is advanced in, among other places, J. L. Austin, *Sense and Sensibilia* 70-79 (1962) and Gilbert Ryle, *Dilemmas* 94 (1954). A more general treatment can be found in Ludwig Wittgenstein, *On Certainty* (1969).

events, and that holdings based on those findings are arbitrary.[19]

This entire position rests on an assumed equivalence. It assumes that judicial truth means just the same thing as truth normally understood. This is wrong, not because there are two very different kinds of truth, but because the truth conditions of an empirical statement are different than those on which first order propositions are based. Under the canonical Tarskian formulation for empirical statements, "M shot L" is true if and only if M shot L.[20] Let S = "M shot L." The skeptics argue that S triggers some first level proposition "p", such as "If A, B, C and S, then p," where A, B and C might be other conditions allowing for p, when for instance, a first-degree murder has taken place. If S is false, then p is either false, or more exactly, does not occur. The fallacy in the skeptic's position is not in the formula "if A, B, C and S, then p." It is in holding that, for S to be true, M did indeed shoot L. In judicial systems, "M shot L" is true if and only if it is found that M shot L. What triggers p is a finding of S, not S itself. The fact that the finding is not truly, empirically S may be a case of injustice or irrationality, but it does not undermine the truth of the relevant first order proposition, p.

The first order skeptic's second claim is that the facts of judicial cases are open to any interpretation, or at least many interpretations, each equally valid. Facts are so vague and ambiguous that their consequences are uncertain, and liable to manipulation. The above formula becomes "if A, B, C, S, and S_i, then p", where S_i represents the additional facts needed to make sense of S and yield a first order proposition. S_i is a subjective matter, varying with the personal preferences of individual judges. In terms of our example, let us suppose that L was a

---

19 The fact-skeptics—Jerome Frank, Leon Green, Max Radin, Thurman Arnold, William O. Douglas, and E. M. Morgan—might well have balked at these being considered the consequences of their position, and would have probably argued that this is not what they had in mind. The actual position of these men is irrelevant here.

20 Tarski's much repeated formula is "s is true in L if and only if p." See Alfred Tarski, "The Concept of Truth in Formalized Languages" in his *Logic, Semantics, Meta-Mathematics* (1956).

trespasser on M's property, shot with an automatically triggered spring gun. The privilege to protect property does not include the right to use deadly force, and thus certain facts—that L was a trespasser, that M had constructed many signs warning of the gun, that L in fact saw the signs, that M's property was in a remote area, both easily and previously vandalized, that L had intended to commit larceny, and that the property involved sentimental considerations—relating to the protection of property ought not to be considered in formulating p. However, they are, in fact, routinely considered, and may mitigate or even excuse blame in the right circumstances. A judge looks to such circumstances, and finds p alone an adequate basis on which to rule. The introduction of p' recognizes this practice.

The plausibility of this position diminishes if it is made clear that the fact that judges actually interpret facts differently is irrelevant to the skeptic's claims. The issue is whether there is a proper method of interpreting facts. The fact that protection of property counts differently with different judges can be seen as indicating disagreement about p, a disagreement perhaps not made explicit in judicial discourse. In order to show that p' rather than p is central, a skeptic needs to argue that there is no correct method of interpreting facts. This entails that S_i is indeterminate, for if S_i had a fixed meaning, then S_i would be just another component of the proposition p, along with A, B, C, *etc.*

If the first order skeptic wishes to distinguish S_i from A, B, C, *etc.*, he must do so by showing S_i to be indeterminate in meaning. That is, in order to fix the sense of S_i, one must appeal to personal preferences not shared by a general public. This is not ordinary (Quinean) indeterminacy, for such ordinary indeterminacy applies equally to all terms found within a natural language, and is thus insufficient to distinguish S_i. It instead must be an indeterminacy based on the fact that interpretation of facts is a personal matter. However, if a judge believes that her interpretation is correct, she ought to redefine p so as to include it. If she believes such redefinition is impossible, it can only be because the facts, rather than her preferences, are elusive. This, however, returns her to the first claim, with the successful concomitant counter-arguments showing its failure.

Many writers, whether or not they claimed the title "legal realist", have engaged in skepticism that varied both in degree and type. Because conceptual clarity has not been their primary purpose, these writers will avow a first or second order skepticism (usually in the guise of suspicion about the relevancy, pedigree or authority of different types of rules) in their more theoretical discussions, often just to back away from it in the legal analysis. Perhaps none has been more influential than Edward Levi.[21]

In his book, *An Introduction to Legal Reasoning*,[22] Levi claimed it was only pretense that the law is a system of known rules.[23] This claim is not based on the fact that there may be other normative contenders (*e.g.* principles) for inclusion in the legal system, and the incompleteness of rules alone would distort the actual fact of how the system worked. Rather, the rules exist

---

21 Although Levi never labels himself a legal realist, there is a strong realist flavor to his book. He repeatedly cites as authority in theoretical matters such realists as Frank, Llewellyn and Arnold. In fact, concerning law being a system of rules, he cites Frank's *Law and the Modern Mind* (1936) as being the "controlling book." Perhaps more revealing, Levi looks to the works of two skeptical pragmatist philosophers as his ultimate authority: John Dewey, *Logic, The Theory of Inquiry* (1938) and George Herbert Mead, *The Philosophy of the Act* (1938). Both men, University of Chicago academics like Levi and Llewellyn, were thinkers rejecting what they considered to be the dry constraints of formal philosophy for the more invigorating air of practical social science. Levi cites Mead at a crucial juncture for the proposition that "It is rather the doctrine of dictum forces him [the judge] to make his own decision." *An Introduction To Legal Reasoning* 3. The freedom unconstrained by rules is part of the general view of Mead that social psychology rather than philosophy is the path to truth. *See, e.g.*, Mead's statement (in the pages Levi cites) that his "rejection sweeps out a vast amount of philosophical riffraff known as epistemology." *The Philosophy of the Act* 94.

22 Hereinafter cited as *"Introduction"*. This work was first published in 1948. However, sometime at least as late as 1961, Levi published a new preface citing certain new work. While it would be unfair to criticize Levi for not including Hart's *The Concept of Law* published that year, and possibly after the new preface was written, it is interesting that none of the criticisms directed by Hart at positions similar to ones Levi advocates is mentioned. See, for example, Hart's "Definition and Theory in Jurisprudence", 70 *Law Q. Rev.* 49 (1953).

23 *Introduction* at 1.

and are the sole relevant normative contenders in judicial reasoning. However, they are too ambiguous and unclear to apply ("legal rules are never clear",[24] "But no such fixed prior rule exists"[25]); they are not binding or of even minimal authority for judges, who have a free choice as to whether or not to apply them ("where case law is considered, and there is no statute, he [the judge] is not bound by the statement of the rule of law made by the prior judge even in the controlling case");[26] and the rules that apply are more or less discovered at the time of or after the outcome of the case is determined ("the rules are discovered in the process of determining similarity or difference [the new case]").[27]

Evidence for Levi's claims is necessarily scant. Clarity proceeds on a continuum. Because some rules are unclear does not mean others are. The rule that "two witnesses are necessary to a valid will" is not unclear, ambiguous, or vague (the concept Levi probably intends when he uses the term "ambiguous"). Cases are factually unalike, but that fact alone does not imply that judges are free (not bound by rationality, judicial role, or any authority) to disregard prior cases or apply the facts as they see fit. Moreover, the factual differences, like the unclarity, are a matter of degree. Any useful theory of adjudication must explain how differences of degree impinge upon a judge's freedom (or discretion).[28] Levi never addresses the issue directly. He indicates that judicial freedom is absolute, at least relative to past decisions, and vaguely bounded by statutes and constitutions: no attempt to tie freedom either to rule clarity or factual similarity is made.

---

24 *Introduction* at 1.

25 *Introduction* at 3.

26 *Introduction* at 2.

27 *Introduction* at 3.

28 Freedom should not be equated with discretion, although Levi appears to do so. Certainly, "discretion" is a concept with severe strictures, as Dworkin explained in "Is Law a System of Rules?", 35 *U. of Chicago L. Rev.* 14 (1967). To what extent such strictures are due to rationality only, and could thus also be attached to freedom of action is an issue Levi does not address. This issue is touched upon in this work at Chapter VI.

Levi does appear, at a too rapid glance, basically to share certain of the tenets of judicial pluralism. Rules (or first order propositions) alone do not govern, but are only part of the explanation of adjudication. Levi spends little time on general theory, preferring to discuss adjudication through an examination of changing concepts and holdings at the hands of successive courts.   Basically, he looks to the evolution of legal doctrines, pointing out repeatedly that the new court bent old rules to reach the results it wanted. What has here been called third order propositions were, in part, responsible. "No one economic or social theory was responsible, although as changes came about in the manner of living, the social theory moved ahead to explain and persuade. The social theory then became useful in explaining connections. The point of view of society changed."[29]

Levi then emphasizes the role of social theory, which, if not identical with legal theory, plays a large part in judicial reasoning.[30] The gap in Levi's picture is that there is no legal theory. As rules are not available to constitute the elements of such a theory, the unbridled discretion Levi calls, correctly under his own explanation, "freedom" allows the judge a choice without guidance. Moreover, it puts into jeopardy the entire legal system every time a judge rules.

This, of course, is (presumably) not Levi's intention (although those who minimize the importance of theory are always in peril). Rather, he spends most of his book illustrating the evolution of certain legal concepts, emphasizing the fact that past decisions, or other legal forms,[31] are used to justify later

---

29 *Introduction* at 102-103.

30 *Introduction* at 104.

31 Levi distinguishes between cases, statutes and constitutions, suggesting that courts are entirely free to disregard cases, somewhat bound by statutes, with constitutions belonging somewhere in the middle. However, as Levi does not explain what being "bound" means, or why past decisions are virtually worthless, his analysis, if interesting, is almost useless to judges, practitioners, and interested observers.

holdings unforeseen by the original decisions' authors.[32]   In attributing much of the evolution to social factors, Levi points to the obvious fact that the bases for rules change as the facts underlying the rules change. Levi's example of alteration in the "inherently dangerous" rule is a clear illustration of this. A society riding covered wagons made by a smith and sold to a buyer capable of fixing defects is quite different from one with automobiles manufactured by a remote vendor with defects hidden, complex, and beyond the capacity of consumers to detect. That a society changes does not (necessarily) dictate how legal rules should change.

Levi's rule skepticism is two-fold: both as to first and second order propositions. No criteria for establishing third order propositions is suggested, nor is the method by which third order justifications determine first order propositions given. It is true that judges are free to decide cases as they want, in that guns are rarely held to their heads. Such an observation, even if true, is not a substitute for conceptual analysis, and does not explain why the change that occurs comes in the form it does.

Second Order Skepticism

The legal realist may be skeptical about the set of second order propositions. This is close to the position taken by most American realists. This position recognizes the authority and validity of judicial pronouncements, but does not believe that any correct criteria exist for selecting these pronouncements. This has given rise to the "sources of law" theory. This theory holds that traditional legal sources—statutes, customs, constitutions, treaties, administrative rulings, and even past cases—have only a contingent relationship to actual judicial decisions. While they can be used in reaching judgment, they are not

---

32 Whether the point is that the original decision's authors did not foresee the uses put to the case or whether their intentions are irrelevant is an important distinction Levi collapses. Decisions, like all language, can only be understood by some reference to the intentionality of the author. Levi's statement that "It is not what the prior judge intended that is of any importance" (*Introduction* at 2-3) is, in its overblown overstatement, both inaccurate and irrational.

necessary to the conclusion. That is, no conclusion necessary from analysis of these sources must follow in a judicial decision. The second order skeptics thus make use of the distinction between "the law" and "sources of the law."[33] Sources are a useful guide to prediction, but they are not determinative of first order questions. Judges can ultimately choose whatever criteria they prefer. This view was expressed in a thrice repeated quotation of Bishop Hoadley in John Chipman Gray's *The Nature and Sources of the Law:*

> Whoever hath an absolute authority to interpret any written or spoken laws, it is he who is truly the Law-giver to all intents and purposes, and not the person who first wrote or spoke them. [34]

The second level skeptic sees decisions as containing justifications or rationalizations. The justifications given may or may not be the ones used. The skeptic's method is prediction, although it is necessary to see that prediction alone does not imply skepticism. One could easily attempt to predict decisions of a culture as an anthropologist might do—with the aim of later constructing the normative propositions which led to decision.

There are points in common between a second order skeptic and a judicial pluralist. For this reason, it is necessary to examine several arguments used against the realists which need not be fatal to the second order skeptic. These arguments are taken from H. L. A. Hart's *The Concept of Law*[35] and while they may have been telling against the actual realist arguments he considered, they fail against the theoretical positions constructed here.

---

33 The distinction was first and most convincingly put forward by John Chipman Gray in his *The Nature and Sources of the Law* (2nd ed. 1921). Gray tempered his skepticism by creating a second order body of rules which judges discover and apply in reading a decision. The status and definition of this body is left obscure. See Chapter IV.

34 Found on pp. 102, 125, and 172 for the second edition.

35 Published in 1961. Hart uses other arguments, but these are tied to a defense of his theory of rules and cannot be examined here. The type of general argument advanced by Hart will be examined more thoroughly in Chapter V.

The first argument of Hart's concerns the distinction made between "sources of law" and "law."[36] Hart is unhappy at separating the two, feeling that rules guide judicial behavior, and that any distinction between the judicial decision and other legal sources is artificial and misleading. His argument is curious. Hart says that judges, upon coming to office, encounter established rules, and adherence to these rules forms the standard of behavior for judges.[37] He then writes:

> Such standards could not indeed continue to exist unless most of the judges of the time adhered to them, for their existence at any given time consists simply in the acceptance and use of them as standards of correct adjudication.[38]

Hart opposes any normative position that allows judges free rein in reaching a decision. But an argument that because judges have followed a set of criteria in the past they a) ought to do so now or b) do in fact do so now is a *non-sequitur*. His position is based on a game analogy he made earlier:[39] if a game has rules established by the scorer at his own discretion, and any statements made by a player or observer as to whether or not the scorer is right are only matters of prediction, then the game is one of scorer's discretion, not an ordinary game. Such a game as scorer's discretion could not make sense of a player following a rule in playing the game. The scorer's rulings are his own, and they are infallible. Yet we know that in most games scorers can make mistakes and players can use rules. The same is true in legal systems.

The argument is pointless against our second order skeptic. He can accept that if there has been consistency in judicial decision-making, and some criteria are available which would (if employed) explain that consistency, then if the criteria are changed and the consistency ends, we can at least say that a

---

36 The arguments are not kept well-separated by Hart, but are embedded in his general treatment of what he believes are rule-extremists (formalists and skeptics) found in Chapter VII of *Concept*.

37 *Concept* at 141-142.

38 *Concept* at 142.

39 *Concept* at 138-140.

different game is being played (or a judicial system has different first order propositions). The skeptic could claim that Hart's analysis begs the question, by assuming that a single game is always being played. If the identity of the game is tied to individuating the criteria, then one needs to argue, not assume, that only one game is allowed. If a number of competing games are possible, then any normative constraint which dictates a following of the rules of the game is without meaning. One must follow some criteria, but just which criteria is left so open as to make a skeptical position viable.

Part of the failure of the Hartian argument is due to its focus on the terms "law" and "sources of law." It is doubtful if as much critical energy would have been spent if "law" were taken to mean (denote) judicial decisions and "sources of law" to mean law. The purpose of employing the distinction was to show that what judges actually decided need not be determined by other legal forms, and that any relationship between the two is contingent. This leads to Hart's second criticism.

Hart's second argument is that skepticism about criteria is really skepticism about rules. His evidence that any realists actually held to a full-blown rule skepticism is based on their labeling themselves as being rule skeptics. Apart from that label, little evidence exists in their arguments of such a complete skepticism about rules. Usually, it is, at most, second order rules that are being questioned. Hart does quote Llewellyn to the effect that "rules are important so far as they help you to predict what judges do. That is all their importance except as pretty playthings."[40] In context, this quotation says no more than, *vis-a-vis* judicial decision-making, rules are only useful as predictors. There is certainly no reason for a second order skeptic to also be a complete rule skeptic. He can believe in moral rules, rules in games, rules of thumb, syntactical and semantic rules, and rules of manners. He can even believe in legal rules. He just does not need to see them as necessary criteria for deciding cases. Ethical rules do not decide cases, yet

---

40 *Concept* at 135 quoting from Karl Llewellyn, *The Bramble Bush* 9 (2nd ed.). Hart does not acknowledge Llewellyn's explanation of what he meant and did not mean by that statement found in the forward of the third edition. (See n. 9.)

they remain rules. Hart argues that theirs is really the position of the disappointed absolutist, for it notices that judges do not always follow rules and falsely moves to the position that they never do.[41] But the second order skeptic does not need to deny that judges follow rules. He only needs to deny that they follow a single discrete set of rules. That is, the skeptic can accept that a judge might follow Rule Set A or Rule Set B or Rule Set C. He would just deny that any particular rule set is correct.

Hart's third argument takes issue with the skeptical assertion that prediction alone fully explains judicial behavior. Hart insists rules are "used."

> Moreover, even where what the rules require is clear to all, the statement of it may often be made in the form of a prediction of the courts' decision. But it is important to notice that predominantly in the latter case, and to a varying degree in the former, the basis for such prediction is the knowledge that the courts regard legal rules not as predictions, but as standards to be followed in decision, determinate enough in spite of their open texture, to limit, though not to exclude, their discretion. [42]

The skeptic could respond to Hart that asserting rule use is not the same thing as showing it. Using a chess analogy immediately following the quotation, Hart emphasizes the non-predictive aspect of rules. Chess players use rules rather than predict what chess officials would hold in case of disputes. The skeptic might respond that this only demonstrates the disanalogy between chess and judicial decision-making. Where rules are controversial and uncertain, prediction operates.

The skeptic might suggest a counter-example, in the form of the liberal judge forced to preside in a fascist courtroom, an example used earlier.[43] That liberal judge was in a position similar to many of his colleagues: he was required to participate in a judicial system that was a component of a political system he abhorred. This particular liberal judge based his decisions

---

41 This argument is generally made on pp. 136-137 of *Concept*.

42 *Concept* at 143.

43 The example was borrowed in large part from Ronald Dworkin, who put it to different uses.

on what he thought the fascist secret police wished to hear. Here is an example of a court regarding legal rules as predictions, contrary to Hart's statement above. The judge predicts what he thinks the fascists want to hear in deciding cases.

Ultimately this is more than a mere counter-example to Hart's position. It undermines the distinction critical to many anti-realists, the distinction between prediction and use. The realists are supposed to be unable to account for rule usage, as theirs is the language of prediction. But the liberal judge employs rule usage in order to predict. In an actual judicial system, there is apt to be a disparity between any set of rules with the results they entail on the one hand, and actual decisions on the other. Rules can be useful as predictors, but the two do not have the same logical extension. (This assumes what a Humean would deny: that constant conjunction implies causation.[44] The conjunction here is between rules and results of predictions. In real judicial systems, divergence is too great, certainly far less than the one hundred percent normally expected, to allow any assumption of causation from conjunction alone.) But although the realist admits rule utility, he does not need to admit to any higher order rule set implying answers to first order questions.

These three arguments of Hart, arguments in some form traditionally applied against legal realism, are thus not fatal to the position of the second order skeptic. The skeptic can still maintain his claim that no objective criteria exist on which first order propositions depend. Justifications are easy to find for first order reasons, but overdetermination is sufficiently prevalent to deny special status to a particular set of justifications.

The skeptic is unhappy with the notion that second order propositions are found or discovered. He sees them nowhere in the empirical universe and knows of no guide for the logical universe.[45] Less abstractly, the skeptic is willing to recognize

---

44 See David Hume, *A Treatise of Human Nature*, Book I, Part III (1734).

45 The argument here is akin to the one John Mackie calls the argument from queerness. It would, plugging in Mackie's terminology, suggest that if there were objective second order propositions, they would be entities of a very strange sort, utterly different from anything else in the universe (the metaphysical objection); and that if we were to be aware of

that there may be agreement on many first order propositions, and this agreement lends them a kind of certainty due any regular occurrence.   However, there are cases of first order disagreement, and in those cases, no criteria exist for selecting an answer. Individuals reason, but they reason differently and imperfectly, and prediction is the best one can hope to do.

The mistake the second order skeptic makes is in equating formalized truth with empirical truth, or put differently, truth within an axiomatized system with truth from correspondence to the exterior world. If I say of a piece of paper before me "This lease is valid," I am making a statement about the social world.[46] The statement refers to a series of relationships between a person sitting peacefully in an apartment (a lessee) and a person somewhere else, who regularly collects money from the apartment dweller (the lessor). The government, the utility companies, the insurance companies, sub-lessees, and zoning boards all alter their behavior in small ways because of the lease. When I justify the statement "This lease is valid", I am no longer making a statement about the social world. I am making a statement about the logical world. I am declaring a logical relationship between the justified and the justifying statements, and appealing to some criteria on which to base that relationship.

Of course, many statements that justify seem also to be statements about the external world. But when these statements function as justifications, they are logical in nature.

---

them, it would have to be by some special faculty of perception, quite different from our ordinary perceptual faculties (the epistemological objection). Mackie's argument is aimed at an objective second order ethical position. Regardless of its force there, it is not telling against a conventionalized system constructed here. See J. L. Mackie, *Ethics: Inventing Right and Wrong* 38-42 (1977).

46 In making a statement, a speaker commonly does more than one thing. He may be trying to persuade or convince, as well as to define or declare. In saying that a statement has reference to the empirical world, I wish to show one use only, and contrast this use with one not necessarily captured by higher order statements. The idea of variant sentence functions is common to speech-act theory. See J. L. Austin, *How to do Things with Words* (1962) and John Searle, *Speech Acts: An Essay in the Philosophy of Language* (1969).

When the second order skeptic doubts the objectivity of second order propositions, he is entertaining a logical, not an empirical, doubt. He can see that first order statements are often undecided, and seem to have a doubtful or controversial empirical existence. A number of possible answers compete. He can discover which one prevails by observation. Second order propositions are not discoverable in the same way. One cannot look about to find the correct set of rules or criteria for judgment. (Those stated in cases are frequently misleading in several ways.)[47] Nor can one even be sure what criteria were used in a single case.

The skeptic here is looking, so to speak, in the wrong place. Judicial reasoning chains are not discovered, they are constructed. The fact that many competing sets of second order propositions exist suggests many different constructs rather than none. The skeptic implicitly accepts this when he allows for overdetermination, a concept he must accept if he is to avoid being attacked by Hart for being a pure rule skeptic. But overdetermination implies determination. However, one is never sure just what the result will be when the criteria fall apart. But if lower order propositions are determinable, then, even if no empirical test is available for selecting the correct criteria, criteria must exist. If they logically exist, then second order skepticism fails.

Third Order Skepticism

The arguments for (and against) second order skepticism can be at least partially applied toward first order propositions. In that the first order propositions take a normative form, and are often uncertain, they are apt to being labeled as subjective. The same interchangeability applies for the third order skeptic's argument in its application to second order propositions.

The third order skeptic denies the viability of third order propositions (judicial views). She cannot deny that a third order set in some sense exists, and that judicial reasoning stops after

---

47 See Chapter IV for a discussion of several of the problems of reading a case.

the second level. This position was shown to be implausible in Chapter I, and our third order skeptic accepts that argument. Instead, she wishes to argue for the subjectivity of the third level *vis-a-vis* the lower levels. That is, the third level set is inadequately formed to yield objective lower order propositions. It would be akin to a geometry where the initial axioms are not well formulated, and thus are unable to serve as a foundation for subsequent theorems and corollaries.

Third level inadequacy occurs in one of two ways. One can be a skeptic about the subjects which form the basis of the third order. For example, one can endorse ethical subjectivism or political relativism and believe that the standards by which to assess the correctness of a moral or political assertion provide no criteria for judicial-assertion validity. Because criteria for standards in these areas are lacking, a structure including propositions dependent on them is faulty. A more tentative skeptic might believe that this position allows that even the most fundamental standards used in any field are completely arbitrary, a difficult position to accept while still making sense of the terms used in speaking of ethics or politics. The tentative skeptic would, however, say that the criteria for choosing standards are so vague and indeterminate that no rigorous schema could be developed using such concepts.

The position of the third order skeptic needs to be distinguished clearly at this point from the position of the judicial pluralist. Both positions hold that third level propositions are a matter of individual choice. Both also hold that the basis for that choice is one's conception of judicial role. The pluralist claims that once one understands judicial role and attempts to construct a judicial view based on judicial role, one is committed to an entire reasoning schema. Although there are standards for what is involved in judicial role, choice (or preference) is not a matter of logical determination. Choice here need not be a conscious, intentional matter. It instead can be taken to denote the set of beliefs and attitudes one possesses on relevant issues. The strong skeptic can hold that even minimal standards for appropriateness of judicial role are absent, but she would be more likely merely to contend that whatever minimal standards apply, they do not affect the essential non-assertability of third order propositions. The tentative skeptic would allow for propositional assertability, but deny that these assertions commit the speaker to specific lower order propositions.

The distinctions that constitute the basis of these separate positions may be made clearer through the use of an illustration. Suppose Z was a prospector for gold who had successfully discovered and laid claim to a gold mine in a remote and frozen wasteland. Shortly after the discovery, Z fell heir to a series of misfortunes and thirty years later found himself destitute and thousands of miles from his property. In order to recover his gold mine, Z borrowed $200 from Y, with the promise to repay it with $10,000 interest. Z used the money to recover and mine his property, which became worth over one million dollars. He refused to repay Y however. Y sues for breach. Z claims unconscionability and usury. [48]

This case presents in an explicit way several third order concerns which are relevant to its eventual resolution: freedom to make bargains, unconscionable agreements, exorbitant loans. The strong skeptic would admit to their relevance. She would see that on the side of Y would be the values of free contract and contractual reliance, while on the side of Z would be the values of equity and fairness. The strong skeptic then could say one of two things. She might argue that one just has no (correct) way to choose between Y and Z. One's conception of judicial role is too weak to allow it to yield propositions on matters of contract altogether. Alternatively, she might say that the conception of role allows for such things as fairness, contractual freedom, equity, *etc.*, but it neither gives us an analogue for choosing between these, nor allows more specific characterizations. [49] How, after all, does one move from the fact that judges ought to decide cases fairly to the specific parame-

---

48 The facts are, with some tinkering, those of *Embola v. Tupella*, 127 Wash. 285, 220 P. 789 (1923). The court there affirmed a judgment in favor of the plaintiff lender, finding that the speculativeness of the loan made it fall outside the range of either the usury or unconscionability defenses.

49 Judicial systems are well-known for yielding a multitude of rights, but are equally well-known for framing many if not most cases as conflicts between competing rights. An analogue is a procedure which would order these rights.

ters of the law of usury? The strong skeptic can admit to the case of *Y v. Z* being resolved in a reasoned way. She would just suggest that the third order reasons have no particular attachment to the judicial role. They were constructed as the individual saw fit from his general stock of ideas. He (that individual) is not committed to the construction as a matter of his view of judicial reasoning.

In order for strong skepticism to be plausible, two things must be true. Only an extremely impoverished notion of judicial role can exist, and the areas that third order propositions draw upon must be very narrow. The notion of judicial role must be too weak to allow for one to begin construction of a third order view. The skeptic might allow that one's conception of a proper role would include settling disputes, settling them fairly, and employing some criteria for their resolution. She would argue that beyond that, role is too uncertain and too weak a concept to yield third order propositions. Thus, in *Y v. Z*, the strong skeptic would allow that there must be a decision, and it ought to be a fair one based on some standards of justice. But she would then say that in regard to any non-arbitrary decision analogue, which is all one can say. There is a type of logical argument that might be made against the skeptic, but it is ultimately unsuccessful. It is a variant of the argument from the paradigm case, and a proponent of it might claim here that if a concept · or term is to be meaningful, there must be instances when the concept or term has a paradigmatic application. While some applications of the concept or term may be a matter for doubt, the occurrence of a central or paradigm instance is necessary to understand what is meant by the concept or term. The concept here is that of "judicial role". If this concept is to be used, there must be some general agreement about what is meant by it.[50] The concept needs to be strong enough to allow for a paradigm case. There need be no actual instances of such a case, but we must be able to recognize what such cases would look like if there were. If "role" is inade-

---

50 Wittgenstein wrote that "if language is to be a means of communication there must be agreement not only in definitions but also (queer as this may sound) in judgments." Ludwig Wittgenstein, *Philosophical Investigations* I, 242 (1953).

quate to answer all cases, it can answer some, and thus tentative skepticism is the strongest skeptical position possible.

The paradigm case argument challenges the skeptical assertion that one can both understand the concept of judicial role, and yet fail to be able to articulate cases of what exactly role entails. If one's concept of judicial role tells how a judge ought to decide cases, it also ought to be able to instantiate a single case that could be so decided.

The simple objection to this argument is that it confuses meaning with use. It assumes that for "judicial role" to be meaningful, it must have a certain kind of application. The skeptic would deny that role has any application of the kind needed to yield propositions, but would accept role as meaningful in that it allows us to make sense of the judicial reasoning schema. The more serious objection is that the argument misses the point of the skeptic. The skeptic can allow for the possibility of a paradigm case. She may say that there is some matter, Q v. R, that could be settled simply by resort to role. But role is too impoverished a concept to decide many cases, and certainly is useless in Y v. Z.

The difficulty in the strong skeptical position is not conceptual, but empirical. It moves from the fact that a conception of role can be extremely limited to the unwarranted and inaccurate position that it is in fact so limited. Let us look at Y v. Z. It presents thorny, ethical issues concerning bargain fairness and one individual using a second individual's misfortune to enrich himself to an extent impossible if the misfortune were less severe. It is easy to imagine groups of judges, say those of a primitive, aboriginal Asian tribe, whose notion of judicial role was inadequate to allow for resolution of such issues. If one assumes that Henry Maine was correct, and history is the story of a movement of societies from status based to contract based, then perhaps the entire notion of contract is alien to these aborigines.[51] But Y v. Z could not arise in an aboriginal society.

---

51 Henry Maine's position can be found in his *Ancient Law* (1861). Henry Maine's view was heavily influenced by the English model, where property was the dominant legal concept, and slow to yield to contract. While the movement from status to contract is somewhat descriptive of England—although there are difficulties even there, where courts of law

The concepts necessary to solve the case are the same concepts that gave rise to it. This is really an explanation for what is an empirical commonplace: enriched concepts of judicial roles. The skeptic is reluctant to imply very much from judicial role, but members of the bench and society generally are not. Y's act of initiating the case, and Z's particular defense demonstrate that some individuals make use of a richer concept of judicial role.

The tentative skeptic may step in and agree with this criticism of the strong skeptic. She could allow that judicial role can be a rich notion. It might allow for a methodology for searching for principles—such as those found in legal forms; and it might provide principles directly. More importantly, such a rich notion is widely held. However, the types of principles it provides are too general to solve specific cases. The kind of fine reasoning needed in $Y v. Z$, for example, is out of reach of even a rich notion of role.

The tentative skeptic mistakes the failure of a conception of judicial role to yield an immediate (complete) analogue for an inability of the propositions yielded to allow for an eventual resolution of first order questions. The moves from fairness to contract fairness to conscionability in matters of consideration disparity to a resolution of $Y v. Z$ are not all easy ones. One does not just contemplate the meaning of judicial role and arrive at the solution to $Y v. Z$. One must analyze one's third order propositions that are relevant to $Y v. Z$. This involves squaring conflicting propositions and determining the scope of concepts embedded within the judicial view. The fact that many of these concepts—such as fairness, justice, freedom, or reasonableness—are extremely vague is only a problem for lower order propositions. If, however, the individual holder of the view can use what may singly be a vague concept in conjunction

---

merchant had a long and ancient stay, and where many contract ideas were imbedded in property concepts, and were in fact hostile to notions of feudalism—it has grave defects as a general thesis. Brazil, which moved from a society of independent Indian tribes engaged in commerce and allowing for personal freedom to a largely regimented society based on wealth and authority, and allowing for virtually no important commerce without government intervention, provides at least one depressing counter-example to Maine.

with others to reach a resolution (to arrive at a unique set of lower order propositions), vagueness need not be a problem. In any case, specific underdetermination in an area is an empirical matter, and its occasional occurrence does not save the skeptic.

The Emotivist Possibility

The final form of skepticism can only be discussed briefly, for any adequate approach leads into an array of problems in the philosophy of language. This form is emotivism, a theory which holds that in the case of certain kinds of judgments, here judicial statements, the meaning of a statement lies in its ability to communicate an attitude or emotion, and thus to inspire an act of will without conveying truth.[52] An emotivist would hold that third level propositions are entirely either emotive or attitudinal in that they are intended to express feeling and stimulate the action of others.

An emotivist position is too insubstantial to begin to account for the complexity found in judicial reasoning. The emotivist wants to take two facts—that role is a matter of individual choice, and that there is an attitudinal component of third level propositions—and build an entire anti-rational theory. These facts do not commit us to such a theory. Pluralism suggests that one needs to consider one's own position toward judicial role as a fact, that one cannot choose but to hold many of the attitudes one does hold. Given an individual's commitment to his own initial position, certain further matters (a judicial view) may be developed. The validity of this commitment need not be, in any sense, objective to be usable, just as the fact that a given postulate is arbitrary is irrelevant to the validity of the theorems one deduces from that postulate. Further, that there is an attitudi-

---

52 The two works most often associated with the propounding of emotivism as a theory which can explain values are A. J. Ayer in the first edition of *Language, Truth and Logic* (1936) and Charles L. Stevenson, *Ethics and Language* (1944). J. O. Urmson's *The Emotive Theory of Ethics* (1968) is the outstanding critical work. Within law, the legal realist Alf Ross endorses the emotivist position throughout his *On Law and Justice* (1958), but in a disorganized way difficult to follow fully.

nal component to a view does not imply that that component constitutes the entire view.[53] The language of judicial reasoning is replete with belief statements that the emotivism which seems attractive in a field as intuitive as aesthetics appears slightly ludicrous in law.

---

53 Richard M. Hare's attack on emotivism for failing to explain all the aspects of moral statements is analogous. He sees moral statements as having both a prescriptive and descriptive content. The emotivists only noticed the prescriptive and falsely deduced that beliefs play no part in moral reasoning. See Richard M. Hare, *The Language of Morals* (1952) and *Freedom and Reason* (1963).

IV

The Concept of the Judicial Decision

Law, says the judge as he looks down his nose,
Speaking clearly and most severely,
Law is as I've told you before,
Law is as you know I suppose,
Law is but let me explain it once more,
Law is The Law.

W.H. Auden

Judicial reasoning finds its focus in the form of the judicial decision. Given the importance of judicial decisions, it is hardly surprising that there is controversy over the proper technique for understanding adjudication. Yet, the nature of the controversy is masked. To assume that a universally accepted proper or canonical way to analyze decisions exists confuses the issue of where the real controversy lies. Some precision in the use of legal terms is essential, as is an understanding that not just bad technique but a difference in one's legal theory causes disagreement. This does not mean simply that individuals disagree on the outcome of decisions, but that differences in belief about what are the important aspects of adjudication lead to different approaches to deciding any case.

The structure of the common law finds its two sided focus in the judicial decision. Looking back, the decision is authority for a set of conclusions reached by or attributed to a previous court. The rule in *Shelley's Case*,[1] the holding of *MacPherson v. Buick Motor Co.*,[2] and the *Erie* doctrine[3] are familiar examples of

---

1   76 Eng. Rep. 206 (1581).

2   217 N.Y. 382, 111 N.E. 1050 (1916).

the authority of a past decision. This authority is complex, as it is not only often difficult to locate the conclusions in the text, but also controversial to select the criteria for location. Should a case have one or a number of conclusions? What happens when the reasons given do not support the stated conclusion? How critical are the facts of the case in limiting the authority or precedential value of the case? In *Erie Railroad Co. v. Tompkins*, the United States Supreme Court overruled *Swift v. Tyson*[4] and stated that the *Swift* Court had wrongly declared that a general federal common law existed for diversity purposes. As *Swift* only discussed negotiable instruments law, did the fact that subsequent decisions construed it more broadly change the holding of *Swift*?[5] Are its commercial paper facts incidental or central?

Of course, decisions are not ordinarily accorded the same authority as statutes or custom. They have a certain fallibility. Decisions can be wrong—the reasons given might not support the conclusions reached, they might misstate or misuse the facts, the reasons themselves might be inappropriate or unsound, or there might be one of a hundred other possible flaws in reasoning. Therefore, the authority is based both on the fact of the decision and on its being well reasoned.

The prospective centrality of the judicial decision comes from its form. Common law lawyers structure all later questions into the hypothetical judicial case form, but it could be otherwise. One might ask, for any particular aspect of the common law, how the case form affects the behavior of those governed by it or the officials who apply the legal rules. Practitioners, however, dissect other forms of legal authority (statutes, constitutions, custom), take reasons, and assemble a new argument

---

3 *Erie Railroad Co. v. Tompkins*, 304 U.S. 64, 58 S. Ct. 817, 82 L.Ed. 1188 (1938).

4 41 U.S. (16 Pet.) 1, 10 L.Ed. 865 (1842).

5 See, *e.g.*, *Black & White Taxicab & Transfer Co. v. Black & Yellow Taxicab & Transfer Co.*, 276 U.S. 518, 532, 48 S. Ct. 404, 72 L.Ed. 681, 57 A.L.R. 426 (1928) (Holmes, J., dissenting); *Salem Trust Co. v. Manufacturers' Fin. Co.*, 264 U.S. 182 (1924); *Oakes v. Mase*, 165 U.S. 363, 17 S. Ct. 345, 41 L.Ed. 746 (1897).

for use as a reason in a judicial decision. This technique or process has well-defined strictures. For instance, only certain forms of authority count. Weighing the reasons is more controversial because measuring the reasons and policies of past decisions against statutes or one another is not just a matter of technical expertise. It is also a matter of stating what is important in the general way one reaches or should reach decisions.

Decisions serve functions other than as precedent. For instance, they provide a record for inspection and appeal and allow a judge an opportunity to state reasons to justify his conclusions. More fundamentally, though, the decision allows for the resolution of disputes. As a result, decisions must be in a form suitable to resolve disputes. In this sense, a decision is more than a mere assertion of ordinary speech, it is also performance, a speech act.[6] If a judge states: "You are now divorced," "Adoption granted," "Guilty," or "There is no valid contract," he cannot, in this one sense, be right or wrong. His statement, like a clergyman's pronouncement of wedlock, makes it so. The answer-providing function of judicial decisions, however, will not be discussed here.

Judicial theories of particular jurisdictions also need to be set aside, but only in part. Theoretical problems of identifying what counts as a decision or precedent and why decisions should count at all, involve difficult areas of individuation, identity, and balancing. We have discussed certain general (non-jurisdiction specific) features of this theory earlier. Each legal system has its own contents for the propositions in the judicial schema. Some legal systems, including the civil law,[7] early English equity,[8] and the original Court of Common Pleas,[9] have

---

6 See generally J. L. Austin, *Philosophical Papers* (1961) for an analysis of the nature of different functions of speech. For a fuller, more recent treatment, see also John R. Searle, *Speech Acts: An Essay in the Philosophy of Language* (1969) and *Intention* (1979).

7 For a general, if oversimplified, description of this system see John Henry Merryman, *The Civil Law Tradition* 24, 35-39, 48, 50-58, 87-91 (1969).

8 Legal scholars do not necessarily agree that early equity greatly differed from the common law in its use of precedent. See, *e.g.*, Frederick Mait-

given past judicial decisions little weight. In the common law, identifying the criteria for selecting a case to carry a certain authority is complex and controversial. Judicial theory sifts the myriad of putative authority and creates an ordering among selected contenders.

Constructing theories for particular legal systems is not the purpose here. Rather, a more fundamental problem needs to be addressed. In constructing a judicial view, it is necessary to include an analogue for locating the sources of authority of the lower order propositional set. This analogue, in the form of a set of related propositions, is a necessary part of the third order propositional set. Legal forms, for example, are not self-evident sources of authority. Nor, once identified as relevant, are they subject to one and only one interpretation. Questions of identity and interpretation are handled differently depending on one's judicial view, but logical distinctions remain regardless of view.

This chapter discusses three related aspects of the concept of the judicial decision. The first section analyzes the use of reasons. Apparent disagreement about what a judgment within a decision "means," "holds," or "stands for" sometimes is not really a disagreement but a confusion. For example, a judge's given reasons need not imply his stated conclusions. If one person claims the decision stands for what the stated reasons imply and another maintains that it stands for what the conclusion states, they may not be disagreeing about anything. To assume a necessary disagreement, as those arguing may suppose, would be to conflate distinct matters unknowingly. The difference lies with conflicting beliefs about how adjudication should work. Eliminating confusion over terms allows for clarity about the dimensions of the real (normative) disagreement.

The second section of this chapter looks at those objects which routinely contain propositions located in the second order: legal forms. These forms operate ambiguously in future

---

land, *Equity* 8, 93-94 (2d ed. 1936). A somewhat different picture is presented by H. D. Hazeltine, in "The Early History of English Equity", in *Essays in Legal History* 261-285 (ed. Paul Vinogradoff 1913).

9 See F. West, *The Justiarship in England* (1966).

decisions.   Once the ambiguity is clarified, there is a further problem: discovering the meaning of the forms. Some resort to intentionality is necessary.

The third section looks briefly at reasoning by analogy. Like "the reason of the case" and the legal form, it is often considered a straight forward tool of adjudication. However, after clarifying certain features of the logic of reasons and of legal forms, reasoning by analogy, at least within judicial reasoning, collapses.

Reasons and Conclusions in Judicial Decisions

There is a vast literature which purports to explain how to read, understand, and use judicial decisions.[10]   Much of it centers on what a holding of a decision entails and how one distinguishes the holding, sometimes in common law called the "*ratio decidendi*," from other conclusions, the "*obiter dicta*".[11] As decisions are authority and arguments from past decisions are arguments from authority (the doctrine of precedent), it is important to understand where the authority is strong (in the form of the *ratio decidendi*) and where it is weak (in the form of

---

10   Although this literature is, in general, of little significance here, see *e.g.*, C. K. Allen, *Law in the Making* (7th ed. 1964); Benjamin Cardozo, *The Nature of the Judicial Process* (1921); Rupert Cross, *Precedent in English Law* (3d ed. 1977); Henry Hart & Albert Sachs, *The Legal Process* 1-206, 367-668 (1958); Edward Levi, *An Introduction to Legal Reasoning* (1948); Karl Llewellyn, *The Common Law Tradition: Deciding Appeals* (1960); Arthur Goodhart, "Determining the *Ratio Decidendi* of a Case," 40 *Yale L.J.* 161 (1930).

11   This distinction between the *ratio* and the *obiter* was once at the heart of jurisprudential discussion, but is now largely out of favor. See, *e.g.*, Karl Llewellyn, *The Common Law Tradition* 36-47 (1960), for a discussion of this distinction. If the categories seem slightly archaic, the idea behind them is still vital. The idea concerns how one understands a case and decides what is critical and what is peripheral to the judgment. The categories are useful as a quick way to enter into discussion of a case without setting up a possibly safer, but certainly more cumbersome and less familiar, system. One still useful analysis can be found in Arthur L. Goodhart, "Determining the *Ratio Decidendi* of a Case," found in his *Essays in Jurisprudence and Common Law* (1931).

obiter dicta).[12] An often ignored prior question involves asking in what way a decision serves as an authority. To answer these questions, several distinctions must be drawn.

The first distinction is between the actual conclusions stated in the decision and the conclusion one can imply from the reasons stated in the opinion. The reasons in the opinion may imply one of five possible things: the conclusion the opinion actually states; a different conclusion, either contrary or contradictory; the conclusion or another conclusion with both being satisfactory (the disjunct here being inclusive); either the conclusion or another conclusion with only one conclusion being satisfactory (the disjunct here being exclusive); or no conclusion. One cannot expect the strict logical implication of the kind found in mathematical statements. The reasons for a certain and widespread imprecision are well-known: judicial reasons often employ vague and ambiguous language, judicial intention is often uncertain, and opinions leave many premises unstated in the reasoning chain; however, the reasons a judge offers in his opinions are not meant to imply (strictly). They are premises in judicial argument and such an argument is employed within a socially shared tradition. Given that tradition and its concomitant common discourse, one can speak of implication of reasons within actual decisions.

Reasons are presumably included in opinions because judges believe that, taken as a set, they imply the stated conclusions. This is certainly sometimes the case. Often though, it is not. If

---

12 The authority of judicial decisions is a dominant common law notion. It is weaker in civil law and many commentators argue that cases do not serve as authority in civil law jurisdictions. Typical is the comment of John Henry Merryman: "[T]he accepted theory of sources of law in the Civil Law tradition recognizes only statutes, regulations, and custom as sources of law. This listing is exclusive." John H. Merryman, *The Civil Law Tradition* note 8, at 25. However, as Merryman points out later, "[t]he civil law is a law of the professors." *Tradition* at 60. These professors often draft the statutes and write the texts which control interpretation. An examination of past decisions is a large part of professorial scholarship. Thus, even here, the judicial case has some importance as authority, although somewhat removed. Of course, the fact that constitutions allow for judicial review of certain cases in some civil law jurisdictions further erodes the idea of the legislature as the sole source of authority.

the judge makes a mistake—such as where he states: "if p, q, r, and s, then t" and "p, q, r, and s" implies either –t or more specifically, u—the two will vary and there will be a wrong determination. More commonly, an underdetermination or overdetermination can occur. Underdetermination occurs when reasons run out; for example, when "if p, q, r, and s, then t" is true, but the judge assumed "if p, q, and s, then t." Overdetermination occurs when both "if p, q, r, and s, then t" and "if m, n, o, and p, then t" are true and the judge uses both of these statements to reach his conclusion—t (is true).

One should not assume that a disparity between reasons and conclusions is necessarily due to fuzzy thinking. It can be personally advantageous for the judge to mask his indecision or uncertainty. In a more basic sense, it can be institutionally advantageous for courts generally to settle disputes in individual cases while not heightening or highlighting the kind of disparity of views which often gives rise to entire dockets of disputes. In that a certain obfuscation is encouraged, ambiguity is sure to follow.

Some commentators apparently dispute the existence of this distinction as they only see an integrated decision with reasons leading to the stated conclusion. For example, Rupert Cross stated, "The *ratio decidendi* of a case is any rule of law expressly or implicitly treated by the judge as a necessary step in reaching his conclusion, having regard to the line of reasoning adopted by him, or a necessary part of his direction to the jury." [13]

---

13 Rupert Cross, *Precedent in English Law* at 76 (3d ed. 1977). Cross does qualify this by noting: "The adoption of one line of reasoning by the judge is not incompatible with his adopting a further line of reasoning. Allowance must be made for the fact that a case may have more than one *ratio decidendi*." *Precedent* at n. 3. What Cross means by more than one *ratio* still involves lines of reasoning tied to the judgment; he merely allows that there may be either more than one judgment or two parallel lines that are compatible and lead to the judgment. He does not recognize a separation between the stated reasons and the given judgment. In Cross' defense, he claims to describe the general usage of "*ratio*" by lawyers rather than the correct usage. Later he wavers in that restriction and seems uncertain about whether his work is a description of certain social data or a recommendation for the use of the data as a basis for improvement. For example, he tells the reader when and to what extent

Rather than assuming that reasons and conclusions coincide, *i.e.*, each implies the same proposition or set of propositions to produce the *ratio*, it is more accurate to say, if one wants to retain the idea of a *ratio*, there are two sets of *rationes* in every case. The reasons stated in the opinion produce the first *ratio* and the opinion's conclusion yields the second. Sometimes the two *rationes* coincide (they each imply the other), but even then, one can individuate the two and each can serve as a check on the other. Of course this division is apart from any other propagation method for a *ratio*, *i.e.*, several issues or several judgments. It is a necessary rather than a contingent division.

A second and more important distinction exists between decisional reasons as reasons and decisional reasons as authority. Each decision contains one or more arguments for the conclusion or conclusions it reaches. Reasons figure as premises in those arguments. In order to put forth a judicial argument, the judge must consider his audience. He assumes a large body of shared knowledge in any case and the scope of that assumption varies depending on such ordinary things as whether the case is one of first instance or an appeal, whether he is sitting alone or *en banc*, whether the type of case is commonplace or esoteric, and whether the situation is straightforward or complicated. In order to advance an argument, it may be just as necessary to employ traditional legal propositions as it is to employ propositions of fact, logic, ethics, or politics.

However, reasons in judicial decisions are taken as authority for future cases.[14] Especially susceptible to this practice are reasons which one can restate as normative propositions. The difficulty arises when one decides to criticize judgment. It is a necessary but often neglected aspect of analysis to decide whether reasons are suspect as logical premises or as authority, as in *Riggs v. Palmer*,[15] the case of the legatee who murdered his testator, but nevertheless sought to enjoy the benefits of the

---

a *ratio* is binding, presumably using the lawyer's description of that term, but treats the subject as if the ambiguities and difficulties did not exist.

14 Although this applies to the common law tradition, evidence exists that it also applies to some extent in civil law.

15 115 N.Y. 506, 22 N.E. 188 (1889).

testator's will. One of the reasons announced by the court for its decision denying the legatee recovery was that no man ought to benefit from his own wrong. One could criticize that reason as being faulty authority. It is vague, it says more than is necessary to reach a conclusion to the case (it is overbroad), and it has a suspicious pedigree (nowhere does the decision clearly state where one could find the reason in previous case law or statutes). In fact, the results of other cases contradict this reason. For example, when an intentional contract breacher violates a contract where there is no benefit to the bargain,[16] the breacher is in a position to benefit from his or her wrong. The "no benefit from wrongdoing" reason could be attacked logically as well. It might not be thought to lead to the conclusion, but merely duplicate it in a more general form. That is, given the counter-reason that disposal of the estate should be in accordance with the testator's written instructions, a statement concerning a reluctance to reward wrongs in the courtroom is of uncertain relevance. Does the reason go toward a reevaluation of the testator's actual or probable intention if he knew about his imminent poisoning? Does it establish a rule which overrides other rules and if so, when?

Both criticisms, from logic and authority, are valid: however, if one rejected the proposition "no man shall benefit from his own wrong" as authority because the argument contains faulty logic, one would commit an error. One commits a complementary error by rejecting the reason as logically invalid merely because it has a suspicious origin. A statement may carry authority regardless of errors of reasoning, just as one may employ a groundless argument in support of a correct and valid conclusion.

A third distinction, and one which generates controversy where controversy does not seem possible, is the distinction between the actual questions raised by the case and the questions stated and addressed in the opinion. Fact situations can produce a complex and initially bewildering number of issues. Judges often address them in the manner suggested by the advocate presenting the case. Appellate courts usually discuss

---

16   See, *e.g.*, Arthur Corbin, 3A *Contracts* Section 707 (1960).

only those issues raised on appeal. At times, courts neglect, overlook, or misunderstand issues.[e17]   The more common occurrence is that perceptions of what is important within a controversy change. Even a slight movement in separating the questions actually addressed from the questions theoretically possible can have dramatic consequences. The shift in products liability cases from the "inherently dangerous rule" to products merely "dangerous" illustrates this principle well.[18]   *Thomas v. Winchester*[19] involved a case of mislabeled poison sold to a remote vendee. The issue for the court was whether the remote vendor's action put life in "imminent danger," the test under relevant precedent.[20]   A subsequent decision, *MacPherson v. Buick Motor Co.*,[21] allowed recovery in a similar case which involved a defective automobile.   In *MacPherson*, the court looked back at *Thomas v. Winchester* and found in the latter case the foundations of general liability for all defective articles. The court simply looked at *Thomas* as raising a general issue never considered by the original court.

When one states that a case stands for a certain proposition, one must be careful to separate the proposition intended by those deciding the case from what other readers, beginning with the facts and ending with the conclusion, may reason that it stands for. This difference between the opinion of the decision's author and future observers' possible, later impressions is also relevant to the fourth distinction—that between judicial intention toward the case and other later parties' intentions.

Karl Llewellyn described this difference as the "distinction between the *ratio decidendi*, the court's own version of the rule

---

17 Cases examining whether a sum of money serves as good consideration for a promise to pay a greatly larger sum exemplify all of these possibilities. These cases virtually never address the issue of usury. See, *e.g.*, *In re Greene*, 45 F.2d 428 (S.D.N.Y. 1930); *American Univ. v. Todd*, 1 A.2d 595 (Del. Super. Ct. 1938); *Schnell v. Neil*, 17 Ind. 29 (1861).

18 See Edward Levi, *An Introduction to Legal Reasoning* at 8-27 (1948).

19 6 N.Y. 397 (1852).

20 See, *e.g.*, *Dixon v. Bell*, 5 Maule & Selwyn 198, 105 Eng. Rep. 1023 (1816). But see *Winterbottom v. Wright*, 10 Meeson & Welsby 109, 152 Eng. Rep. 402 (1842).

21 217 N.Y. 382, 111 N.E. 1050 (1916).

of the case and the *true* rule of the case, to wit *what it will be made to stand for by another later court.*"[22]   One can restate Llewellyn's distinction in general terms and distinguish between the deciding judge's view of the case and later observers' assessment of the judgment. A difference can arise when just interpreting a previous decision involves deviations from the original intention of its authors. This may occur when a decision is of alien or ancient origin (borrowed from another or predecessor legal system) or when one tries to fit a troublesome decision into an otherwise tidy line of past cases. Interpretation can also range wider afield and these wide discrepancies may occur when a later court or observer fastens onto an earlier decision's ambiguity or vagueness and proceeds to gloss or rereason the previous case.[23]

A. W. B. Simpson contests this distinction. He speaks in terms of the *ratio decidendi,*[24] but one can generalize his position. Simpson writes:

---

22   Karl Llewellyn, *Bramble Bush* at 52. Llewellyn continues by saying that:

> One of the vital elements of our doctrine of precedent is this: that any later court can always reexamine a prior case, and under the principle that the court could decide only what was before it, and that the older case must now be read with that in view, can arrive at the conclusion that the dispute before the earlier court was much narrower than that court thought it was, called therefore for the application of a much narrower rule. Indeed, the argument goes further. It goes on to state that no broader rule could have been laid down *ex cathedra*, because to do that would have transcended the powers of the earlier court.

Karl Llewellyn does not fully accept the third distinction. He fails to see that a subsequent reading of a case can broaden as well as narrow the conclusions. This process occurs routinely in constitutional law cases and generally takes place when there is an attempt to eliminate an overcrowded classification.

23   Perhaps Glanville Williams had this phenomenon in mind when he said that the phrase "*ratio decidendi*" is slightly ambiguous. See Glanville Williams, *Learning the Law* 80 (8th ed. 1969).

24   A. W. B. Simpson, "The *Ratio Decidendi* of a Case and the Doctrine of Binding Precedent," in *Oxford Essays in Jurisprudence* 148 (ed. A. Guest 1961).

The *reductio ad absurdum* of this confusion is to be found expressed in the theory that the *ratio decidendi* of a case is a rule which is constructed by a later court when called upon to consider the case. To *define* the *ratio* in this way is surely perverse—if it were correct to do so a number of oddities would follow. For example, it would be a contradiction to say that a court had misunderstood an earlier case's *ratio*, for by definition this could not be so; it could neither be understood nor misunderstood; confronted with two variant judicial decisions as to the *ratio* of an earlier case one would have to say that the case had two different *rationes decidendi*; analyses of cases which had not yet been considered by a court would have to be portrayed as prophecies as to what in the future would be the *ratio decidendi* of a case already decided. [25]

Given the divergent use of "*ratio*," Simpson might want to offer his own definition of the term. He could also argue, as Cross does in places,[26] that the accepted usage of the phrase "*ratio decidendi*" lies in the original court's expression of its intended interpretation. Instead Simpson uses a logical argument that suggests that the point discussed above is untenable because the idea of a later construction of the *ratio* is not logically viable. He uses three arguments to support this idea. None of them is satisfactory. [27]

First, he suggests that allowing for a later interpretation of a case's *ratio*, we are prevented from asserting that a court misunderstood an earlier court's *ratio*. If this were true, one could only echo Simpson and state that it is odd. It is not incoherent and, in fact, one can see advantages to such an approach. Where neither the decision's stated reasons nor the court's actions imply the earlier decision's stated conclusions, one can simply disregard the inconsistent and usually irrational conclusion. However, Simpson's objection fails for another reason. One can recognize parallel types of approaches to case analysis as useful and use them without a commitment to any single approach. Even if one is committed to the approach of later construction, one can speak of wrongly interpreting an earlier *ratio*. Strictly speaking, this would not constitute an assertion of an incorrect *ratio*, but a statement that the court reached an incorrect conclusion. This, however, is a small matter of termi-

---

25 *Id.* at 169.

26 Rupert Cross, *Precedent in English Law* 35-101 (2d ed. 1961).

27 A. W. B. Simpson, *Ratio, op. cit.* note 26, at 169.

nology. In any case, the type of analysis and criticism under Simpson's preferred approach would still be available.

Simpson's second argument maintains that if later cases interpret an earlier case differently, then one is placed in the unhappy position of having to say that the earlier case has two or more *rationes decidendi*. This, however, confuses conditions for asserting a proposition with conditions for that proposition being true. Suppose two later courts seek to discover whether a previous decision's conclusions are justified. That they may disagree on the answer does not suggest that either is without grounds for its assertions. If both later courts have authority to declare judgment, then presumably there is some method for deciding which of the cases' judgments is superior. As for whether the original conclusion was justifiable, anyone who analyzes it is equally able (if not equally competent) to comment upon this question. Disagreement does not indicate that subsequent analysis is impossible. One can make the same argument for the *ratio*. That courts may disagree about where to locate it does not suggest that any contradiction need arise. If the original decision is a social fact to be observed, then one can settle the subsequent disagreement about its *ratio decidendi* in the same way as one settles any dispute.

Simpson's third argument is that, until a decision is reexamined, if a *ratio* is subsequently constructed, then one can only predict its holding. This is exactly what occurs as a normal aspect of the concept of precedent anyway. When one looks to judicial decisions, or statutes for that matter, their application in subsequent cases is a matter of concern. Some normative standard may exist which will tell what the answer ought to be and such a standard may serve as the controlling element in a prediction. If judges use standards, not only can one predict the holding, but one can also predict it with some confidence. Stating that a method employs prediction is not a criticism if the expectations of persons interested in court opinions focus upon prediction, and the construction of a method which allows success in predicting future court judgments is possible at least in theory.

The final distinction drawn is between a canonical or formula-bound way of presenting reasons and the judge's peculiar and individual method of presentation. Legal scholars have always recognized style as an important component in a case. The American Realists particularly have pointed to schools of style and their effects on a decision's presentation.[28] Given a set of facts and a set of competing arguments, one might devise an analogue for ordering facts and arguments in such a way to reach a determination. If one were then to criticize an individual's or judge's ordering, one could have a standard by which to measure it. Suppose that use of this analogue depended upon information that was occasionally missing. In addition, suppose that one could find the method for attaining this information, whether missing or incomplete, in the ordering that the analogue meant to criticize. Then any criticism leveled at a judge's treatment would be suspect, for the criteria that produced the analogue are themselves a function of criticism of the case. An illustration will clarify this point.

Suppose that D and P are adjoining landowners. D is a plant biologist who performs regular and extensive experiments on her property. She has devised a spray which causes normal grass to mutate into a giant cereal—woody, fast-growing, pungent, and high in protein when applied regularly. Because of the prevailing wind and the fact that P took down a high fence which once separated their properties, P's yard has become a cereal jungle. P is unhappy and therefore sues D.

---

28 For example, Karl Llewellyn saw the development of Anglo-American common law as a battle between two types of judicial style. The "Grand Style" allowed for growth through the incorporation of new concepts into lines of precedent. The "Formal Style" allowed for a system of increasing internal consistency at the expense of adequately shaping decisions for solving societal problems. Karl Llewellyn recognized both styles as equally legitimate *vis-a-vis* the law, but criticized the Formal Style as socially and politically inadequate, intellectually moribund, and aesthetically cumbersome and inelegant. In this sense, he embraces the judicial pluralism position. Karl Llewellyn, *The Common Law Tradition: Deciding Appeals* at 62-120 (1960). Llewellyn uses the term "style" not merely to refer to "literary quality or tone, but to the manner of doing the job, to the way of craftsmanship in office, to a functioning harmonization of vision with tradition, of continuity with growth, of machinery with purpose, of measure with need." *Id.* at 37. While this description is a bit overblown for our purposes, style does denote a personal approach to cases as well as a literary tone.

The judge, sitting in an American jurisdiction, finds for D. He reasons that D's work is socially useful,[29] that P could have taken steps to prevent the growth by simply not removing the fence,[30] and that P came to the property knowing of D's operations.[31]

An observer would note that the judge treated the matter as a private nuisance. While examining the case's main proposition, this observer would note (at least) two facts. First, the reasoning of the judge is ambiguous. The reader does not know whether each of the stated reasons alone mandates a holding against P or whether all are necessary to the decision. The reasons themselves are closely tied to certain facts but the generality of the reasons or the number of fact situations they cover is not knnown. Under the court's opinion, given a replica of *P v. D*, D wins. but given cases like, but not exaclty like, *P v. D*, we cannot say how P or D might do. Second, an alternate basis of liability might exist: that of trespass.[32] We do not know from the actual case of *P v. D* whether or not trespass was barred because the

---

29   Assuming that the court treats the case as one of private nuisance, one well-recognized defense arises when the alleged creator of the nuisance is conducting an activity of great social worth or value. See, *e.g.*, *Richard's Appeal*, 57 Pa. 105, 111-14 (1868).

30   If a plaintiff can easily prevent the nuisance, his failure to do so may cut off liability. See, *e.g.*, *Keeney & Wood Mfg. Co. v. Union Mfg. Co.*, 39 Conn. 576 (1873); *Carroll Springs Distilling Co. v. Schnepfe*, 111 Md. 420, 74 A. 828 (1909).

31   Courts sometimes hold that "coming to the nuisance" bars liability when the public has a major interest in the nuisance. See, *e.g.*, *East St. Johns Shingle Co. v. City of Portland*, 195 Or. 505, 524-25, 246 P.2d 554, 562 (1952); *Powell v. Superior Portland Cement*, 15 Wash. 2d 14, 19, 129 P.2d 536, 538 (1942).

32   The difference between trespass and nuisance is historically obscure, but the *Restatement of Torts* provides the modern view which states that trespass is an invasion of a plaintiff's interest in the exclusive possession of the land, while nuisance is an interference with the use and enjoyment of the land. Obviously, the two are not mutually exclusive. *Restatement of Torts*, Scope and Introductory Note to Ch. 40 preceding Section 822 (1939). See also *Ryan v. City of Emmetsburg*, 232 Iowa 600, 603-04, 4 N.W.2d 435, 438 (1942) (describing the historical difference between trespass and nuisance).

jungle growth did not constitute interference with possession, because the statute of limitations ran,[33] because of another good reason, or because no one thought of trespass as a basis for liability.

The style of the judge's opinion prevents us from knowing which lines of reasoning he considered necessary and which lines sufficient. It also prevents a full understanding of which other possible causes of action might lie in similar cases. One might wish to criticize *P v. D*, claiming that trespass ought to have been considered or that one or another line of reasoning was irrelevant. Criticism might require an analogue based in part on the holdings of past decisions.[34] In theory, these past decisions are as vulnerable as *P v. D* to the objection that style shaped their meaning. The analogue is uncertain to the degree that style allows for ambiguities. There is, thus, a considerable measure of indeterminacy of intention in evaluating decisions, an indeterminacy that undermines any attempt to use past decisions precisely to assess the validity of future decisions.

These five distinctions made, we can now say something about the role of a case in judicial reasoning. All five distinctions suggest that reliance on previous decisions as authority is far from an uncomplicated matter. One's judicial view provides a method for approaching a past decision as well as for answering questions in a present case. However, there is a logical space between giving judgment and understanding an already-answered case.

A judge lists reasons in his judgment, but these reasons are not necessarily the ones which brought him to the conclusion. He may not know or remember these and others may not have the ability to offer a satisfactory account of his reasons. The judge does not look at his own psychological reasons as relevant

---

33   Traditionally, an action for trespass becomes complete upon entry onto the land, while nuisance begins when substantial harm occurs. If D had stopped spraying but the growth continued, a difference in actions could be significant. See William Prosser, *Handbook of the Law of Torts* 89, 595-96 (4th ed. 1971).

34   In this context, analogue connotes an ordered procedure for solving a problem, *e.g.*, a statistical method or a computer program. Analogue in the sense of "paradigm" or "model" is not intended.

for inclusion in his decision. Rather, he looks to reasons which are appropriate and justify a decision. In this important sense, judicial decisions are reconstructions. Once the judge arrives at a decision, he employs an analogue yielded by his judicial view and reconstructs his decision on a rational basis. (One should not impute duplicity to judges in this context. In their reconstruction, judges may employ the reasons which motivated their decision or at least those that they believe motivated their decision. However, they use these reasons differently when they employ them as justifications.) The actual reasons for his decision are outside the purview of any propositional set, as are the reasons which consciously or unconsciously motivated his decision. The reasons stated are evidence of his judicial view.

To understand what a judge meant by his stated reasoning, one must have some notion of his judicial view. This will explain why he put forth his stated reasons. But it is one's own view which determines how one assesses the meaning of judicial decisions. One can look at the earlier distinctions and see them as competing alternatives for inclusion within a judicial view. In this sense, when one speaks of a case standing for some proposition or holding some position, the case is a reconstructed reconstruction, what one might call a "re-reconstruction." One's own judicial view tells one how to read the case—whether one looks to reasons or conclusions, whether one takes questions as they appear to be or actually were raised, whether one looks at the judge's intention as central, and how one treats the individual style of reasoning in past cases—and puts in an orderly basis the disparate elements of individual cases, and allows classification of the variety of cases.

The distinctions discussed might also suggest methods of adjudication. Third order commitments govern one's approach to a case. For instance, a commitment will dictate whether one looks to all of the reasons stated in a previous decision or just to the stated conclusion. The same logic holds for other legal forms—strict versus revisionary interpretations of written constitutions, or statutes interpreted on their face versus statutes interpreted according to legislative intent as evidenced by committee records and floor debates. These are competing positions based on competing views and debate over whether one's choice of position is constitutive of view disparities.

Of course, the various positions only occasionally produce different results. This is a general characteristic of judicial views. Identity of conclusions between competing views on so many questions lull one into believing that only a single view predominates. However, if intersubjective agreement does not imply an objective standard, neither should agreement between different views suggest that only one view is operating.

Legal Forms

Judicial decisions are central to a discussion of judicial reasoning. Within the context of legal systems, they are one of several objects labeled "legal forms". Individually, these forms have their own nuances, but they share several formal features. Certain difficulties inherent in interpreting the meaning of cases are common to all legal forms and have received quicker recognition as problematic in other forms. Both statutory and constitutional interpretations are usually considered troublesome matters and controversy surrounds the selection of criteria for settlement. Like cases, other legal forms often exhibit a certain logic intended to persuade. Thus, they collapse an otherwise clear distinction between sources which argue from authority and sources which argue from reason. There is the problem in all legal forms of deciding which concept of intention to employ.[35] This determination must take into account numerous factors including who originally generates the legal form—customs originating with no individual; cases decided by a certain, ascertainable individual; statutes enacted by a discrete, corporate body of individuals with a range of

---

35 This chapter employs "intention" here in the ordinary language sense— one's purpose or meaning concerning a future act. This use is not the special denotation of the term found in law, which at times differentiates "intention" from "motive" or "presuming the natural consequences of one's acts." The ordinary language sense is closer to the meaning discussed in philosophical literature. See, *e.g.*, Elizabeth Anscombe, *Intention* (2d ed. 1963); Donald Davidson, "Belief and the Basis of Meaning", 27 *Synthese* 309 (1974) and "Truth and Meaning", 17 *Synthese* 304 (1967).

competing views; and constitutions promulgated by several corporate bodies, often without a certain, ascertainable membership. If intention is a well-accepted, necessary component in any theory of meaning,[36] then the construction of a concept of intention broad enough to interpret legal forms is a general difficulty in this area.[37]

There is a popular picture of legal forms. Practitioners employ forms, usually called sources of law, as authoritative reasons for determining a certain judicial proposition. If a question arises before a court, attorneys turn to legal forms which are first, complete or nearly complete; second, easily selected as relevant from the universe of possible sources; and third, authoritative according to some not too difficult preference ordering (*e.g.*, if a case and a statute conflict, choose the statute; if an earlier statute conflicts with a final court's gloss on it, choose the case). A great deal of debate among legal theorists centers on just how well forms fulfill the task described above. Do they answer all questions or most?[38] Are things such as customs, international agreements, or administrative rulings

---

36 See Christopher Peacocke, "Truth Definitions and Actual Languages", in *Truth and Meaning* 162 (eds. Gareth Evans and John McDowell, 1976). Many commentators have tried to characterize the role of intention, but all have had at best limited success. H. P. Grice made the most ambitious attempt and defines the meaning of an expression in terms of the intentions of the majority of individuals who commonly use it. He defines the meaning a particular speaker gives that expression in terms of the effect he intends to bring about in the mind of the listener. See H. P. Grice, "Utterer's Meaning and Intentions," 78 *Philosophical Rev.* 147 (1969) and "Meaning," 66 *Philosophical Rev.* 378 (1957).

37 For a good illustration of how a deviant model of intention illuminates a particular type of utterance or statement, see Gerald MacCallum, "Legislative Intent," 75 *Yale L.J.* 754 (1966), reprinted in *Essays in Legal Philosophy* 237 (ed. Robert Summers, 1968). MacCallum argues that legislatures are not capable of ordinary intention. Therefore, in order to understand the meaning of statutes, one needs to construct an institutional model which interprets the workings of a corporate body when it enacts legislation.

38 This controversy concerns completeness and centers on when, if ever, one can look beyond legal forms for assistance in decision-making. Further, if one must go beyond legal forms, does the decision have as much authority as it would if it only employed legal forms?

properly considered legal forms in themselves, or do they merely figure derivatively, so that, for example, administrative rulings are authoritative only because statutes prescribe them?[39] Are judicial interpretations of constitutions subject to alteration by legislatures or future courts?[40] Does the repeal of a statute give life to prior case law inconsistent with that statute, even though that case law has neither evolved nor been tempered by other cases subsequent to the statute's enactment?[41] All of these kinds of questions assume that the popular picture is true. That picture, however, is incomplete and, depending on how one completes it, either becomes nearly accurate or quite misleading.

Practitioners introduce legal forms at two distinct steps in the judicial reasoning process: the definitional occurrence and the resolution occurrence.[42] The definitional occurrence indicates the role of legal forms in defining the judicial role. The resolution occurrence indicates the part played by legal forms in reaching an actual decision in a case. Legal forms are social facts, evidence of individual or group practices or intentions. They contain propositions but are themselves largely documentary (and occasionally, unwritten but easily recognized social, business, or religious customs). The ties between legal forms and the judicial decision are so strong that it is easy to forget that they are not a necessary but a contingent element in judicial decision making. One could imagine a system, perhaps not unlike early English equity, where legal forms would exist as facts but judges largely ignore them. Under such a system, the

---

39 This question exemplifies the inclusion controversy, which focuses upon what should be included within the set of legal forms.

40 This is an example within the ordering controversy, which centers on how one should settle formal disputes. See, *e.g.*, William O. Douglas, "Stare Decisis", 49 *Columbia L. Rev.* 735 (1949) (a practical ordering controversy which focuses on judicial interpretations of written constitutions).

41 This second order example of an ordering controversy illustrates how the difficulty in ordering can escalate.

42 One should not assume that individuals retain these distinctions when constructing a judicial view, but only that they are logically distinguishable.

judge (or Chancellor) might claim not to be governed by central court cases, past equity cases, custom, and certainly local regulations and pronouncements.[43] The intimacy of legal forms with the judicial decision also obscures the fact that forms enter twice into the judicial equation.

The initial intrusion of legal forms comes with the definitional occurrence. As the entire structure of judicial reasoning rests on the concept of role, the formulation of judicial questions thus takes on an altered, contextual flavor. Many of the kinds of questions found in courtrooms are also found, perhaps in slightly altered terminology, in other settings. Conflicts make for judicial cases and their characterization and resolution depends upon the type of forum resolving the conflicts. The judicial form depends on the role of the judge. The question of what he should do arises in every conflict which comes into court.

Formulating a concept of role involves constructing a procedure for deciding cases. That is, a part of role involves making decisions on what types of things a judge ought to use to resolve cases. A likely set of possible factors would include a notion of justice, a notion of fairness or equity, a certain political and social philosophy, and loyalty or adherence to certain legal forms. A conflict at this point between, for instance, a statute (a legal form) and some fairness principle is not an argument about how to resolve specific cases. It is, rather, an argument about what things are proper considerations for judges. One might believe that judges should consider the pronouncements

---

43 This is the common picture of early English equity. See generally William Holdsworth, "The Relation of the Equity Administered by the Common Law Judges to the Equity Administered by the Chancellor," 26 *Yale L.J.* 1 (1916) (defending this view). However, given England's common law backdrop and the small size of its bench and bar (which allowed all to know the same, shared body of past cases), it appears that from an early time equity may have looked to past decisions as authority *de facto* if not *de jure*. This suggests that the case is important here, as in civil law, despite an orthodoxy that follows the contrary view. See generally Charles Dickens, *Bleak House* (1853) for the classic, if notorious, caricature of the narrowness and relative smallness of the equity bench and bar. The accuracy of Dickens' picture is defended in William Holdsworth, *Charles Dickens as a Legal Historian* (1928).

of legislatures without being committed to any position concerning competition between statutes and equity principles. This position only states that a judge is not behaving as a judge if he does not consider statutes.

Legal forms are among the objects examined when one constructs a concept of judicial role, as role entails a method of proceeding for the judge. Here, the popular picture is misleading, as it suggests that one turns to legal forms and more or less finds answers to the issues raised in cases. In the case of the definitional occurrence, however, one uses legal forms to determine role. The determination involves whether to look to legal forms and deciding to what extent they are the concern (or a concern) in defining role. One has to determine the exact direct scope of forms in the definition and then analyze the derivative part which arises upon practical application. This can be seen more clearly with an example.

In *Williams v. Walker-Thomas Furniture Co.*,[44] a plaintiff furniture company sold household items to the defendant on credit.[45] The sales and credit involved a complicated contract whereby Walker-Thomas added each purchase price to the general amount owed and credited *pro rata* each payment toward paying off all past purchases. Purchases were deemed to be leases until the customer paid all outstanding debts to the company. The appellate court stated, "As a result, the debt incurred at the time of purchase of each item was secured by the right to repossess all the items previously purchased by the same purchaser, and each new item purchased automatically became subject to a security interest arising out of the previous dealings."[46] Five years after initiating the contract relationship, the defendant, Ms. Williams, made and defaulted on a final purchase. Plaintiff sued in replevin to repossess all the items defendant ever purchased. Defendant claimed the contract was

---

44   350 F.2d 445 (D.C. Cir. 1965).

45   Actually, the case on appeal joined two lower court cases with a common plaintiff but unrelated defendants. The other joined case will be disregarded here.

46   350 F.2d at 447.

unconscionable by reason of past cases[47] and a recently enacted statute of limited relevancy.[48] The trial court upheld the contract, but the appellate court reversed and remanded the case on the grounds of the possible unconscionability of the contract, in large part because of the defendant's weak bargaining position owing to economic duress which gave her no real choice but to sign an unfair contract. Further, unconscionability was a concern relevant to the court and a factor which the lower court could use to overturn otherwise valid contracts, but one which it failed to exercise.

The main disagreement between the majority and the dissent concerned competing conceptions of judicial role and the exact place of legal forms in constructing that role.[49] The dissent thought that looking to legal forms provides a more or less complete description of judicial role, at least in terms of how a judge ought to proceed. It did not argue that the contract was fair or that general considerations of public policy prevented a finding of duress in the bargaining situation. Further and more basically, it did not argue that the majority disregarded precedent, ignored statutes, or abused any legal form. The dissent did argue, although not in these terms, that it was not part of the judge's task to assess fairness in agreements, or more gener-

---

47 *Id.* at 448. The cases cited were from other jurisdictions. Even *Scott v. United States,* 79 U.S. (12 Wall.) 443, 20 L.Ed. 438 (1871), although a United States Supreme Court case, was not binding on the federal circuits. The reliance on these cases was largely due to relevant case authority within the jurisdiction rejecting unconscionability as a defense in a liquidated damages contract case. See, *e.g.,* *District of Columbia v. Harlan & Hollingsworth Co.,* 30 App. D.C. 270 (1908).

48 D.C. CODE ANN. Section 2-302 (Supp. IV 1965), *amended by* D.C. CODE ANN. Section 28:2-302 (1981). The District of Columbia amended this version of Section 2-302 of the UNIFORM COMMERCIAL CODE after the parties had entered into the instant contract. The section provides that a court may refuse to enforce a contract which was unconscionable at the time it was made.

49 A secondary disagreement involved the lower court's failure to find unconscionability. The dissent recognized that failure was an indication of a finding of conscionability. *Id.* at 450. The majority believed the trial court made no finding on the issue, one way or the other. We shall assume for the purposes of this discussion that the majority is correct.

ally, that judges may not look outside legal forms for criteria to make decisions, at least in the case of otherwise binding contracts.

The majority presented a slightly more complicated argument. At first glance, it also appeared to hold that a judge may not go beyond legal forms when reaching a decision. The court stated that no controlling authority existed on the points raised in the case and thus, the congressional adoption of Section 2-302 of the Uniform Commercial Code became "persuasive authority for following the rationale of the cases from which the section is explicitly derived."[50] This argument is untenable, its difficulties numerous. First, subsequent statutes are generally considered irrelevant to the resolution of cases arising prior to their enactment, especially in contract matters where reliance of the parties is a major concern. Second, statutes are more often taken as changing case law, which suggests that the legislature believed that the case law did not remedy unconscionable contracts. Third, relevant precedents existed which favored the plaintiff. Four hundred years of contract law suggests that courts should enforce bargains, unless they are illegal, formally faulty, or subject to some other recognized excusing defense. Despite a plethora of case citations and discussion of the Uniform Commercial Code, the court simply argued that the contract was in fact unfair. It was apparently self-evident to the court that, if a contract was unfair, it could not be enforced. These cases and the Code agreed with this conclusion, but they were not (according to the opinion) the basis of it. Legal forms here figured in that they evidenced a fairness principle: their consideration in looking to role was derivative. The court recognized that its perception of the proper conception of judicial role might be a minority view and thus recommended that Congress codify the decision. Nevertheless, the holding demonstrated that the court's own position on judicial role obviously did not require codification to allow a conscionability test in any case involving a challenged contract.

The *Williams* case suggests how the popular picture of legal forms can be misleading. The dissent argued not merely within

---

50   350 F.2d at 449.

the context of legal forms, it implicitly argued for their primacy. The majority is either arguing for forms to be one consideration among many or that forms serve a token primacy, but one which should not obscure the extent to which they are only one factor among several.   If the popular picture suggests that courts can always or ever reach a judicial decision solely by resorting to legal forms, it misleads by failing to state that how one considers legal forms depends upon one's view of judicial role.   Depending on the answers to the prior questions of role, solutions suggested by legal forms may be more or less relevant or important.   This is why, for example, a computer could not solve cases satisfactorily even if its memory bank included a thorough knowledge of legal forms.   Judges hold competing positions about the place of legal forms and no single analogue would duplicate the varieties of judicial behavior. [51]

Williams further illustrates how, even when controversy exists over the definitional occurrence, the resolution occurrence can be straightforward.   The entire court agreed on how, given certain assumptions about role, one would reach a decision. The professional education of the bench and the bar focuses primarily on the study and employment of legal forms.   Once forms are considered relevant, debate about their workings is extremely narrow.   The popular picture is a simple one, and the shared universe of knowledge allows the simplicity to endure and be perceived as accurate.   When conflicts come before courts, the *modus operandi* is apparent and consistent.   Both the majority and the dissent in *Williams* looked to cases and statutes and found almost the same thing.   Although their procedure was almost identical, their use of procedure differed.

A brief word might be helpful in ascertaining the meaning of the statement that legal forms contain propositions but are not themselves part of the chain of judicial reasoning.   One identi-

---

51   This is not to say that a computer could not do as good a job, *vis-a-vis* legal forms, as any particular judge.   The assertion merely suggests that no single program could duplicate the workings of a judicial system, even in the matter of narrow legal questions.   Nevertheless, in stating that a computer could not duplicate a judicial system, one should not imply that it necessarily would always operate more poorly or achieve less satisfactory results.

fies legal forms by their pedigree.[52]   They are public objects generally taken as having a special relevance to judicial decision making.   This relevance results partially because of their authority as standards for decision and also because of their pedigree, as these were intended uses.   This does not mean that the actual or imputed intentions of a form's author toward legal forms are reasons for attributing authority to those forms. This is a quite unsupportable assertion.   Rather, one can believe that the form's author realized that practitioners would take his work as authority and that he produced his form with that realization in mind.   The reader manufactures the intention which makes no pretense of being identical to the actual intentions of the author.   Statutes, published cases, and constitutions may be intended as authority for future decisions.   Customs (or commercial practice) rarely carry this intention, but practitioners and judges read or gloss an intention into each legal form. Thus, the propositions which one can extract from legal forms have an immediate relevance to making a judicial decision, but they are only important when employed propositionally.   The legal realists recognized this and said that forms are not law but evidence of law.   A clearer interpretation, depending on one's judicial view, is that forms are not law but one may use their propositional contents as law.

Reasoning by Analogy

Judicial reasoning is often thought to be primarily reasoning by analogy.   At least in the case of the common law, a judge is expected to look to specific previous decisions to decide a specific instant case.   A movement from the general to the specific involves deductive reasoning, from the specific to the general inductive reasoning, and from the specific to the specific, so-called reasoning by analogy. [53]

---

52   See Ronald Dworkin, *Taking Rights Seriously* 17 (1977).   According to Dworkin, pedigree refers to the manner of adoption or development of such forms (or in other contexts, rules).

53   Strictly speaking, this is not the way the terms would appeal to a logician, but it is the way lawyers would probably define them.   Some lawyers do not speak of analogous reasoning but see statutes as involving deductive

The movement from specific to specific often involves making a generalization after analyzing the first case. This, in turn forms the basis for deciding the next case. It thus resembles an induction followed by a deduction. Edward Levi, though a skeptic, states well the idea of the mechanics of reasoning from precedent:

> A three-step process described by the doctrine of precedent in which a proposition descriptive of the first case is made into a rule of law then applied to a next similar situation. The steps are these: similarity is seen between cases; next the rule of law inherent in the first case is announced; then the rule of law is made applicable to the second case. [54]

Nevertheless, one should consider analogy as a separate kind of reasoning from induction, as it characterizes those cases where there is not the already established rule provided in the case of induction. Thus, it is necessary to look to a specific case to generate a rule. In reasoning by analogy, one can impeach the second case if the first case is faulty, while the case of induction followed by a deduction, normally one only attacks as far back as the rule. An attack on a specific application of that rule is not fully sufficient to impeach the rule but only weakens its scope or creates an exception. Analogy brings to mind Dr. Johnson's observation that the thirteenth chime of the clock throws the validity of the first twelve into doubt.

It is important to understand clearly that induction is not the logic of law. Essential to any inductive logic is a method of testing the correctness of hypotheses or putative conclusions. Thus, planetary behavior could disconfirm an astronomical hypothesis, a native speaker could inform a language learner of misuse of a concept, or weather could determine the accuracy of a theory of meteorological forecasting.[55] Predicting right

---

reasoning and cases as involving inductive reasoning. The terminology is erratic in much of the literature and one can think of this section as applying to reasoning from case to case, rather than pertaining to reasoning under a certain, tagged category.

54 Edward Levi, *Introduction* at 1-2 (1948).

55 Whether one can confirm or disconfirm any hypothesis or theory is a question within the philosophy of science which is irrelevant here. The method of confirmation typifies inductive reasoning regardless of the

answers or results becomes the focus of any inductive logic, both methodologically and for purposes of establishing its soundness. If the criteria for being right are unavailable, such a logic amounts to no more than random guesses.[56] Given that testing is not a method of judging the appropriateness (truth, correctness, verisimilitude) of judicial assertions, such a fact at least would suggest that one cannot regard induction in any ordinary sense as logic.

In fact, reasoning by analogy is not a distinct matter from reasoning by deduction.[57] Instead, analogy is a method of proceeding when certain premises in a deductive argument are hidden or obscure. When one employs a truly nondeductive method, it is more aptly called argument by metaphor than argument by analogy.

This view can be construed with the one presented by Joseph Raz in *The Authority of Law*.[58] Raz begins by suggesting that a court can be in two positions, one where a statute or past decision is binding, and one where it is not.[59] Only in the latter case does reasoning by analogy come into play. According to Raz, "A court relies on analogy whenever it draws on similarities or dissimilarities between the present case and previous cases

---

difficulties of empiricism, verificationism, or theory formation. The point is that method, whatever form it takes and whatever general value it possesses, is not descriptive of judicial reasoning. For a discussion of certain difficulties in constructing a method of confirming inductive hypotheses, see R. M. Chisholm, *Perceiving* (1957).

56 Predicting judicial results fails on two well-known accounts. Prediction would not help judges reach decisions because, even if one believed that judges predict what other judges do, one would need to engage either in circular thinking or in a search for some objective psychological standard of correctness. More basically, judicial reasoning has a normative component, with court results capable of fallibility. Absent this, the bench and the bar could not accomplish their routine tasks, *e.g.*, discuss and assess whether decisions are correctly decided.

57 Deduction here denotes a standard zero and a first order logic which allows for implication and equivalence.

58 Joseph Raz, *Authority* 201-09 (1979).

59 *Authority* at 85, 90-97, 102, 111-15 (discussing the division of cases into two categories, those where the judge can exercise discretion and those where the judge is bound).

which are not binding precedents applying to the present case."[60] Thus, in cases where a court is not bound, it uses analogy, which allows it to discover new rules.[61] These new rules are not binding; however, they are persuasive. Raz sees this position as a compromise between that held by Ronald Dworkin, whom he characterizes as holding that analogies are binding,[62] and that held by those who "have concluded that analogical argument is mere window dressing, a form of argument without legal or other force resorted to for cosmetic reasons."[63] Analogies for Raz "are always morally relevant. . . . [But] there is no point in saying judges are *legally* obliged to use analogical arguments."[64] He sees analogies as a reforming aspect of adjudication, one where new ideas, brought in as new rules via old cases, are used differently.

Raz sees the actual procedure of applying analogy as this: one looks at the series of relevant features the instant case possesses, then looks at a past case sharing some but not all of these features, somehow sees that past case as relevant, and finally borrows the conclusion of the past decision and uses it in the instant case.

---

60 *Authority* at 202.

61 *Authority* at 202, 204-05. Joseph Raz explains that argument by analogy "is not a method of discovering which rules are legally binding because of the doctrine of precedent; [rather, it is] a form of justification of new rules laid down by the courts in the exercise of their lawmaking discretion." *Authority* at 202.

62 *Authority* at 205. It might appear at first glance that the position taken here is the same as the one held by Dworkin. There are, however, two important differences. First, Dworkin believes that the third order is objective and thus analogy will not only reveal a commitment but a truth. "Third order" is the term Raz uses to describe the group of legal rules which include beliefs about legal rules. Second, Dworkin believes that the analogical process is itself an objective matter, rather than one where different but equally valid positions are available. See Chapter VI for a more detailed analysis and criticism of Dworkin's position.

63 *Authority* at 205 (1979).

64 *Authority* at 206 (morally relevant in the sense that such arguments "should be assigned the weight which it is morally right to give them").

The major difficulty with Raz's position is that it confuses cases with propositions or, using his own terminology, rules. Raz appears committed to the view of a past case as binding authority for only one thing, and that thing is intimately connected with the factual background of the specific case. Let us imagine a case, case F, where, for the first time, a defendant raises the justification of self-defense in a civil suit for assault and battery. Prior cases allowed self-defense as a defense in criminal cases, but the civil case F is one of first impression. According to Raz, a judge is under no obligation to consider the criminal cases; if he did, he would be engaging in a moral activity.

Earlier, it was suggested that interpreting the *ratio decidendi* of a case is a matter which can vary according to one's judicial view. Certainly, one can imagine judicial views where reasons provided in one context are always considered relevant, if not determinative, in others. Under such views, there would be no "new rules" (as Raz calls them) but merely the discovered implications of existing propositions. However, even under a judicial view with a narrower notion of intercontextual relevancy, one needs to consider the premises of any argument as part of the *ratio*, according to the rule of logical implication. One element in the criminal propositional set would necessarily specify the scope of the criminal self-defense claim and would offer a higher order reason which justifies that claim. Cases can state or imply reasons, such as discouraging violence, allowing for just deserts for assailants, protecting potential third-party innocent victims, providing a cost efficient method of imposing punishment to those who should be punished, or allowing for the spending of the retributive inclinations of a society in a fruitful and circumscribed manner. Raz would argue that higher order reasons are never obligatory in the related civil cases, because of the disparity of factual context.

Let us consider a second case of first impression, case N, which involves the prosecution of a wife for criminally assaulting her husband. The wife claims self-defense. N would be the first instance of the use of self-defense within a marriage, allowing that marriage is a legal relationship which permits certain kinds of contacts between persons which are sometimes impermissible outside that relationship.

Raz at this point has a choice: he may claim either that a new rule is needed to decide F but not N or that new rules are needed to decide both F and N.[65] If he chooses the first option, he must distinguish F from N. Certainly, he cannot say that N shares more features with the traditional self-defense case than does F, because they each share all relevant features but one—a lack of criminal proceedings versus a lack of other than marital proceedings. In fact, given the possible variations and complications—involving such matters as prior history, ability to escape, psychological state, the presence of others including children, the physical strength of assailant and potential victim, or the proximity and immediacy of the threat—it would be difficult to know how to measure similarity of particular factual situations. Moreover, it is far from self-evident why greater similarity alone is a reason for allowing precedent to govern N and applying analogy to F.

Raz could say that the difference between N and the traditional cases is not significant. The circumstances of marriage should not make a difference in an assault and self-defense case. That is, the reasons for allowing self-defense in normal circumstances also apply to N. Raz, however, cannot distinguish N from F on these grounds. The reasons for allowing self-defense in F might be compelling and certainly are likely to be the same reasons found in criminal cases. Looking at reasons rather than facts logically requires a court to apply reasons from analogous cases to determine the result, even in new factual situations. Raz seems to reject this position.

One might believe that N is obviously distinguishable from F because the "old rule" that one can protect oneself from deadly assault applies only to N and not F; however, assuming that past decisions enunciated this formulation of the rule, it covers both N and F. Of course, one can formulate the rule in such a way as to exclude F, but we are, *ex hypothesi*, not so formulating it. One

---

65 Joseph Raz actually makes a third type of objection. He claims that the kind of position taken here is indistinguishable from (or collapses into) Ronald Dworkin's position and is thus defective for the same reasons which he criticized Ronald Dworkin's position.

can assume a general formulation of the rule where subsequent exceptions have been previously introduced. In other words, one can assume what does occur: courts, not overly careful about the implications their statements may have on future difficult cases, leave the determination of those cases and the reformulation of the rule to future courts.

Raz's other option is to suggest that a new rule is necessary in both F and N. The obvious difficulty with this position is that if one can freely decide case N as one sees fit, then when is one ever compelled to decide cases in accordance with old rules? Each case presents a unique factual situation. For a rule to be useful, it must cover diverse cases with common features. Specifying in advance which cases a rule covers involves understanding the reasons why one applies a given rule. These higher order reasons compel the use of the given rule when no rational differences exist between the instant situation and the type of situation that the rule was meant to cover. This is just the type of situation, however, that Raz claims analogy covers. If the rule is not applied, an irrationality exists in the rule system; if it is applied, then the instant case is not one outside the purview of existing propositions.

One might object that the categories of criminal and civil are so basic, that whatever difficulty might surround delineating the scope of specific rules, the criminal/civil distinction is easy to trace throughout the case law. Given this fact, one could see how to distinguish F from N. Such a distinction ignores the numerous intermediate cases between criminal and tort categories which include cases in tort with punitive damages, criminal proceedings where the defendant must pay restitution to the victim, and declaratory judgment actions where the plaintiff asks for advice on some contemplated action which may eventually sound in either tort or criminal law.

Raz schematically tries to show when an argument from analogy holds. Let us assume two cases, case 1 and case 2.[66] Each has facts shown by lower case letters, implications of facts

---

66 For purposes of clarity, we shall use the designation sign "Case 1" and "Case 2", instead of Joseph Raz's symbols, P and Q.

shown by upper case letters. The precedent case used for analogy by Raz is:

Case 1: a, b, c, d, e, g/A, B, C → X (which means A, B, C yield the holding X)

The instant case is:

Case 2: $a_1, b_1, c_1, d_1, -e_1, f_1$/A, B, D → ?

Raz says that we know A, B, C → X, but we do not know if A, B → X or A, B, D → X. If one introduces Case 1 as an analogy, it is for the proposition that A, B → X, which would solve Case 2.

The problem is that long before one needs to settle Case 2, it is appropriate to ask what is meant by case 1 yielding X. Suppose the issue in Case 1 is whether a contract exists. We see bilaterally uncoerced assent (or consent), consideration, and an exchange of promises, that is, A, B, and C. The numerous facts involved would at least include: a, b, c, d, e, and g. What does the case stand for? It certainly does stand for "A, B, C → X" where X means the contract is valid, but it strictly applies only where there is exactly A, B, and C. Suppose "a" is the fact that Smith consented and "A" denotes consent. If "A" is a broad concept of legal consent—freely entered into approval with certain kinds of knowledge of the bargain, *etc.*—then "a" does not imply A. No "a" can be that complex.[67] Here A's meaning will derive from propositions outside the facts of the case. In order to work out the logic of A, an investigation of the criteria which yield its parameters is eventually necessary. When Case 2 arises, perhaps a consent case where, say, economic duress is explicitly at issue, the scope of A will be determined for both Case 1 and Case 2. But one's commitment to Case 1 also serves as a commitment to a certain line on Case 2. On the other hand, if "a → A", then each case stands only for its facts. This seems to make each case unique and to yield a degenerate notion of implication in case law.

---

67 A partial difficulty is that Joseph Raz's use of the stroke function ("/") is deviant and the reader is left to ponder just what he might intend.

The problem with Raz's explanation of analogy largely lies with its allowing for only two kinds of cases, those where past decisions bind the court and those where they do not. One is bound, however, by reasons rather than decisional judgments. This process begins with the construction of the tertiary propositional schema where one has a commitment to the implications of one's judicial view. This means that a number of conclusions can be generated, each of which is binding, that are not normally associated with the holdings of past decisions. For example, suppose that in reaching a judgment in a property case, one needs to hold that "if p, then q." Regardless of the general relevancy of that property case in a subsequent commercial paper dispute, if p arises in the course of resolving the commercial paper case, then if one is committed to p, one is also committed to q. If a judge is to have a rational judicial view, one can envision her looking to other cases to investigate the nature of her commitments, unless, of course, the judge finds that "if p, then q" is irrelevant. In that sense, it can be said that analogies intrude rather than entice. [68]

One should note that this is not Ronald Dworkin's view.[69] Because judicial views are partly a matter of choice, no analogue exists for settling disputes among those with different views. Thus analogy, as it is part of the process that begins with higher order propositions, is not uniform. It seeks internal consistency, but allows for change even in the third order propositional set as consequences are revealed. Thus, in Raz's terms, it is "reformative" rather than "conservative", a tag he gives to Dworkin's theory.

---

68 This position is at odds with John Wisdom's well-known analysis of analogies. John Wisdom, "Gods," I *Logic and Language* 187, 195-96 (ed. Anthony Flew 1951). Wisdom claims that the process of reasoning by analogy does not involve a chain of reasoning. "The reasons are like the legs of a chair, not the links of a chain." *Id.* at 195. But if one reaches for an analogy and that analogy fails, a critical support for one's argument is missing. This can result in more than a tipsy chair; it can result in a failed argument. This chapter does not contest Wisdom's argument that analogical discussion is *a priori* and not a matter of probabilities (a matter of experience).

69 Dworkin's view is discussed at length in Chapter VI of this work.

Raz might object that he could admit everything said, but still be able to say that certain cases involve neither deduction, nor a search for hidden premises and deduction from them once they are found. These other cases employ a method whereby a rule from one case is applied to another case, even though it does not strictly apply. These cases sometimes use a method labeled "legal fictions."[70] In other cases, the new rule is such an obvious change from the old rule that the court employs a different tag, as in cases of tacit consent or constructive eviction. The cases, though, share the feature of holding some proposition which the judges know is not (strictly) true. Therefore, they use metaphor, a rhetorical device, to transpose a term from its original concept. Metaphor allows the transposition even when there is no preservation of truth. "All the world's a stage" may be evocative, interesting, poetic, dramatic and perceptive, but unless one changes the meanings of certain terms, it is false. The metaphor as a linguistic device is inoffensive to a concept of truth. It allows for the deviant predication of names without evoking literal truth. To say within a system such as the common law that metaphor compels a result is not only logically and methodologically untrue, but wrong, because the suggested result is the wrong result under the existing principles of the system. Metaphor suggests future reform or perhaps that it is time to reconsider one's judicial view.

Raz's sole example of a case which reasons by analogy can best be interpreted this way. In *D v. National Society for the Prevention of Cruelty to Children*,[71] the House of Lords held that, in an action for negligence against the National Society for

---

70 Scholars often criticize legal fictions unfairly. Jeremy Bentham's famous remarks on legal fictions are not atypical: "Fiction of use to justice? Exactly as swindling is to trade. . . . It affords presumptive and conclusive evidence of moral turpitude in those by whom it was invented and first employed." Jeremy Bentham, "Constitutional Code," in 9 *Works* 77 (ed. J. Bowring 1843). Fictions merely allow an alteration of the propositional set. Even in a Benthamite, utilitarian analysis, if the positive effect of the change is greater than the negative effects of the disruption and slight ruse, one can say that fictions are useful. For our purposes, one can view fictions as just another form of judicial metaphor.

71 [1977] 1 All E.R. 589 (H.L.).

Prevention of Cruelty to Children (NSPCC), the defendant was allowed to hide the identity of one of its informants, even though that identity was relevant to the case. Existing rules seemed flatly to compel the NSPCC to reveal its source. However, a rule (or proposition) allowed government agencies to keep similar information secret if revealing it would be contrary to the public interest or the efficient function of government. The Lords held that in cases where the NSPCC serves a public function, it is entitled to the protections of privilege afforded to government agencies.

It seems unlikely that a desire for propositional consistency motivated the Lords' holding, as no instances of a separation between an agency's governmental aspect and its public function aspect previously had arisen. If one supposes, however, that courts granted the privilege to government agencies because they serve a public function, this does not help Raz. This supposition would make the case one of deduction, where a judge should be bound to view the NSPCC as having the privilege.

Normally, private agencies do not enjoy the privilege. For Raz to claim that one can freely choose whether or not to grant the privilege to the NSPCC, he would have to allow that cases which withheld the privilege as a matter of course from private agencies, before the instant case, did not endorse the rule that they appeared to use. Ruling for the NSPCC not only expanded the rule of privilege for those meeting the revised test, it reduced the scope of the rule which allows for the discovery of information in ordinary circumstances. If later courts can cut back rules, when are they ever binding? If one can articulate reasons for reading in exceptions later, then the distinction between binding and nonbinding situations upon which Raz bases his argument falls apart.

A more reasonable explanation of *D v. National Society for the Prevention of Cruelty to Children* involves seeing the case as an instance of metaphor. Metaphor allows one to alter propositional sets not merely by adding new propositions, but by changing unsatisfactory old ones. In the instant case, the House of Lords separated the factor of "public function" from its governmental usage home. The two were no longer synonymous. Thus, certain cases which were previously outside the purview of governmental rules can be brought in without destroying the concept of "governmental" or the content of a large quantity of previous case law.

How metaphor comes into play is a function of one's judicial view. Metaphor is not merely whim or whimsy, and how and when reasoning is extended through metaphor is not just a matter of license and preference of the individual suggesting the metaphor. More broadly, unlike deduction, where the propositional scheme determines an answer to a given first order question, metaphor can involve an entire shift of the propositional schema. It can call for a re-evaluation of the weight and relevancy of different pre-existing propositions, and can reflect shifts in the elements of a general judicial view, including politics, ethics, and the very role of judges.

The extent of the re-evaluation can be easily seen by the fact that the metaphor itself can change the meaning of rules or principles in the legal system, as when the metaphor brings its own conceptual baggage. For example, the well known case of *Henningsen v. Bloomfield Motors, Inc.*[72] raised the issue of whether a manufacturer is liable to a foreseeable user of a defective product under a warranty theory absent privity of contract; and concomitantly, whether that manufacturer may limit liability for its breach by asking its customers to sign disclaimers, waiving the right to sue beyond the terms of the warranty. Under the clear terms of the contract, the customer waived certain rights to sue for defects in an automobile. While the court's analysis is complex and involves a number of so-called policy factors, one fundamental issue was whether the tug of tort or the tug of contract would draw the court. That is, if the court fundamentally believed the analysis involved should be one of contract alone, then the failure of privity would be dispositive. Given that determination, mutual assent, consideration, the language of the agreement, and other formalities of contract law would be involved, and standard contractual analysis would bar recovery under the disclaimer. Although the degree of real freedom of bargain may have been suspect, this

---

72   32 N.J. 358, 161 A.2d 69 (1960).

alone would hardly have been sufficient to overturn a basically sound agreement. However, the court saw contract analysis as less than dispositive, and turned to the possible tort aspects, particularly the implications of allowing tort-feasors the freedom to continue manufacturing a harmful product without providing a remedy to the victim. More specifically, the difficulty of pinpointing causation (or at least proximate causation, with some link between a breach of the duty of care and the circumstances of the particular accident) made negligence impossible, and yet the type of facts involved—a new automobile swerving off the road when an erratic steering wheel spun wildly following a loud crack under the hood—caused the court to believe that some protection and recovery be afforded the injured user of an apparently defective product, regardless of privity. Believing that contractual warranty should give rise to a duty, but that limitations on standing to sue and the type of recovery for damages should be based on tort, the court reversed and allowed the matter to proceed to trial. In so doing, not only was the basic contract analysis for embedded and implied warranties changed, but the additional baggage of tort became the rule in such cases. Thus, the entire area of consequential damages and particularly damages for emotional distress, along with widened notions of foreseeability and the lack of the procedural hindrances such as privity and the statute of frauds became the rule in product liability cases based on warranty law. The metaphor itself brought along with it not only a decision in the case but additional notions which shaped the law in future cases.

The same court recently addressed a similar issue of problematic categorization in the case of *Matter of Baby M.*[73] There, the natural father and his wife brought suit to enforce a contract whereby a so-called surrogate mother—a natural mother who had agreed to artificial insemination pursuant to a contract—agreed, in exchange for a sum of money, to carry and bear a child for the natural father and then release all rights to that child back to the natural father and the father's wife.

---

73   109 N.J. 396, 537 A.2d 1227 (1988).

The court needed to decide if the surrogate contract should be upheld. It struck down the particular contract on both contractual common law and statutory grounds regulating adoption. In finding the surrogate contract improper based on the common law, the court held that the transaction was just like selling a baby, or slavery, and thus improper. Further, the surrogate contract violated the statutory grounds, because it was just like unsupervised, irrevocable, private adoption. Because of this, the issue of consent, more closely scrutinized in adoption than contract cases, was pushed to the front, and made revocable.

The court was faced with a number of difficult issues of comparison in the *Baby M* case. Certainly, a surrogate contract is not the same as adoption, and thus the pull of metaphor. Moreover, analogy in the manner suggested by Raz, where some terms are the same and some are different, is hardly adequate. The entire issue of which terms count more, and which terms count at all, is itself controversial, difficult and to some extent open, requiring a shift in the judicial view. The issue of whether there were existing binding precedents was a question solved by use of metaphor, not a question examined initially and then found determinative of the issue of the need to consult further (by way of analogy or metaphor).

The choice of appropriate comparison is not determined, and thus any simple recitation of analogy without seeing disguised metaphor is inadequate. Simple, putatative analogies, unaccepted, often unconsidered by the *Baby M* court, abound. Take property law. An individual considering a building, might think that the joint contribution of materials would allow sharing of an ultimate construction. D's use of P's bricks to build D's house gives P some right in D's house or, in property terms, its component parts. Thus, because the biological mother contributed an egg while the natural father sperm, the natural mother ought to have the right to consider the baby her child in some legally significant way. (Rights here might include visitation rights, custodial rights, rights to make decisions about the child's future, *etc.*) However, if that were the case, then an anonymous sperm donor to a sperm bank might have rights to a child conceived months or years later unbeknownst to the donor. This (metaphor) the court rejects.

Full property ownership is not required. One can look at Hohfeldian right to a use, or more simply, a lease. The court puts great stock in the nurturing or bonding aspect during pregnancy. Would that matter if a couple had planted a fertilized egg in an unrelated womb, thus making the birth mother other than the natural mother: a womb for rent arrangement? If the female carrier has no property right in a womb once leased, and a contributor (sperm donor) has none either, what property right would a natural mother who is party to a surrogate contract have? Would the area (and law) of organ donation be an apt or relevant metaphor? The court stays far away from those or other property metaphors. Why it does so has little to do with either the dictates of deduction or the requirements of analogy, and quite a lot to do with the pull of the metaphor.

In fact, the entire analysis of the *Baby M* case involves a categorization of just what kind of transaction is involved. If the court sees a surrogate contract as just like other contracts, then the analysis would follow those transactions normally associated with freely entered into bargains. Certainly, there is the initial problem in that what appears to be the good or chattel involved is a human being and the assent or consent involved appear to be protected and worthy of scrutiny because of the special bonding relationship between a parent and an embryo-turned-child; however, personal service contracts are valid, even if not always specifically enforced, and attachments to one's projects are often disregarded by courts. One may have formed bonding attachments as a grandparent, as a pet owner, as an architect or artist who created a beautiful work, as a scientist working in a particular lab, as a football coach for a particular team or school, as a priest under the direction of a transferring bishop devoted to his present congregation, or as any individual who forms emotional ties during the course of performance of a contract. In fact, it is unclear from the court's analysis why the special bonding relationship of a birth mother should even enter into the agreement: after all, that relationship appears to have been freely contracted away. The concern of the court in a confused sense is the potential bonding of the child to the missing birth mother, not the mother to the child. This is hardly a matter of contract, as that child never consented to anything. It is clear that the contractual foundations involved in a surrogatehood relationship differ markedly from those of an ordinary contract, although what implications one would draw from noticing that difference are not so clear.

Equally, the entire analysis of adoption and slavery is inadequate. Under the contract, the child remains with one of its natural parents. The child is at least as well off as any adopted child (all other things being equal), is not being sold, and, at least in one important sense, owes its entire being to the existence of a contract of surrogatehood. If there had been no contract, there would be no child. Certainly, in that sense, it would be difficult for the child or its court-appointed guardian to complain about the existence of the surrogate contract, as absent that contract, there would be no child.

The crucial terms in any judicial argument or reasoning chain able to solve the issues raised by *Baby M*, then, are not ones merely of deduction from traditional judicial propositions, where historically such a contract was neither technologically feasible nor conceptually or emotionally considered. Rather, what is involved are reconsiderations of one's entire view, and the borrowing of concepts from personal identity, freedom of expression, parenthood, freedom to procreate, the right to contract, consent, privacy, property, and the nature of society, elements which normally populate the third order propositional set. It does not matter that contract law may make the case a settled one, or that some single missing term remains to be found. Moreover, no particular other instance is borrowed which requires, by the entire force of precedent, a certain determination. Metaphor pulls us away from that past force, and redirects our judicial view.

In that any particular metaphors are used, then, they are hardly randomly chosen. The theory here is not at odds with, if perhaps less broadly stated than, that proposed by Lakoff and Johnson,[74] who write:

---

74 George Lakoff and Mark Johnson, *Metaphors We Live By* (1980).

We have offered evidence that metaphors and metonymies are not random but instead form coherent systems in terms of which we conceptualize our experience.[75]

Thus, deductive reasoning through resort to prior standards evident in judicial sources may directly determine a result. But where the suggestion appears to be one of the attraction of a similar situation—surrogatehood is like adoption, warranty violations are like negligent acts—analogy as metaphor comes into play. Metaphor is a possibility, but only that, not a requirement. Metaphors change the meaning and scope of legal doctrine, and enter when pertinent and reflective of other third order values which solve problematic first order questions. The great utility of both analogy as metaphor and deduction masked as analogy is that they allow judicial growth and refinement without offending notions of consistency, fairness, disinterestedness, or justice.

---

75 *Id.* at 41.

V

Rules and Rulings

Yet law-abiding scholars write:
Law is neither wrong nor right,
Law is only crimes
Punished by places and by times,
Law is the clothes men wear
Anytime, anywhere,
Law is Good morning and Good night.

W.H. Auden

There is a prevalent idea within the legal profession that complicated theory has only a marginal role to play in discussions of judicial decision-making, for most of the time a judge simply applies the existing law to the case at hand with little room for complicated analysis. Facts may be elusive, styles may vary, cases may defy ready classification. All this makes the ability to apply law to facts more valuable. It is a value readily marketable, and it is squarely the task of the bar. The bar needs to find the law, and apply it to the great majority of cases where it uncontestably fits. Occasionally, the fit is problematic, controversy appears, and judicial discretion is required. This discretion is limited, though, by the backdrop of the ubiquitous easy cases, and thus one can speak of gaps or leeways where the easy cases run out, and a limited liberty to create new law becomes possible.

This picture has attracted many theorists, most of whom belong to a school of thought called "legal positivism". If positivism cannot be discredited, then pluralism is invalid, and the picture of judicial reasoning is both simpler and more mechanical than has been suggested here. The claim of the seminal place of rules in adjudication, and the theory of legal positivism that makes the claim, must be examined; however, several limitations in the examination need to be made clear. First, legal positivism is a label applied to such disparate writers as Jeremy Bentham, John Austin, T. E. Holland, J. N. Salmond, John Chipman Gray, Oliver Wendell Holmes, Hans Kelsen, H. L. A. Hart, Joseph Raz and Neil MacCormick.[1] These writers generally shared little except a distaste for their ghostly opponent, the natural lawyer. Therefore, little can be gained from discussing them as a group.[2] Instead, several points taken from three closely aligned writers within the positivist tradition must be analyzed. These three, H. L. A. Hart, Neil MacCormick, and Joseph Raz, have the advantage of sharing many basic ideas and of having revised and improved upon their predecessors.

Second, the legal positivists have written on a wide number of topics, from rule-utilitarianism to the structure of norms. Only one aspect of their work—the structure and status of higher order judicial propositions—will be discussed here. Although the status of judicial propositions is in many ways central to much of their writings, no opinion on the remainder of their work ought to be read into this limited discussion. Finally, the positivists addressed the issue of higher order judicial proposi-

---

1 Positivists tend to be prolific in their writings. However, the most important works of the authors mentioned, at least in their commitment to legal positivism, are: Jeremy Bentham, *Of Laws in General* (ed. H. L. A. Hart, 1970); *Introduction to the Principles of Morals and Legislation* (1789); John Austin, *The Province of Jurisprudence Determined* (1832), and *Lectures on Jurisprudence or the Philosophy of Positive Law* (1863); T. E. Holland, *Elements of Jurisprudence* (10th edition, 1906); John Salmond, *Jurisprudence* (1902; John Chipman Gray, *The Nature and Sources of the Law* (1909); Hans Kelsen, *General Theory of Law and State* (1945) and *The Pure Theory of Law* (1967); H. L. A. Hart, *The Concept of Law* (1961); Joseph Raz, *The Concept of a Legal System* (1970), *Practical Reason and Norms* (1975), *The Authority of Law* (1979); Neil MacCormick, *Legal Reasoning and Legal Theory* (1978).

2 H. L. A. Hart himself does not claim to attack natural law, merely all natural law theorists. He states that, properly viewed and stripped of virtually all meaningful claims, there remains a core of good sense. *The Concept of Law* at 181-195. Whether H. L. A. Hart's form of natural law is worth having, and, more importantly, whether a full bodied natural law can be constructed to meet the criticism of the positivists, are questions eloquently addressed by John Finnis in his *Natural Law and Natural Rights* (1980).

tional status only derivatively and often casually. Thus, some completion of the positivist picture is needed. In that this will be done throughout this chapter, one should perhaps be speaking of a Hartian or Razian idea, rather than an idea actually held by Hart or Raz.

Perhaps its most important present contributor, Joseph Raz, has attempted to define positivism. He writes that it rests on three conditions or theses.[3] The first condition he calls the "social thesis", which holds basically that what is or is not law is a matter of social fact. Social conditions are thus the necessary and sufficient criteria for identifying the existence and content of law. The second condition, the "moral thesis", holds that the moral value of a legal system or its components is a contingent matter. There can be no necessary connection between law and any particular conception of ethics. Taken to its extreme, no moral benefit necessarily inures to a society because there is a legal system in place. While contingently that is unlikely to occur, one could find just as much (or as little) to be commended in a Hobbesian state of nature as in any particular legal system.[4] The third condition, the "semantic thesis", holds that certain central terms like "rights", "duties", and "guilt" have different meanings in legal and moral contexts. One may earn moral opprobrium, but have committed no legal breach. Assuming Raz's description to be accurate, why is it important, relative to a discussion of the foundations of judicial reasoning, to contest such a seemingly benign, if somewhat vague and general, theory?

Certainly, neither the social nor the semantic theses are exceptionable. (Something akin to the moral thesis was presented in Chapter I of this work.) The main objection to Raz's statement of it is a correctable one. There may well be certain necessary moral implications to the fact of a legal system. The changes in authority, dispute resolution and the

---

3 See Joseph Raz, *The Authority of Law* 37-52 (1979). This definition is a refinement of the picture he presented earlier in Chapter 5 of *Practical Reason and Norms* (1975).

4 Thomas Hobbes' discussion of life in the state of nature is found in his classic work, *Leviathan: or the Matter, Forme and Power of a Commonwealth Ecclesiaticall and Civil* (1651).

norms of behavior may carry certain necessary moral implications. That said, however, in any consequentialist weighing (of the moral good and the bad), one would have to know the design of the system to know the moral outcome. Necessity would occur, but only to input, not outcome.

The semantic thesis can also be made valid when two exceptions to it are noted. First, the social thesis does not apply in those societies where law, religion, and ethics are not well-differentiated. This occurs in primitive societies where superstition overshadows science; in countries, such as those found in medieval, Catholic Europe and the present day Islamic Middle East, where government and large sections of the population fail to differentiate between law and religion, and their concomitant rules and values; and in revolutionary states, whether Thermidor France or Maoist China, where ethics are held to be embodied without change in legal standards and rulings.[5] It would not be an adequate response for Raz to suggest that because the existence of this type of legal system is contingent rather than necessary, such examples are not a problem for positivism. Law itself is contingent. Properties or conditions can attach to law only by the fact that it is contingently, conventionally organized in actual times and places. One cannot speak of necessary conditions of uninstantiated legal systems in the same way as one can of the necessary condition of uninstantiated mathematical systems.[6] Some legal systems violate the semantic thesis because individuals, those who employ semantics, do not distinguish what can, but need

---

5   Much of the vast literature of anthropology is concerned with the overlap of science, superstition and authority. Emile Durkheim's *Elementary Forms of Religious Life* (1915) was the precursor of a great deal of this work. The recurrence of this overlap, even where distinctions have been clearly drawn, appears to be a regular (although certainly not constant) companion of revolutionary change.

6   Even an intuitionist, with the most nominal commitment to more problematic mathematical entities, hardly can be said to worry about instantiation. See, for a general introduction to intuitionism and nominalism in mathematics, L. E. J. Brower, "The Effect of Intuitionism on the Classical Algebra of Logic," found in 1 *Collected Works* (ed. A. Heyting, 1975); Ludwig Wittgenstein, *Remarks on the Foundations of Mathematics* (1967); Crispin Wright, *Wittgenstein on the Foundations of Mathematics* (1980).

not necessarily, be distinguished: law from morality and religion. The thesis should be changed: from law and ethics are necessarily different, to law and ethics are not necessarily the same.[7]

The second exception is similar, but on a conceptual rather than social level. Even where law, religion and ethics are well distinguished, there will be areas of semantic overlap. Certain concepts, such as "adultery", "murder", or "wrong", may share meanings, or have users who fail to distinguish their legal from their religious meaning. "Oath" may be the most widespread of those concepts.[8]

---

7 In considering a social, contingent, empirical enterprise, the notion of necessity may always be considered to be out of place. However, as "law" is generally employed, there is room to allow a weakened concept of necessity to apply to law in actual societies having already existed.

8 Traditionally, oaths require a promise to a deity. (Affirmations do not.) Triers of fact, usually jurors, are *de facto* third party beneficiaries of oaths made in the setting of a law suit.

Perhaps the most eloquent statement of the traditional view of an oath is attributed to the common law lawyer Thomas More in Robert Bolt's drama of More's fall:

Roper: Yes ... Meg's under oath to
persuade you.
More (coldly): That was silly, Meg.
How did you come to do that?
Margaret: I wanted to!
More: You want me to swear to the Act
of Succession?
Margaret: "God more regards the
thoughts of the heart than the words of
the mouth" or so you've always told me.
More: Yes.
Margaret: Then say the words of the
oath and in your heart think otherwise.
More: What is an oath then but words
we say to God?
Maragret: That's very neat.
More: Do you mean it isn't true?
Margaret: No, it's true.
More: Then it's a poor argument to
call it "neat", Meg. When a man takes an
oath, Meg, he's holding his own self in

The semantic thesis thus has certain limitations. It is doubly contingent, applying only in certain societies, and to a limited number of concepts within those societies.

While the social thesis, as Raz stated it, is no doubt susceptible to different interpretations, the standard one held by most positivists begins by seeing rules as socially sanctioned and the basis for legal obligations. (Arguably, this even applies to John Austin, who, although he spoke of obedience rather than rules, appeared to mean a kind of habit more binding than that which Hart later stated inheres in the term.)[9] Law is the central notion; rules are the components of law; and some kind of consensus (shared social rules) identifies the particular rules which are pertinent.

The talk of rules and law is quite different from that of propositions and judicial views employed here. It is not the positivist's idiolect that is objectionable, although talk of "law" and "rules of law" appears to multiply the difficulties just because it tries to bridge the chasm between behavior and justifications for that behavior. The main problem with this conception of rules and law, a conception which presupposes both a certain unity of belief relative to the idea of a judge's role and a certain ready criteria for determining when rules either apply or do not apply based on some consensus, is exactly what this conception denies.

Three objections will be made concerning possible different versions of the social thesis. These notions overlap, but the advantage of examining them by type rather than breaking them into components is that we can look at ideas held by three

---

his own hands. Like water (cups hands)
and if he opens his fingers then—he
needn't hope to find himself again. Some
men aren't capable of this, but I'd be
loathe to think your father one of them.
Margaret: So should I... .

Bolt, *A Man for All Seasons* 83 (1960).

9 John Austin's well-known jurisprudential works include *The Province of Jurisprudence Determined* (1832) and *Lectures on Jurisprudence or the Philosophy of Positive Law* (1863).

leading positivists, and try more sympathetically to understand their basic arguments.

Rules and Criteria

In *The Concept of Law*, H. L. A. Hart introduces the idea that all legal systems contain a mechanism for deciding which standards or rules constitute the law of a society. This mechanism recognizes the correct rules, and is called, appropriately, the "rule of recognition". Hart argues that every legal system consists of a simple set of rules identified by reference to a discrete set of criteria, and that what determines that criteria of recognition is a shared acceptance by the officials of that system of the content of the rule-determining criteria. The criteria can be identified through observation: they are a discoverable, social fact. Every system has exactly one rule of recognition, although it may be complicated and consist of a related set of separate rules.[10] Hart states further that:

> In this respect, however, as in others a rule of recognition is unlike other rules of the system. The assertion that it exists can only be an external statement of fact. For whereas a subordinate rule of a system may be valid and in that sense "exist" even if it is generally disregarded, the rule of recognition exists only as a complex, but normally concordant, practice of the courts, officials, and private persons in identifying the law by reference to certain criteria. Its existence is a matter of fact.[11]

Hart's concept of the rule of recognition is part of a complex scheme tied in particular to the distinction between habit and obligation, internal and external point of view, and primary and secondary rules. These distinctions are not always clear or convincing, and any use of the concept of a rule of recognition would have to include modification.[12] (There are difficulties as

---

10 H. L. A. Hart's analysis is found throughout *The Concept of Law*. See particularly Chapters V and VI.

11 *Concept* at 107.

12 The criticisms of H. L. A. Hart's theory have been voluminous. Hart himself includes a partial listing in his corrected edition of *The Concept of Law*, published in 1967, at pp. 257-258. The muddle in H. L. A. Hart's scheme is exposed clearly in Rolf Sartorius, "The Concept of Law" 52

to what exactly are the grounds for dividing primary from secondary rules, whether a rule of recognition is necessary for the existence of a legal system, whether that rule is necessarily primary or secondary. Also, Hart is unclear about what divides the internal from the external point of view. A consequence of this lack of clarity is that he leaves up in the air what constitutes the connection between constitutional law and the rule of recognition.) Moreover, Hart speaks only of rules, with the rule of recognition being a master rule. Dworkin's well-known criticism[13] that a rule-based structure neither allows for nor can take account of the legal principles that are an integral part of judicial decision-making is telling against Hart's formulation of the rule of recognition, and would require a major revision of the thesis.[14] However, assuming all these faults can be remedied, there is still a problem with any formulation similar to Hart's as the basis of judicial propositions. This problem is one of locating the source of the rule of recognition.

Hart states that only rules of a certain pedigree are valid. Which rules these are is a matter of social fact: we can look to the officials of a legal system and see what set of rules they employ to establish what rules have the proper pedigree. The set of valid rules can be identified by whatever criteria these officials accept. There is a trivial and a deep circularity to such a test. The trivial circularity, (noticed by MacCormick[15]), is that the valid rules are necessarily determined by reference to the officials of a legal system, but who is a proper official within a legal system is a matter determined by reference to certain of the valid rules. If one is genuinely puzzled about the location of

---

Archiv fur Rechts-und Sozialphilophie 161 (1966), reprinted in *More Essays in Legal Philosophy* 131 (ed. Robert S. Summers, 1971). His view is endorsed here. Joseph Raz attempts to modify Hart's rule of recognition without destroying it, in *Practical Reason and Norms* 146-148 (1975).

13 See Ronald Dworkin, *Taking Rights Seriously* 14-130 (1977).

14 Both Joseph Raz and Neil MacCormick attempt to save the rule against Ronald Dworkin's criticism, but it is questionable as to whether their salvation is successful.

15 See Neil MacCormick, *Legal Reasoning and Legal Theory* 54-54 (1978). Neil MacCormick labels the problem one of apparent circularity, but he does not adequately explain how to break the circle.

legal rules (where one might find their proper application), one might be equally puzzled as to which officials are the proper officials. This would most clearly be seen when serious social unrest, such as rebellion or civil war, gives rise to parallel systems of both rules and officials. However, officials may always be located by reference to certain notions of power, coercion and obedience—even though Hart is unhappy with collapsing the distinction between laws and order.

There is, however, good reason to locate officials in this way. One could refer to individuals' holding of power and their use of coercion, or threat of coercion, and then fill in the authority network through some analogue involving staying-power, claims, legitimacy, and loyalty. This would involve collapsing Hart's distinction between laws and officials on the one hand, and orders and gunmen on the other. [16]

This distinction is important for Hart, as he bases his entire idea of law as a set of rules rather than a series of commands upon it. One argument he finds telling in favor of the distinction is that in a complex, large society, there are few occasions when an individual is actually confronted by an official issuing a direct order. Hart argues that no society could support the number of officials necessary to guarantee direct compliance. Thus, law and officials utter statements of a generality to yield obligations, while gunmen utter orders only, giving rise to someone being obliged but not obligated. Obligations require regular conduct and social rules.

Hart's circularity concerning rules and officials is recapitulated in his distinction between gunmen and officials. Only social rules which distinguish the behavior of the two in general —not in every instance, as a Robin Hood would do what is expected of officials, while a Mussolini would do what is expected of a gunman—can define obligation, but obligation is a social fact reflected by behavior. In that it is the apparently identical behavior of one obeying a gunman and an official which needs explaining, the distinction is of little use.

This is a difficult distinction to maintain in any case. Social phenomena such as vigilante groups, rebels, invaders, warlords,

---

16 See *Concept* at 20-21.

organized crime, political machines, lawful elite-status hierar-
chies, and *de facto* anarchy (abandonment of a sphere by a
central authority) are situations suggesting the distinction blurs.
Even where the distinction is clear, the officials may be required
to give orders backed by threats, while an outlaw group may be
able to call upon felt obligations (*e.g.*, where an outlawed theoc-
racy operates clandestinely, or where the government is run by
people widely felt to be morally derelict).

There is, however, a deep circularity or regress with Hart's
test for the rule of recognition in an actual society. Hart argues
that a rule of recognition can be spotted by its internal acceptance by members or officials of a society.

> The use of unstated rules of recognition, by courts and others, in identi-
> fying particular rules of the system is characteristic of the internal point
> of view. Those who use them this way thereby manifest their own accep-
> tance of them as guiding rules and with this attitude there goes a charac-
> teristic vocabulary different from the natural expressions of the external
> point of view. Perhaps the simplest of these is the expression, "It is the
> law that ...", which we may find on the lips not only of judges, but of
> ordinary men living under a legal system, when they identify a given rule
> of the system ... . The first of these forms of expression we shall call an
> internal statement because it manifests the internal point of view and is
> naturally used by one who, accepting the rule of recognition and without
> stating the fact that it is accepted, applies the rule in recognizing some
> particular rule of the system as valid, ... To say that a given rule is valid
> is to recognize it as passing all the tests provided by the rule of recogni-
> tion and so as a rule of the system.[17]

The circularity arises when one inquires what criteria a judge
should use in reaching a decision. Putting aside the peripheral
cases of hypocrisy and inconsistency, one might take it to be a
truism that judges use the criteria they feel that they ought to
use. Under this formulation, if judges look to the rule of
recognition as a criterion for deciding individual cases, then
they must use the criteria they think that they must use. The
test is self-referential, and as such, provides no more guidance
that if there were no such rule. If we try to unpack the formulation and put the problem in terms of a single case, we could say
that a judge using the rule of recognition decides cases as she

---

17 Quotations are from *Concept* at 99-100.

thinks other judges would decide them. More precisely, this refers her to the standards officials would use if they were in her position. As the judge is herself the official in the relevant position, *ex hypothesi*, she is referred to the standards she believes she should use. This leaves her without guidance, and fails to establish that there is an independent set of rules followed by officials which characterizes legal systems, for how could one, in theory, verify or falsify such a position? The self-referential aspect of the judge's inquiry remains. She merely uses the rules she uses, without an independent test for establishing whether or not they are right, correct, or appropriate. Hart admits as much when he writes that rules are inadequate to ensure solution of the cases at hand.

> The truth may be that, when courts settle previously unenvisaged questions concerning the most fundamental constitutional rules, they get their authority to decide them accepted after the questions have arisen and the decision has been given. Here all that succeeds is success. [18]

Hart wishes to limit to "previously unenvisaged" cases those situations where the individual judge does not employ the rule of recognition to find an answer, but, why ought that limitation to apply? Hart would no doubt answer that courts in ordinary cases do behave just as though they are bound (bound usually to follow rules as found in legal forms); that is part of their taking the internal point of view. Hart sees unenvisaged cases as ones where the courts have a limited freedom to choose among competing formulations of rules, as, for example, where the language of a statute is vague and statutory interpretation becomes a matter forced upon the courts. However, the criteria the judge uses to settle a case involving the vague statute are as much a part of a rule of recognition for that judge as the criteria she uses in clear cases. That a judge normally employs a certain set of criteria should not lead us to imply that she ought to continue using that set. Once a judge asks herself why she is using the criteria she has been using—a situation found often, but not exclusively, in previously unenvisaged cases—reference to past practice alone is no longer sufficient. The rule of recog-

---

18 *Concept* at 149.

nition will not itself tell a judge whether or not she is right—when she avoids Hart's horror of behaving as though the game of scorer's discretion (rather than a game where a scorer follows rules) is being played—and thus fails to identify the criteria for judgment independently of that judgment. In short, the rule of recognition utterly fails to offer the judge guidance. Put in Hart's terms, the rule recognizes nothing.

The well-known American case of *Erie Railroad Company v. Tompkins,*[19] illustrates this point. The case involved a Pennsylvania citizen walking along the right of way of a New York railroad when he was hit by a projecting door. Tompkins, although hurt in Pennsylvania, brought suit in federal court in New York under diversity jurisdiction.[20] The ultimate question was whether Pennsylvania state or general federal law should apply.[21] On appeal, the United States Supreme Court held that a direct precedent, *Swift v. Tyson,*[22] stating that general federal law ought to apply to an act of Congress[23] in such diversity

---

19 304 U.S. 64, 58 S. Ct. 817, 82 L.Ed. 1188 (1938).

20 Under Article III, Section 2 of the United States Constitution, the judicial power of the federal government is extended to controversies between citizens of different states. The defendant railroad was a New York corporation and Tompkins was a citizen of Pennsylvania.

21 More specifically, the issue concerned choice or conflict of law. The (forum) court was federal, but the issue was whether the forum court should apply its own law or the law of the Commonwealth of Pennsylvania. In any case where there is a choice of forum, courts are faced with the question of which court's law should apply. Choice of law rules are thus secondary rules which determine which primary rules of substantive law a court should apply.

22 16 Pet. 1, 41 U.S. 1, 10 L.Ed. 865, (1842). Actually, the case was reversed only on the jurisdictional issue. It remained as authority for the fact that a pre-existing debt was a good consideration for an endorsement of a bill of exchange, so that the endorsee would be a holder in due course.

23 The statute was Section 34 of the JUDICIARY ACT OF 1789, 2 Stat. 92, now in slightly altered condition, 28 U.S.C.A. 1652. Called the RULES OF DECISION ACT, it provided that "the laws of the several states, except where the constitution, treaties, or statutes of the United States shall otherwise require or provide, shall be regarded as rules of decision in trials at common law in the courts of the United States in cases where they apply."

cases, was applicable but wrongly decided. Instead, state law ought to apply. *Swift* was reversed, the statute reinterpreted, the case remanded to determine the parameters of Pennsylvania law, and the doctrine of general federal law in diversity cases abolished.

What would Hart say of *Erie*? At the time the case was pending, there had been a strong case-in-point holding, written by Justice Story (acknowledged to be the leading federal scholar and jurist of the century), and ninety-six years of massive and confirming case law on the matter. It would seem that this is not a previously unenvisaged case, nor is it one where reference to the consensus among officials or judges would have successfully forecast a solution. The judges in *Erie* looked to the existing rule, and found it wanting. Hart might argue either that *Erie* changed the pre-existing rule of recognition or that it did not. If it did not, then the rule in this instance would be something of the sort that Supreme Court judgments are supreme, and that that court declares the primary rules. However, if the court is not bound, then the need for rule of recognition is gone. That court does what it wishes without restraint. The finality of a judgment becomes equivalent to its validity. If the rule is supposed changed, on the other hand, then consistency is preserved at the cost of utility. Every overturning and even modifying of a rule becomes cause for changing the rule of recognition, and such a rule becomes merely descriptive of the legal system for a brief duration. The difficulty is general. Every change or every modification throws into doubt the validity of the rule of recognition.

The problem lies clearly with Hart's desire for a single, unified rule, one adhered to by the officials of a society, to explain how a legal system works. In fact, such a rule needs to provide existence conditions for a legal system.[24] Hart states that there are two minimum (existence) conditions for a legal system: valid rules must be obeyed; and society's rule of recognition, specifying the criteria of legal validity and its rules of change and adjudication, must be effectively accepted as common public standards of official behavior by its officials.

---

24 *Concept* at 113.

He argues that a system tends to break down (becomes more or less pathological) to the extent that these conditions are not strictly met.

Hart fails to see that a society can operate quite well with several rules of recognition vying for ascendancy. In such a society, the requirement that the officials all or mainly agree is loosened, and a rule of recognition may exist even if held by a minority of officials. The decision in *Erie* represented a different view of the doctrine of precedent, of the reach of state decisions, of federalism and the sharing of power, and of statutory and constitutional interpretation. It was a view at times present in earlier courts, where it was always outnumbered.[25] No single rule of recognition can capture such different views, rooted often in competing political and ethical beliefs, but such diversity is characteristic of legal systems generally.

Hart could claim at this point that a legal system implies a single rule of recognition, and thus the most that the above argument suggests is that at the time of *Erie*, several legal systems operated within the United States. In that case, however, the rule of recognition loses much of its explanatory force. One cannot simply look to a given set of officials and automatically secure a rule of recognition, for it is possible for such officials to disagree in basic ways. Disagreement, then, would not imply the absence of a legal system, but the existence of several legal systems. All this is far from the tone of Hart's discussion of legal systems. Hart speaks of the possibility of more than one legal system in a society at the same time, in those situations when revolutions or civil wars occur. He speaks of the "breakdowns" of such systems. That is quite different from the type of variety of normative schemata discussed here. (It is also far afield from the normal use of "legal system", which, in ordinary language, does not extend to the case of many distinct instances within an ordinary society). The pluralist claim is that many different judicial views (or Hartian legal

---

25 Judge Field argued against *Swift v. Tyson* in his dissent in *Baltimore and O.R. Co. v. Baugh*, 149 U.S. 368, 13 S. Ct. 914, 923, 37 L.Ed. 772 (1893); as did Justice Holmes in his dissent in *Black and White Taxicab Co. v. Brown and Yellow Taxicab Co.*, 276 U.S. 518, 532-536, 48 S. Ct. 404, 408-410, 72 L.Ed. 681, 57 A.L.R. 426 (1928).

systems) can co-exist and are likely to co-exist within a given society. It is necessary to see why Hart consistently fails to notice this.

First, he confuses consensus with convergence, a distinction made in Chapter II. "Consensus" was taken to denote an agreement on first and second order propositions due to shared beliefs. This use seems to agree with Hart's, as when he looks to a consensus of officials on which to base his rule of recognition. Of course, in a system such as the one Hart has always before him, modern England, agreement has long been widespread. But this is because the convergence of lower order propositions between competing views is great. Hart sees the seminal cases as marking the boundaries of consensus. Rather, they are better seen as demonstrating the failure of presumed consensus. One interesting feature of the *Erie* case is that it allowed expression of differences on issues that typically would not be allowed to surface. The court held that scholarship could be used to impeach a statutory construction given by a previous final court, that constitutional questions may be discussed even when they had not been briefed by counsel, and that state decisions have a diminished role in constitutional issues, all positions on which there was dissent. If one were determining the law of the United States federal courts in the first half of the twentieth century, and the *Erie* case had not arisen, one might well have agreed with the dissent as to what the law was (what first and second order propositions were true). Yet the members of the court, in writing opinions prior to *Erie*, and usually reaching agreement with the members of the *Erie* dissent, had been for sometime holding beliefs opposed to the dissent. There existed intersubjective agreement which a Hartian might easily mistake for true consensus of judicial view.

Hart cannot remedy the flaws in the rule of recognition without abandoning his fundamental thesis that a single master rule exists, embodied among the shared set of beliefs among a society's officials. One purpose of a recognition rule is to settle most judicial issues that arise and turn them into easy cases. Such a large body of easy cases allows for the open-texture that makes possible the only creative, rather than erudite, aspect of judicial reasoning.[26] More importantly, the certain distinctions between law and ethics, legal duties and moral imperatives, being obligated and being obliged all rest on the ability readily to locate uncontroversial rules which constitute a society's law. Hart thus needs a recognition rule which yields a unified set of rules in a given society. As long as the contingent fact that a society is homogeneous in its beliefs occurs, consensus can arise and one can find such a rule. However, there is no reason either that officials must agree prior to their official appointment or that such agreement cannot fall apart. Allowing for different recognition rules not only begins to look like pluralism, it eliminates the idea of easy cases with a certain semantic open-texture to handle problem cases. Moreover, truth becomes tied to certain third order beliefs and attitudes normally anathema to Hart and the positivists. [27]

Judicial Discretion

A central point of disagreement between the positivist and the pluralist position concerns the problem of judicial discretion. Discretion is a complicated concept and will be taken up at some length in Chapter VI. What we will discuss here is the problem of whether the positivist conception of discretion is viable, and whether it can be made attractive without collapsing into the pluralist conception.

It might be well to state the competing conceptions of discretion. The positivist position begins its analysis with a set of rules, unified in origin and consensually agreed upon, as the basis for settling most potential judicial problems. Most cases fall under this set of rules, and are thus easy cases, for once the

---

26 H. L. A. Hart generally uses the concept of open-texture to mean vagueness. He allows courts the freedom, presumably within the bounds of semantic sanity, to give definition to general rules, usually legislative. Whether a narrow theory of vagueness is sufficient to yield answers to judicial questions, without resort to individual beliefs and attitudes, is just what is being here contested.

27 This is, of course, because of H. L. A. Hart's (and other positivists') insistence on separating law from individual beliefs, and rooting it in social rules.

rules are identified, then solution of the issues within the case is an easy matter. Some cases are not covered by this set of rules, and here discretion must be invoked to settle them. In these hard cases, the judge employs a different method for solution. The pluralist position begins with a judicial view, one individually held, unified in theory rather than by origin, and thus possibly eclectic (*vis-a-vis* other judicial views). Cases generally can be brought under ascertainable rules and the occurrence of indecision as to whether or not rules govern is rare. Hard cases occur only when anomalies, contradiction, or unforeseen and distasteful consequences arise from the imposition of the view on individual cases.

As stated, the positivist position is open to a number of criticisms. It appears to ignore the actual decisions of a court: these decisions are written and reasoned in much the same manner in all cases, without regard to a case's difficulty. One sees the same reference to past cases, incorporation of relevant norms, and legal reasoning chains in virtually all cases. The positivist position, moreover, fails to aid in the recognition of potentially hard cases, just because the criteria for determining inclusion in the set of hard cases are themselves a matter of controversy. It also fails to give sufficient guidance for the resolution of hard cases. If the social thesis holds, then regarding these cases, there is no answer to the first order judicial questions raised, making judges the double villians as unguided dictators of outcome and confounders of the two-valued logic rules they use to justify their decisions as being legally correct. [28]

Finally, the positivist position allows for neither a continuum of difficulty among cases nor for logically different kinds of difficulty being encountered. Cases are either easy or they are not. Two and only two types of analysis are called for, despite a range of either hybrid types that might benefit from a combined analysis, and despite cases being hard for different reasons— because they are *de novo*, are controversial, involve a contradiction between existing rules or conflicting past decisions, or fall

---

28 Raz defends a three-valued logic—truth, falsity, and indeterminancy—as a better way of evaluating judicial statements (*The Authority of Law* 53-55). Ronald Dworkin has attacked the viability of such a logic in *Taking Rights Seriously* 279-290 (1977) and *A Matter of Principle* 119-145 (1985).

outside any rules—not necessarily being susceptible to a single type of analysis.

These, and other criticisms,[29] have led to restating the positivist position by Neil MacCormick in his *Legal Reasoning and Legal Theory*.[30] While MacCormick has other aims in the book (he sets out to explain the relevance of practical reasoning to legal theory and "to advance an explanation of the nature of legal argumentation as manifested in the public process of litigation and adjudication upon disputed matters of law"[31]), he engages in a serious effort to make tenable a positivist position on discretion in the face of criticism by Dworkin and others. He does this by setting up a twofold test for judging whether a case is easy. If both criteria are met, a case is easy, and not in need of discretion to resolve it. Meanwhile, the two criteria involve different uses of discretion if they are not met.

MacCormick, in the positivist tradition, begins his analysis with a system of rules, and defines hard cases as those not falling under those rules. However, he adds that if a case falls under a rule susceptible of various interpretations, it too is a hard case.

> What makes a case clear in law is that facts can (it is believed) be proved which are unequivocal instances of an established rule; but the established rules are susceptible of variant interpretations depending on the pressure of consequentialist arguments and arguments of principle. To be confident in advance that one has a clear case, one must be sure both that it is "covered" by a rule, and indeed by that interpretation of the rule which is best justified by consequentialist arguments and arguments of principle - whose application will not offend judicial conceptions of the justice and common sense of the law. [32]

The two criteria are intended to be complimentary, despite the wording of the quotation. A hard case can either fall outside the rules or it can involve a controversial rule. That the

---

29 For a partial listing of works containing well-known criticisms, see note 12.

30 Published in 1978.

31 *Legal Reasoning and Legal Theory* at page 7.

32 *Legal Reasoning and Legal Theory* 277-228.

two criteria can conflict is a problem MacCormick does not discuss.

Let us suppose that a case arises well within existing rules. The rules in this case had been considered susceptible of only one interpretation. This is a paradigm easy case. Such a case might have been thought to be *Allegheny College v. National Chautauqua County Bank of Jamestown*.[33] The case involved a suit upon a charitable subscription. A promise was made for payment upon the death of the subscriber. The executor bank refused to pay the balance due, claiming that the transaction was neither a gift nor a valid contract, and the college, the charitable beneficiary, brought suit.

Two well-established rules were relevant to the case. The gift rule stated that a valid gift occurs when the donor has capacity, intention to make a gift, has completed delivery to or for the donee, and acceptance has been made by the donee.[34] Under this rule, there was no doubt that Allegheny College did not receive a gift, for no delivery was made. The offeror claimed that the subscription was no more than a putative gift, and it seems, under the rule, to be a failed one. The other relevant rule was one of contract. Under that rule, promises made without consideration or detrimental reliance are not enforceable. More specifically, bilateral contracts require an exchange of promises. Under the facts of *Allegheny*, the consideration was "in consideration of my interest in Christian education, and in consideration of others subscribing", considerations not normally sufficient at law. Certainly, no binding promise was made by the college to do some act, as the offer was never accepted; nor was an act done by the college that would constitute performance. Under the contract rule, no contract was made.

If it is clear that the case falls under those two rules, it is also equally certain that the rules were not considered susceptible to various (relevant) interpretations. There can be no debate about whether delivery is necessary or what the term means. There is further no question as to the certainty of considera-

---

33   246 N.Y. 369, 159 N.E. 173, 57 A.L.R. 980 (1927).

34   See *In re Greenberg's Will*, 286 N.Y.S. 56, 58, 158 Misc. 446 (1936).

tion, or the fact that, under traditional interpretations, it is not met here. However, the court in *Allegheny*, while recognizing all this, decided in favor of the college. It held that the acceptance of the subscription on the part of the college implied a promise to execute the work contemplated and to carry out the purposes for which the subscription was pledged. The implied promise was held to furnish a sufficient consideration for the subscriber's promise.

MacCormick has two possible responses open to him regarding the *Allegheny* case. He could say that it is an easy case: it is just wrongly decided. Clear rules were disregarded. There are difficulties in taking this position. The case was decided by Justice Cardozo, and has been widely acclaimed[35] and widely followed as persuasive authority in other jurisdictions.[36] More telling, perhaps, is the ordinariness of the decision in modifying a body of case law. A general rule, announced in many past contract cases, had an exception for charitable subscriptions read into it. Reworking of general rules to fit situations unforeseen at the times the rules were formulated is a general feature of case law. If MacCormick's classification of hard and easy cases is meant to reflect how case law develops, characterizing decisions like *Allegheny* as wrong leaves a gap in his description. It also leaves MacCormick with a burgeoning set of wrongly decided cases. The consistency principles he invokes throughout his work[37] would force him either to call for sharp and repeated reversals of members of the set of positivist rules, or make him turn his back on the social thesis of recognizing followed decisions, in favor of an embedded body of outlaw decisions.

---

35 See, for example, Arthur L. Corbin, "Mr. Justice Cardozo and the Law of Contracts," 39 *Colum. L. Rev.* 56, 60, 52 *Harv. L. Rev.* 408, 412, 48 *Yale L.J.* 426, 430 (1939).

36 See *Danby v. Osteopathic Hospital Association of Delaware*, 34 Del. Ch. 427, 104 A.2d 903 (1954).

37 This is sometimes referred to as the "validity thesis", at other times merely as logical consistency. See *Legal Reasoning and Legal Theory* 195-228.

However, one could classify *Allegheny* as a hard case.[38] Both the majority opinion and subsequent commentators present novel approaches to resolution of the case of charity subscriptions, and make convincing arguments why such subscriptions ought to be distinguished from ordinary cases of gratuitous contracts or undelivered gifts. Although the language of the bequest was vague and general, it did specify certain limited uses for the money. The majority found the acceptance of the subscription by the college to imply a promise on its part to execute the work contemplated and carry out the terms of the bequest. The college's implied promise was said to be sufficient consideration to balance the subscriber's promise.[39] Certainly it can be argued that, in such cases, the promises of the subscribers mutually support each other. The subscription contract is thus a bilateral contract between subscribers of which the charitable organization is a donee beneficiary. This holds despite the fact that the subscribers themselves never bargained. This interpretation would suggest that the case was not covered by the "consideration" rule. The court's reasoning would argue for the "consideration" rule applying, but not with its traditional interpretation.

The problem with such an analysis is that it allows any case rationally argued by two sides to become a hard case. Past

---

38 Neil MacCormick states that cases move along a continuum from easy to hard (page 228), but in his analysis, cases are hard if they meet certain criteria only, and for such cases, discretion applies and a different analysis than rule-following is required.

39 "The promisor wished to have a memorial to perpetuate her name. She imposed a condition that the "gift" should be known as the Mary Yates Johnston Memorial Fund. The moment that the college accepted $2,000 as a payment on account, there was an assumption of a duty to do whatever acts were customary or reasonably necessary to maintain the memorial fairly and justly in the spirit of its creation. The college could not accept the money and hold itself free thereafter from personal responsibility to give effect to the condition," (from the majority opinion of *Allegheny*). It is unclear what offer is being accepted by this implied promise, however. Certainly, the offeror asked for no such promise, merely performance. Moreover, it seems certain that the college undertook no such open-ended commitment to forever do everything necessary to maintain such a memorial. What if only $.02 had thus far been paid by the late Mary Johnston?

framings of the contract rules established general rules for *Allegheny*, and the court disregarded them. New rules, similar to the old rules, can be formulated, but they are not the same as the old rules.

Reference needs to be made to MacCormick's requirement of consistency, touched on above. He labels this requirement, generally, the validity thesis, and claims it is a necessary tenet in any positivistic scheme. This requirement:

> Presents law as comprising or at least including a set of valid rules for the conduct of affairs: such rules must satisfy the requirements of consistency, at least by including procedures for resolving conflict. [40]

There is a specific corollary, according to MacCormick, to this rather vague requirement: "Thou shalt not controvert established and binding rules of law."[41] One ought not to disregard rules merely because of policy considerations or desirable consequentialist-determined goals.

The validity thesis affirms the primacy of rules, and establishes the scope of hard case discretion: namely, the conceptual space between rules. It is quite different in approach from the pluralist position. Rules may be expendable for the pluralist. However, upon scrutiny, it can be seen that the validity thesis is either self-contradictory or trivial, and further, that any attempt to see *Allegheny* as a hard case results in compromising the validity thesis.

According to a straightforward interpretation of the validity thesis, *Allegheny* violated existing rules and was thus wrongly decided. However, after the decision, *Allegheny* became a basis for further decisions. This would mean that the rule of charitable subscriptions would be altered, but also altered, just as surely, would be at least one rule of precedent. *Allegheny* would stand for the proposition that exceptions could be carved out of clear and controlling rules when certain unnamed conditions are met. Thus, once *Allegheny* is handed down and followed, the validity thesis as a rule of the system no longer holds. This indicates the perhaps obvious point that positivism is only a

---

40 *Legal Reasoning and Legal Theory* at 107.

41 *Legal Reasoning and Legal Theory* at 195.

contingent property within a judicial system, and false within certain actual systems. If it is argued that *Allegheny* does not impair the validity thesis as a second order proposition about judicial statements, it may be asked what counter-example could? At any time, a system can be thought consistent and rules be defined and binding, but rules would here take on a fatal ambiguity. A rule would not be a normative proposition guiding action, but a proposition that would be impossible to contravene. Such an interpretation of the validity thesis renders it of no interest for understanding judicial reasoning.

Hard cases are those meant to be outside disposal by a reference to the validity thesis. Something like the validity thesis is common, as MacCormick points out, to all positivist or rule-bound theories. As *Allegheny* is obviously covered by a rule—the rule of contract consideration—it is a hard case for MacCormick only because interpretation of the rule is difficult or ambiguous. We saw, however, that the validity thesis is not a guarantee that rule-following is sufficient to duplicate the results reached in actual cases. Thus, in settling a hard case, both the rule and the interpretation always remain open. MacCormick instructs us to use consequentialist arguments to settle hard cases. But these are surely not meant to be purely consequentialist without resort to the judicial rules. If that were so, he would be endorsing a pluralist position of putting judicial view before rules. But if this consequence is to be avoided, MacCormick must find a way to limit the category of hard cases. A principle of rule-following sufficient to define a set of clear cases is not easily formulated, as seen from the fortune of the validity thesis. An appeal to consensus only works as long as the sides agree. The fact that a reasonable challenge arises as to the difficulty of a once-considered-to-be easy case itself negates the possibility of consensus.

Two final points need to be made. First, there has been an implicit appeal to reasonableness as a concept for assessing how a decision ought to be decided. Reasonableness is meant here as a weak concept, sufficient to screen out any arbitrary, trivial, or irrational challenge which might be made to a rule, a case, or a position, but not strong enough to support a theory as to how cases should be classified. As one's views change with new political, social, and ethical practices in society, what is or is not reasonable also changes. A more profound look at a position or simple observation of some of the consequences that have arisen from it can also change one's idea of what is reasonable.

The second point concerns starting place. The positivist begins with rules and continues with a way to supplement but not displace these rules. MacCormick suggests consequentialist arguments to supply the supplementation. A pluralist may endorse a consequentialist view, and use judicial rules along with general means/ends analysis to formulate first order propositions. However, the pluralist position uses rules consequentially, while the positivist accepts rules regardless of his opinion of their consequences. If MacCormick is forced to see all cases as hard, he effectively has given up the fundamental positivist premise.

The Social Thesis

The positivist tradition has always included a broad empirical streak. This has been expressed by the statement that law is a social fact. Joseph Raz, in *The Authority of Law*,[42] explains the social fact slogan.

> The view of law as a social fact, as a method of organization and regulation of social life, stands or falls with the two theses mentioned. At its core lie the theses that (1) the existence of a legal system is a function of its social efficacy, and that (2) every law has a source. [43]

The first thesis requires objects denoted as laws to be those actually obeyed, while the second limits membership in the set constituted by the first thesis to those originating from a certain source. Positivists look to social practices to avoid ephemeral theories or constructs. The sources thesis is essential to locating the correct social practices, to giving certainty to the structure of rules. If one cannot locate the source of the prescriptions on which Raz bases the legal system he describes, then one is lost.

---

42 Published in 1979.

43 *The Authority of Law: Essays on Law and Morality* (hereinafter called "*Authority*") 152.

Early in his book, Raz points out that there is a potential ambiguity in adopting the social thesis. One measure of law, say a particular statute or series of statutes, may require that disputes be settled with reference to moral considerations. Moral argument is not a traditional source of law for positivists. Raz calls the thesis that sources may multiply derivatively the weak thesis.

> The difference between the weak and the strong social thesis is that the strong one insists, whereas the weak one does not, that the existence and content of every law is fully determined by social sources. [44]

Thus, for Raz,

> a law has a source if its contents and existence can be determined without using moral arguments (but allowing for arguments about people's moral views and intentions, which are necessary for interpretation, for example).[45]

Raz endorses the strong thesis, and it is this one which we shall examine. He gives two related arguments in its favor. The first is that the strong or social thesis "reflects and explicates our conception of the law."[46] Raz runs through a series of distinctions—legal expertise versus moral enlightenment, applying law versus creating law, settled law versus unsettled law—and suggests such distinctions are integral to our understanding of judicial systems. The first members of each distinguished set are related. They refer to and help explain both the certainty of law, and the method of investigating legal contests through the use of technical skills. The sources thesis suggests that one looks to certain sources to find this certainty.

When there is no source, the second member of each distinction comes into play. Raz's second argument is that these distinctions and the conception they support reflect a deep truth, and one ascertainable through exploration of the sources thesis, about the function of the judicial system in society. The

---

44 *Authority* at 46.

45 *Authority* at 47.

46 *Authority* at 48.

argument is that societies distinguish between authoritative rulings and non-authoritative expressions.

> This marking-off of authoritative rulings indicates the existence in that society of an institution or organization claiming authority. [47]

> Since it is of the very essence of the alleged authority that it issues rulings which are binding regardless of any other justification, it follows that it must be possible to identify those rulings without engaging in a justificatory (moral) argument. [48]

Thus Raz wishes to separate what is essential in authoritative (and legal) expressions from what might also (contingently) happen to characterize specific authoritative statements. In so doing, Raz wants to eliminate moral or value considerations from authoritative rulings. His suggestion that the sources thesis reflects ordinary conceptions assumes that ordinary conceptions do not, rather than cannot, include value-laden reasoning within them. The sources thesis is a contingent thesis, falsifiable when societies employ value-laden behavior and label it as such.

One problem with the sources thesis is that it seems to concede too much. Hard cases, however decided, fall outside the normal purview of authoritative decision-making. Raz admits that "the sources thesis makes them (gaps or hard cases) unavoidable since it makes law dependent on human action with its attendant indeterminacies."[49] For these hard cases, he argues there are no correct answers. Presumably, one might settle these cases through resort to value reasoning. Raz points out two instances of such cases, those "where the law speaks with an uncertain voice (simple indeterminacy) or where it speaks with many voices (unresolved conflicts)."[50]

---

47 *Authority* at 51.

48 *Authority* at 51-52.

49 *Authority* at 73.

50 *Authority* at 77. An example of an uncertain voice might be product liability law in England prior to *Donoghue v. Stevenson* [1932] A.C. 562; 1932 S.C. (H.L.) 31; of many voices might be product liability law in New York State prior to *MacPherson v. Buick Motor Co.*, 217 N.Y. 382, 111 N.E. 1050 (1916).

If a certain decision is correctly decided, for Raz it must be so because of its agreement with the answer dictated by the sources thesis. A hard case cannot be rightly or wrongly decided, but is left open, exempt from determination by the sources thesis, and capable of being settled through moral reasoning. After a hard case is decided, does such a case become part of the general body of law and a source of further decisions? It is at this point that Raz is faced with a contradiction. The new judicial decision is an authoritative source for future decisions and thus must be obeyed. Yet the decision incorporates illegitimate moral reasoning and stands for, among other things, moral reasoning as allowable in reaching judicial decisions. If allowed, the hard cases serve as a counter-example to the sources thesis. If rejected, the sources thesis does not incorporate the decisions it claims to incorporate.

Even if one were to avoid those hard cases which involve disputes between different sets of authoritative or putatively authoritative standards, Raz is still left with those hard cases which appear to involve no clear prior standards. For instance, take the 19th Century English case of *Dawkins v. Antrobus*[51], a matter apparently of first impression.

Dawkins involved an action brought by an expelled member of a private club seeking legal redress for what he believed to be an improper and unwarranted action against him. In that case, Colonel Dawkins was accused of printing and circulating a pamphlet which "severely reflected on" the conduct of a Lieutenant General Stephenson, also a member of the club. A copy of the pamphlet was sent to General Stephenson's official address, the Guards' Orderly Room at the Horse Guards, but never to the Travellers' Club. However, under a club rule initially passed after Dawkins had become a member but before the pamphlet had been written, members could be expelled from the club should their conduct "be injurious to the character and interests of the club". When Colonel Dawkins was questioned about the pamphlet, he basically refused to reply and later indicated that the club rules were "never intended to settle personal disputes, nor to enable members of the Travellers

---

51   17 Ch. D. 615 (Ct. App. 1879).

Club to transfer the guardianship of their honour to the committee." He instead suggested that the only gentlemanly method to settle any disputes between him and the general was by a duel. Faced with Dawkins' position, the majority of the present members, including a significant number who had served under the general's command specifically or were military men generally, voted for expulsion.

Of particular significance here is the fact that apparently the court could find no relevant authority of any kind, at least in the traditional sense of authority recognized by Hart or Raz—including prior decisions, legislative acts or other standards deemed authoritative by any rule of recognition—which would bear on the decision the court faced. The colonel sought reinstatement, and the court heard his case—that is, allowed that there was jurisdiction over the matter—but decided it on grounds other than those unconnected with morality. The court held that the club's decision did not violate natural justice, was not a departure from the rules of the club, and was one that the club had reached in a *bona fide* manner. The court appeared quite willing to use the positivist's bugaboo of natural law or natural justice to decide the case unhampered by any prior relevant decisions or legislation on settling the internal disputes of private associations.

Lord Justice Brett, in his opinion, fashioned the issues quite clearly in terms of moral judgments:

> The only question which a Court can properly consider is whether the members of the club, under such circumstances, have acted *ultra vires* or not, and it seems to me the only questions which a Court can properly entertain for that purpose are, whether anything has been done which is contrary to natural justice, although it is within the rules of a club—in other words, whether the rules of the club are contrary to natural justice, secondly, whether a person who has not condoned the departure from them has been acted against contrary to the rules of the club; and thirdly whether the decision of the club has been come to *bona fide* or not.

The decision, then, is for Raz one without a legitimate source. However, it can hardly be ignored. First, as Raz and other positivists are hard-core empiricists, it would be difficult to overlook the simple, brute fact of cases like *Dawkins v. Antrobus*, decisions which populate the law reports and are heard daily in the courtrooms. Every issue was originally one of first impression. Second, as a practical matter, it is easy to see why courts, when faced with a choice between taking jurisdiction over a novel issue or allowing private remedies including dueling to the death, choose to hear such cases. Certainly, from a jurisdictional standpoint, a number of possible reasons to entertain such a case exists, including ruling on the property rights of club members which are forfeited upon expulsion, deciphering the contract of membership which was arguably altered after the original agreement, or analyzing the peculiar personal relationship which occurs between private associations and their members.

In any case, the court in *Dawkins* used natural reasoning; and the long line of subsequent cases which, in the next hundred years resolved disputes within such associations, relied on *Dawkins* incorporated the moral reasoning so objectionable to Raz.[52]

Raz, if unable to analyze the new case situation found in *Dawkins* directly, resorts to a curious argument in defense of his theory, and one he might reiterate in the face of both *Dawkins* and the criticism above.[53] He claims that it is an essential part of the function of law in society to provide publicly ascertainable ways of guiding one's behavior and regulating aspects of one's social life in conformity with the prevailing authority. The public nature of legal standards prevents members of society from being excused from non-conformity by challenging the justification of the standard. Thus a distinction must be made and enforced between the activity of extracting from public sources legal standards and that of engaging in moral reasoning in a limited number of peripheral cases. That part of a hard case which endorses moral reasoning is thus rejected, while stricter holdings or *rationes decidendi* would be allowed to stand.

---

52 See, for example, *James v. Marinship Corp.*, 25 Cal.2d 721, 155 P.2d 329 (1944). For a general discussion of the problems of the internal settlement of disputes in private associations, see Zechariah Chafee, Jr., "The Internal Affairs of Associations Not for Profit", 43 *Harv. L. Rev.* 993 (1930).

53 This argument is found in *Authority*, Chapter 3.

Such a response would be entirely inadequate. Aside from excluding the *Dawkins* situation from law by definition rather than argument, it would require a rethinking of the concept of precedent and a reworking of the notion of "public" to account for all the secret laws and proceedings found in political history.

Raz concedes that not all laws are open. He states that "Secret laws are possible provided they are not altogether secret. Someone must know their content some of the time."[54] Every law meets this test as does every putative law. Someone must have known of it to express it. A further stipulation saying that secret laws must be known to certain officials only moves the problem back a step. In every society, many individuals and some officials (including judges, as is evinced by the number of successful appeals which reverse lower court holdings) are ignorant of legal standards. Further, if moral reasoning is to be considered as part of judicial reasoning, then, one can be knowledgeable of that part of judicial reasoning, in that such reasoning can be duplicated. To a limited extent, this type of reasoning is public, and unable to be kept fully secret.

Raz's response also emphasizes the importance of access to authoritative standards, when it is conformity to such standards that is important. In a society with rational laws and a rational citizenry, access will aid in making conformity possible, but one can imagine other social situations. A society with many ignorant members may have laws which are designed to reflect their mores and customs, and can thus achieve a high degree of conformity, as with, possibly, a protectorate state governing a backward archipelago. We can also imagine a repressive regime where highly educated persons routinely and knowingly break the law. Finally, where a society and its concomitant set of rules are large and complex, almost everyone will be ignorant of a significant portion of the law. If in none of these situations fairness is achieved, this ought to be irrelevant to the positivist.

There is a different kind of mistake in Raz's hypothetical response. He would be suggesting that moral argument is susceptible to a kind of criticism not good against expressions of authority: namely, if the moral argument is shown to be

---

54 *Authority* at 51, n.9.

faulty, it can be challenged. Thus, if moral argument were allowed on a regular basis in judicial decision-making, it would incorporate this vulnerability into the judicial decision. Raz seriously overestimates the invulnerability of authority while arguing incorrectly that value statements are peculiarly more impeachable than other statements. Courts are often wrong in their reasoning. They commit errors in inference and implication, make category mistakes, and adopt faulty premises. The United States Supreme Court decisions holding that tomatoes are not fruit[55] or that women are not persons[56] were acknowledged at the time to be biologically incorrect. Neither the incompetency, irrationality, prejudice or stupidity of the courts, nor their lack of scientific expertise affected their authority or necessarily the obedience paid to either decision. One can challenge the scientific basis of the decision, just as Raz worries that if moral reasoning were allowed, one can attack the ethics of those decisions. Repeated incompetency in reasoning could eventually undermine the authority of the judicial system, but this would occur regardless of whether the incompetency was value-laden, scientific, or logical.

It should be noted in conclusion that the impetus for the sources thesis would be preserved under pluralism. The distinctions between settled versus unsettled law, legal versus moral talk, and creating versus applying law would remain, although perhaps within a different terminology. The last distinction would be the most altered. As one would not be limited to legal forms, but could draw upon the larger set of third order propositions. Then, given a sophisticated, consistent judicial view, a unique answer could always be found to first order questions. However, one could still distinguish, if one wanted, between first order propositions traceable back to legal forms and those not so traceable. Given that vagueness, overdetermination, and inconsistencies would still occur, cases could be considered to

---

55 *Nix v. Hedden*, 149 U.S. 304, 13 Sup. Ct. 881, 37 L.Ed. 745 (1893).

56 *Bradwell v. Illinois*, 83 U.S. (16 Wall.) 130, 21 L.Ed. 442 (1873). This belief was reiterated in another context by the Massachusetts Supreme Judicial Court in *Commonwealth v. Welosky*, 276 Mass. 398, 177 N.E. 656 (Mass. 1931).

be either harder or easier. However, when a hard decision requires that such vagueness, overdetermination or inconsistencies be resolved, at least in part, one would strictly speaking not just be applying law. The shifting property could be called indeterminancy, but as mentioned earlier, it is a shifting indeterminancy, one whose resolution is an individual matter. One can be inconsistent in first order propositions without the justification of conflicting larger social principles. Thus, an easy case could be wrongly decided, and a failure to apply law would occur.

The purpose in criticizing these three positivist ideas—the rule of recognition, the distinction between binding easy cases and non-binding hard cases, and Raz's social thesis—is not to suggest that the positivist picture of adjudication is irreparably wrong. Rather, it is meant to suggest that an inter-personal, rule-based approach is difficult, misguided, and unhelpful. The positivist assumes a unity of belief among the bench that is contingent at best, and seemingly false everywhere upon examination. By looking at judicial decision-making in terms of individual conceptions of judicial role and view, one is able to explain legal change, and simultaneously able to understand why there is normative regularity in the case law. The judicial pluralist thus can reject the positivist assumption that there is a discoverable set of rules which characterizes a society's legal system without abandoning the empirical approach of observation that the positivist cherishes.

More concretely, the situation of the easy case turned hard is one beyond the analytic power of positivism, or rule-based theory generally. An individual may be content to formulate (first and second order) rules, seeing them as disposing of the judicial questions that arise; however, one day those rules will lead to unsatisfactory results. The fault is not with the rules' existence or their scope. It is with their authority. The new situation is one where they will not do. Their application will be sufficiently unjust, unfair, impolitic, absurd, catastrophic, or far-reaching that the individual must reject their application. He does this not because the rules tell him so, but because his third order beliefs and attitudes demand it. Thus, the apparent authority of the rules may at any time dissipate. Values and preferences intercede, for the holder of a particular view will find that there are limits to his respect for following narrow rules strictly. This is not a problem which can be solved by adding simply a new layer of rules sterilized of politics and values. Ultimately, these politics and values will intrude, defeat a positivist conception and demonstrate the pluralistic flavor of judicial decision-making.

VI

Truth and the Solution to Judicial Cases

Law, say the gardeners, is the sun,
Law is the one
All gardeners obey
To-morrow, yesterday, to-day.

And always the loud angry crowd
Very angry and very loud
Law is We,
And always the soft idiot softly Me.

W.H. Auden

We have been, up to this point, examining several of the problems inherent in determining the status of judicial state-ments. Part of the time has been taken criticizing two types of theory which purport to answer the question: what are the grounds for making judicial statements. These theories—skep-ticism and positivism—imply, respectively, that there are no belief grounds for judicial assertions and that grounds exist according to a master rule socially ascertainable within each society. We now shall turn to the logic of, rather than the grounds for, judicial statements. This involves several of the same questions refocused rather than an entirely new set of questions.

Judges, lawyers, parties to law suits, and members of the general public all make putative judicial assertions. They say "this contract is valid" or "x is guilty of theft" or "such-and-such state of affairs constitutes tortious negligence". Regardless of the justification for such statements, some understanding of their meanings may be garnered from an analysis of the indi-

viduals' intentions who made them. For example, some understanding may be had of pre-Copernican astronomical statements, even if these statements were often or invariably wrong,
by knowing what their speakers intended.[1] Of course, the sense
or meaning of a statement is closely tied to the way it can be
found to be called true or false,[2] but the grounds for assertion
are initially based on what the speaker intends to assert.[3]
Words which are scientifically false may be aesthetically
compelling or brilliantly humorous. Meaning is contextual and
context is connected to intention.

The first part of this chapter examines a theory which says
that judicial assertions are virtually always able to have the predicates "true" or "false" applied to them. That is, this theory
suggests that for each judicial question, one and only one right
answer exists. When a speaker utters a judicial statement, he
has in mind this truth, and judicial argument and discussion can
proceed only because there exists an answer to be found. The
second part of this chapter will outline a pluralist approach to
the question, drawing on the analysis of the theory discussed in
part one.

Overall, this chapter will assert the position that truth predicates can be meaningfully applied to judicial statements, but not
in any simple way. Judicial statements are true or false only in
lieu of an individual's own judicial view, and that view is not, in

---

1   See Thomas S. Kuhn, *The Copernican Revolution: Planetary Astronomy in
    the Development of Western Thought* (1957) for a discussion of pre-Coperni-
    can and post-Copernican language.

2   This idea can be traced back to Frege's notion that truth values are the
    referents of sentences. "How does a thought act? By being appre-
    hended and taken to be true." Gottlob Frege, "The Thought: A Logical
    Inquiry" in *Philosophical Logic* 38 (ed. P. F. Strawson, 1967). See
    generally Michael Dummett, *Frege: Philosophy of Language* 152-203 (1973).

3   The role of intention in a theory of meaning is widely discussed. Well-
    known works include Elizabeth Anscombe, *Intention* (1957); John Searle,
    Intentionality (1983); and various essays of Donald Davidson, including
    "Freedom to Act" in *Essays on Freedom of Action* (ed. T. Honderich, 1973);
    and "Actions, Reasons and Causes", *The Philosophy of Action* (ed. A. R.
    White, 1968). The connection between utterance and intention is also
    discussed in Stanley Cavell, *Must We Mean What We Say* 1-43 (1969).

its basic premises, susceptible to bivalent truth conditional analysis. One can thus make a mistake or be wrong about some assertion relative to commitments, but no proposition is true for a legal system merely because it is implied by a theory or master rule which is necessarily valid.

It should be mentioned why no attempt will be made here to discuss judicial statements in the larger context of normative language. Certainly, judicial talk is largely concentrated on rules and rule behavior, and many writers have found discussion of the normative category useful in their analysis of judicial statements.[4] However, the variety of norms makes any general grouping weak and, perhaps, confusing. For our purposes, it is necessary to keep in mind two distinctions between judicial statements and certain other types of norms. First, judicial statements are conventional, while ethical statements, at least arguably, are not.[5] The practices of the community are thus critical to understanding judicial language. Second, judicial statements carry an authority which rules of games, for example, do not. Games often make sense only when seen as voluntary (consensually entered) activities. Law is not a voluntary activity, and thus reasons for obedience as well as objections to past interpretations of standards (custom and precedent) are weighed differently than in game situations. In general, the category of normative statements is to be too broad to be useful here.

---

4 The works of Hans Kelsen, *General Theory of Law and State* (1945), *The Pure Theory of Law* (1967); Alf Ross, *On Law and Justice* (1958); and Joseph Raz, *The Concept of a Legal System* (1970) and *Practical Reason and Norms* (1975) are typical, prominent examples of this phenomenon. See also Georg Henrik Von Wright, *Norm and Action: A Logical Inquiry* (1963).

5 It is a matter of some controversy whether moral statements are objective. However, even those who deny the objective status of ethical statements admit that a case can be made against the conventionality of ethics. Even such a *prima facie* argument against most judicial statements is not possible. The two most convincing writers who challenge the objectivity of ethics are John Mackie, *Ethics: Inventing Right and Wrong* (1977) and Gilbert Harman, *The Nature of Morality* (1977).

The "One Right Answer" Theory

In a series of papers, Ronald Dworkin has developed a powerful theory concerning the meaning of judicial statements.[6] While his theory involved an evolution which allowed for certain alterations and thus inconsistencies when taken as a whole,[7] his theory might generally be stated in terms of the following four propositions:

1) For every actual and potential question faced by a sitting judge, there exists an answer to settle that question;

2) That answer is discoverable;

3) That answer is exclusive;

4) That answer is correct, it is the right answer.

These propositions will in turn be examined, reconstructing the whole of his theory along the way. [8]

---

6   The most important of Dworkin's papers are collected in *Taking Rights Seriously*, published in 1977 (hereinafter referred to as "*TRS*"), *A Matter of Principle*, published in 1985, and *Law's Empire*, published in 1986. On the whole, *A Matter of Principle* is mainly concerned with political and constitutional theory. In that either *Principle* or *Law's Empire* cover judicial reasoning and jurisprudence, they generally reiterate and defend, (although occasionally with some refinement), the positions taken in *TRS*, which will thus be the main focus here. Generally, any paper published elsewhere which is collected in that work will be cited to the book only.

7   The only shift in Dworkin's theory relevant here is his early belief that one source in the form of a master rule could not capture all standards needed in adjudication, to his position that such a source can be found in a political theory. Whether this latter position is actually precluded in his early papers, discouraged, or just not discussed is a matter of scholarly exegesis not pertinent here.

8   The theory being reconstructed is Dworkin's theory of the status of judicial statements. In his work, this theory is mingled with his theory of rights, his larger theory of adjudication (which is both normative and descriptive) and his political and ethical positions. The particular theory extracted here may, in being stripped of the related theoretical impedimenta, not be one Dworkin himself would wish to accept.

Dworkin's major point in his early papers was that every potential and actual question which a court faces has an answer.[9] His analysis was conducted through a critique of H. L. A. Hart's rule-based positivistic legal theory, particularly his theory of judicial discretion. Dworkin claimed that the standards employed in judicial reasoning are of two kinds: rules and principles. These are logically distinguishable, in that rules either apply to a particular case or they do not, while principles are weighed one against another. Principles individually do not require a specific outcome, but can modify the course of an argument. Dworkin doubted that Hart accounted for principles as a standard used in adjudication; thus his (Hart's) model of rules was inadequate. Besides being a descriptive failure, it left a Hartian unable to handle hard cases, those not within the purview of rules alone.[10] Principles were Dworkin's tool for settling the hard cases. He wrote that in those cases, a judge has discretion to reach judgment. This discretion is not mere license. It requires the employment of principled reasoning, and this reasoning always guarantees an answer.

There are great difficulties in enumerating the relevant principles, although strictly speaking, it is unnecessary for Dworkin to do so. One might only be able to locate their sources generally and in an *ad hoc* manner. By Dworkin's own definition, the sources of the principles are eclectic, and no single pedigree captures them all. However, if one is uncertain of the extent of the full set of principles, it is unclear how one can be certain that every possible case is covered within the scope of these principles. The vast number of principles is not of itself a sufficient condition to imply completeness. After all, Dworkin has

---

9 These early papers include "Judicial Discretion," 60 *J. of Phil.* 624 (1963); "Wasserstrom: The Judicial Decision," 75 *Ethics* 47 (1964), reprinted as "Does Law Have a Function?", 74 *Yale L. J.* 640 (1965); and "Is Law a System of Rules?", 35 *U. of Chicago L. Rev.* 14 (1967), reprinted as Chapter 2 of *TRS* 14-45.

10 Ronald Dworkin assumes that cases where the rules are clear are easy cases. He says, for example, "But if the case at hand is a hard case, when no settled rule dictates a decision either way, then it might seem that a proper decision could be generated by either policy or principle." *TRS at 83.*

rejected as incomplete the set of rules that Hart discusses, a set both large and extensive. Yet this latter set is well-known, through inspection, to be incomplete. Without such inspection, it might seem risky to believe, *a priori*, the set of principles to be complete.[11] As principles are tied to particular legal systems, the fact that certain systems have extremely broad and numerous principles does not guarantee that every system will contain such principles. It is difficult to see how, in theory, such completeness could be insured in advance.

Dworkin's second proposition is that the answer to every judicial controversy is discoverable.[12] This is an epistemological rather than a logical assertion. Dworkin sees the set of principles as both sufficient to solve every potential problem and manageable according to some algorithm for actually using them. Of course, principles play a prominent role for Dworkin only in hard cases. While he never delineates the distinction between hard cases and easy cases, the test he seems to be using is that of the positivists: if a case falls squarely under a clear rule, then it is easy. While Dworkin denies the existence of a master rule or rule of recognition,[13] clearly rules somehow play a part in ordinary cases, and these rules are ascertainable. Resort to legal forms (past decisions, statutes, constitutions, treaties, edicts, and custom) might be the likely source. While principles always figure in deciding a case, when rules "run out" or "leave gaps", principles become the dominant factor.

Not just any principle will do in adjudication. Dworkin outlines a procedure for finding the right principles, and thus arriving at the right answer. He requires an examination of all past legal forms, with their embedded rules and principles. This may involve certain inconsistencies when taken as a whole.

---

11   Since the time of Kurt Godel's Theorem, it has become common-place that many axiomatized systems are incomplete. Dworkin's assertion that this legal system he postulates, with its rules and principles, is complete cannot, without some proof, be accepted as true. See Ernest Nagel and James R. Newman, *Godel's Proof* (1959) for a philosophical discussion of the limitations of consistent axiomatized systems in generating truths.

12   Ronald Dworkin's main discussion of the discoverability of answers to judicial questions is his chapter entitled "Hard Cases" in *TRS* 81-130.

13   This is the thrust of his argument in "The Model of Rules", in *TRS* 14-45.

Instead of using propositions contained in past forms directly, one must seek a unifying political theory which justifies the legal forms when surveyed in their entirety. There is, however, a central ambiguity in Dworkin's theory. Take a favorite case of Dworkin's, *Riggs v. Palmer*,[14] the case of the legatee who, having murdered his testator, defended a civil suit to deprive him of the benefits of the will. Dworkin speaks both of principles found directly in cases, such as the unjustly-gained benefits principle of *Riggs* and principles which are implied by the political theory. These sets of principles may potentially conflict. The principle of *Riggs*, for example, is unlikely to remain as broad in a political theory which must be based on cases where contract breachers, accused criminals improperly arrested, adverse possessors, negligent defamers protected by free speech legislation, sellers of real property who sales pitch is geared to the doctrine of *caveat emptor*, and tortious governments operating under the cloak of sovereign immunity all benefit well and regularly by their own wrongs.

A theory must meet a minimal threshold degree of fit to be considered, although how this threshold is determined is not discussed by Dworkin. Then if several theories meet this degree of "fit", that theory which best justifies the whole is the one to be accepted. This theory will locate both the apparent principles that derive from it, and even any hidden principles—such as the principle guaranteeing a right to privacy in tort law[15]—which were latent in past decisions or statutes. [16]

There are a number of technical difficulties with this method. A great deal rests on the point at which an easy case turns into a hard one, a point difficult to locate.[17] Moreover, within Dworkin's theory, there is an argument to be made that one could see every decision either as hard or as easy. As easy cases

---

14   115 N.Y. 506, 22 N.E. 188 (1889).

15   The argument for an embedded, implicit principle guaranteeing a right to privacy being lodged in the American common law of torts was put forth initially by Samuel Warren and Louis Brandeis, "The Right to Privacy", 4 *Harv. L. Rev. 193* (1890).

16   Ronald Dworkin discusses this in *TRS* 118-120.

17   This point was discussed at some length in the previous chapter.

are those with clear, self-applying rules without interfering principles, it is hard to find a member of this category.   Dworkin
suggests *Riggs v. Palmer*[18] as a typical hard case.[19]   Dworkin
begins his discussion by quoting what the court recognizes as
the rule applicable in the case:

> It is quite true that statutes regulating the making, proof and effect of
> wills, and the devolution of property, if literally construed, and if their
> force and effect can in no way and under no circumstances be controlled
> or modified, give this property to the murderer. [20]

Both Dworkin and the court give the rule short shrift, but it is a
paradigm example of a rule that is clear, self-applying, relevant,
and uncontradicted by any other rule.   Such a rule should make
for an easy case.

The fact that a principle does apply to *Riggs* and adequately,
in both Dworkin's and the court's opinions, disposes of the case,
appears to make it, in a different way, an easy case: it mirrors
the structure of paradigmatically easy cases.   One looks to the
relevant standards, be they rules or principles, and simply
applies them to the case.   One is required to do so, and
"discretion" as a relevant concept seems only to mean that more
than rules needs to be considered.   Certainly, no special freedom ought to be inferred, nor is any special mental acuity
needed.   Dworkin's choice of a perfect judge, Hercules, is thus
apt.[21]   Hercules' great physical strength allowed him to labor
successfully to examine all relevant standards, and his unex-
traordinary judgment appeared to be sufficient to solve any
case.[22]   The ubiquity of standards and their automatic application appears to make all cases easy.

There is a larger difficulty for Dworkin in the demarcation
between easy and hard cases.   Dworkin's method for construct-

---

18   115 N.Y. 506, 22 N.E.188 (1889)

19   *TRS* 23-45.

20   *TRS* 23; *Riggs v. Palmer*, 115 N.Y. 506, 509, 22 N.E.188, 189 (1889).

21   *TRS* 105-130.

22   For one account of the laboring Hercules and his adventures, see Robert
      Graves, 2 *The Greek Myths* 100-206 (1955).

ing a political theory to handle what are, at the least, controversial cases relies on a large residue of easy cases being available. The two part claim for the political theory is not that it is equitable, just, or politically efficacious, but that it justified by past cases and statutes. In order for a justification to be measured, there must exist a substantial set of straightforward easy cases, a condition Dworkin implicitly recognizes, among other places, in his discussion of the gravitational force of precedent.[23] The easy cases, or at least their *rationes decidendi*, serve as propositions on which the political theory rests. For the theory to be sustained, to have enough data to draw on, there must be this large set of easy cases. If only a few cases are in that set, theory construction would largely be a matter of political and ethical preferences alone. The few cases available would underdetermine the political theory, such that Dworkin's third proposition would be impossible.

The third proposition states that there is a single, exclusive answer to every judicial question.[24] He advances this proposition through two quite different arguments. The first is the argument from logical negation. While the argument involves symbolic manipulation, it can be stated as claiming that once it

---

23   See *TRS* 110-123.

24   This claim is made in *TRS* 81-130, 279-290 and in "No Right Answer?" in *Law, Morality, and Society: Essays in Honour of H. L. A. Hart* 58-84 (eds. P.M.S. Hacker and J. Raz, 1977). This article has also appeared, with minor differences, in 53 *New York L. Rev. 1* (1978) and as Chapter 5 of *A Matter of Principle* (1985). Citations here will be to the Hart *Festschrift*. Ronald Dworkin allows that it is possible for that answer to be a tie between two competing positions, but those occasions will be extremely rare, and virtually non-existent in advanced legal systems. There is also the:

> Possibility that the political theory that provides the best justification for the settled law is for some reason entirely neutral . . . We must also concede the theoretical possibility that two different political theories, which suggest different answers to that question, for some reason each provide exactly as good a justification of the settled law as the other.

Law, Morality, and Society at 83. Such possibilities will be discounted for purposes of the analysis here, as they are not counted except as asides in Ronald Dworkin's own treatment.

is recognized that judicial judgments may be made which allow for truth values being assigned to propositions of law, then it is not possible to restrict the assigned set of judgments. Thus, for any proposition, to deny that that proposition is either true or false is to engage in a contradiction. (This argument shall not be taken up directly, as it claims only to be refuting Hartian positivism[25] and is, in any case, linked in more accessible terms to the argument from the best evidence and Dworkin's fourth proposition). The argument focuses on the difficulty in keeping separate negation within a system of propositions ("it is not true that p") and negation outside such a system (for some system S, it is true that not-S(p)).

A component of this first argument, but one we shall consider separately, is the argument from the best evidence.[26] This argument states that once one looks to the relevant rules and principles, a single answer to judicial questions can be found. Even where any particular outcome is controversial, one merely looks to the evidence presently available, and that evidence is able to serve as the sole basis for decision. In effect, an answer cannot be denied because of underdetermination: whatever reasons are listed are sufficient. The reason that an answer is guaranteed is due to what Dworkin calls the terms of the judicial enterprise. Parties to a suit are participants in a common enterprise which by its rules requires a single answer. They, the judges, are not given the luxury of waiting until a conclusive line of reasoning is put forward: they must always decide cases, and they must use the best evidence which they presently have available.

Dworkin collapses the distinction between the external observer to a judicial system and the judge. The distinction would be this: the judge is required by some type of institutional responsibility to adjudicate the cases before him. His duty is to sift the evidence given him and decide the case immediately.

---

25 Joseph Raz does have a rebuttal against the argument in *Authority* 53-77. While I am not entirely persuaded by Joseph Raz, I am sympathetic to his conclusions, for reasons which do not lie within the scope of this work.

26 Ronald Dworkin labels it a refutation of the argument from controversy. See "No Right Answer?" in *Law, Morality, and Society* 76-84.

Thus, the judge must decide on the basis of the best available rather than the best possible evidence. The external observer, on the other hand, can suspend judgment until a sufficient case is made in favor of a certain position. If we hypothesize a situation where a theoretical issue is being discussed, and the evidence underdetermines the conclusion, then no single answer would be assertable by the external observer, although it would be so assertable by the theoretical judge. Dworkin, to be consistent, would need to claim that even for the external observer, as in observing he participates in a certain type of answer-requiring enterprise, a conclusion on the question is mandated. This conclusion is not merely exclusive, though. It is correct. Dworkin's fourth proposition is that "right" is not an inappropriate predicate to apply to the answers to judicial cases.[27] He suggests that lawyers commonly speak of cases being rightly or wrongly decided, and that this language is justified, as long as their assertions are grounded in a theory of law (captured in a larger political theory) which justifies the relevant cases and statutes.

> A proposition of law may be asserted as true if it is more consistent with the theory of law that best justifies settled law than the contrary proposition of law. It may be denied as false if it is less consistent with that theory of law than the contrary. Suppose that this enterprise proceeds with the ordinary success of modern legal systems. Judges often agree about the truth values of propositions of law, and when they disagree they understand the arguments of their opponents sufficiently well to be able to locate the level of disagreement, and to rank these arguments in rough order of plausibility.[28]

Judges thus agree about what they are disagreeing about, and within this common frame of discourse are in fact arguing about what is right and wrong.

Dworkin states that it is common for lawyers to argue about whether a case has been rightly decided, and suggests that for those whose philosophical skepticism resists such usage, a short time spent actually studying law would cure them of their reluc-

---

27 This point is put forward in *TRS* 81-130, 279-290; and in "No Right Answer?" in *Law, Morality and Society* 58-84.

28 *TRS* at 283.

tance to endorse a single answer.[29] He says that anyone who
studies law will find himself wanting to assert the correctness of
certain propositions, and will feel that these propositions must
have a two ordered truth value. While he does not use the term
"convention", it is the conventionality of judicial statements
which gives them their truth value, and the convention itself
requires exactly one answer to every question.

Dworkin is here appealing to a common enterprise, one in
which all who make judicial assertions must participate. This, as
we saw in Chapter II, is a fundamental error. One can appear
to be arguing about a proposition within a common enterprise,
but actually be arguing from the perspective of quite different
enterprises. This is not because of wide semantic divergencies,
for the terms can have similar extensions when used by
different parties.[30] Further, the parties to a dispute may believe
they are right, that the others are wrong, and that it is the
correctness of the outcome which is central to the dispute.
Parties' beliefs are fallible, and the fact that they believe they are
arguing about p does not imply that they are arguing about p
(rather than conflating p with p'). Some pseudo-arguments
imitate real arguments in appearing to focus on a single point,
when the parties are using a parallel discourse to advance unlike
propositions. (An example of this phenomenon elsewhere can
be found in discussions on counter-factuals, which exhibit this
characteristic generally).[31]

There is a more fundamental reason why Dworkin's reliance
on a common enterprise is misplaced. A common enterprise
consists of two distinct sets of standards. The external set is
that which organizes the enterprise itself. Included would be
the minimum criteria of individuation (such that an enterprise x

---

29 *TRS* at 283-284.

30 It is not clear that even for a Dworkinian, extension would remain the
    same for those using the same terms within a common enterprise.
    Certainly, different intentions would have to be allowed. Convergence
    rather than consensus would be sufficient to allow for direct
    disagreement under Dworkin's model.

31 See David Lewis, *Counterfactuals* (1973) for one discussion of this prob-
    lem.

could be recognized as an x rather than a y) and standards delineating how the enterprise is to be carried out. The set of propositions which provides answers to judicial questions and allows that whatever solution has the best current evidence in its favor is a member of this external set. The internal set of standards are, here, the set of propositions of law or put in normative terms, the operative rules and principles. They are answers to the questions which the external standards require to be answered. The discussion in specific cases always centers on members of the internal set. Individuals assert the truth of p, where p is some proposition such as "this contract is valid" or "B's activity constituted an attractive nuisance". That truth is conventional, and is truth condition dependent upon the common enterprise. Dworkin uses the symbol $L(p)$ to indicate this. The actual argument does not usually include talk of the enterprise, merely of the internal propositions. If one hypothesized the existence of the series $L_1(p), L_2(p), L_3(p),...L_o(p)$, one could imagine those engaged in controversy regarding the outcome of a case to assume that they are discussing the truth value of $L(p)$, without imagining that competitors (as symbolized by the above series) for the designation of "common enterprise" exist, or specifying the identity of $L_o(p)$.

Consider, for example, a case before a judge in which each side cites a different set of precedents for its authority. Such a case might be one where a landlord P brings suit against his tenant D for non-payment of rent.[32] D claims that P violated the implied warranty of habitability of the lease by failing to keep a secure lock on the building entrance. The flimsy lock in place was inadequate to keep potential assailants from wandering into the common areas of the apartment house, thus making D's own apartment unsafe. P claims that the apartment is in a dangerous neighborhood, that D knew this when she moved there, and that she pays less rent because of it. P further claims that D assumed the risk of the dangerous neighborhood in choosing to live in P's building, and that it would be unrea-

---

32 This example is entirely hypothetical and ought not, despite its amalgam of a number of viable common law doctrines, to be considered legally tenable in any jurisdiction. Moreover, it assumes that no legislation governs the rights and duties of the parties.

sonable of the court to demand that P install better and stronger locks and doors as part of a mental combat against the wiles of potential trespassers and assailants. D counters that an assumption of risk argument has no place in a property action, and points out its novelty. P cites a number of other instances where property law borrowed from tort law certain concepts, and notes that the whole idea of an implied warranty of habitability is itself an example of this borrowing.

The proposition being disputed is whether or not assumption of risk is a valid defense in a property suit to a claim of breach of warranty. The dispute will focus on certain precedents and the appropriateness of analogical argument from tort to property or possibly contract. It appears to be a controversy about the truth of p, much in the same way as two geologists might argue about the truth of some proposition, q, which dates a piece of shale. However, Dworkin admits that p, unlike q, is not a proposition which can stand alone (outside the rules of the enterprise). It is true or false in lieu of the external rules which define $L(p_o)$.[33] Do P and D necessarily agree on the definition of $L(p_o)$?

It is certainly true that they agree on many of its general features. Let us suppose, however, that they disagree on how limited the analogical reasoning ought to be, on whether categories such as property, tort, and contract are indicative of isolated concepts which need to be kept separated or are merely shorthand for distinctive groups of cases, and to what degree a concept of justice has been employed to restrict the property rights of landlords. P, who sees the case law as moving toward systemic consistency and denies that ethical notions of justice are an important factor in this movement, has ample evidence for his position. This is not just because the case is easy (with no evidence for D's position, for some evidence does exist) or because the case is hard (for when a new theory of liability or new line of defense is presented, the case is in some ways to be

---

33 As a point of symbology, the subscript in the phrases "$L_o(p)$" and "$L(p_o)$" is used to indicate just where the controversy lies. In "$L_o(p)$", we are discussing competing legal enterprises, in "$L(p_o)$" different propositions within a given enterprise. The complete terminology is "$L_o(p_o)$" for all propositions in all legal enterprises.

considered easy, because without this novel approach it would be), for the case is, in its disagreement about precedent, quite ordinary. P's evidence is partly a function of the way he defines $L(p_o)$. P believes that notions of property rights ought to be upheld while incursions of imposed responsibility for the welfare of others ought to be limited. In sifting the ambiguous and inconsistent legal forms, (and as a prior move, judging contenders from the set of putative legal forms), P employs these two (and other) beliefs to construct the set of valid judicial propositions, or in Dworkin's terms, to construct $L(p_o)$. As P's beliefs differ from D's, even if the suit *P v. D* had never arisen, P would assess the criteria for judging the outcome to a hypothetical *P v. D* differently from D. His political beliefs might suggest that property rights are paramount in the pantheon of rights, while his ethical beliefs might suggest that responsibility for a person's safety ought, in normal circumstances, to rest squarely and solely with the said person. P may see the judicial system as generally supporting him, and treat counter-examples as mistaken aberrations. Finally, he may see systemic consistency as a central tenet of judicial decision-making.

P and D seem to be engaging in a single argument, but they are in fact engaging in two distinct arguments. They disagree over the truth of p, the internal proposition which allows a defense of assumption of the risk to the breach of warranty of habitability claim. They also disagree over what common enterprise or convention ought to be used to settle the question of truth of p: should the convention emphasize property rights, inter-conceptual consistency, or judicial deference to the legislature in creating new defenses and claims. Regardless of the outcome of *P v. D*, this latter question or set of questions will not be directly decided.

It is now easy to see where Dworkin's argument goes wrong. He is anxious to show that the law of excluded middle is violated when an indeterminate, or third, truth value is allowed in a convention which requires an answer.[34] However, the fact

---

34 In fairness to Ronald Dworkin, it must be added that his claim is limited to positivists (as represented by Hart in *The Concept of Law*) and the arguments he thinks they might make.

that parallel and similar conventions may address the same questions and use the same criteria can mislead one into believing a single, authoritative, right, true answer exists, when such an answer exists only within the bounds of an entirely subjective convention.

There is an additional caveat here. It is Dworkin's assertion that a single answer is almost always required by the ground rules of the common enterprise.[35] This is an external claim, or claim about the parameters of the convention or enterprise. (In being "external" as we have defined it, there is no reason why a judicial view cannot incorporate into its propositional schema the "external" claims. It is a commonplace of logic that higher orders can be collapsed into lower ones). It is a contingent claim, but one nevertheless which might be found to be true. For it to be valid, there must be little difference between finding an answer to an easy case and finding an answer to a hard case except for physical exertion. Dworkin simply has the judge apply an analogue (either rule-based for easy cases or rule and principle-based for hard cases) to arrive at a decision. Judges and lawyers talk of an answer and an answer is the outcome of adjudication.

Some of Dworkin's critics have felt that for certain cases, while an answer might be offered, it should not have quite the

---

35 Dworkin states:

> Each of these judgments about the truth value of propositions of law is one that a judge might sensibly make, under certain conditions, *within the ground rules of the enterprise.* Suppose a judge thinks that the case for a theory of the relevant law that makes the defendant liable for economic damage is exactly as strong as the case for a theory that frees him from that liability. The rules of the enterprise, as so far described, acknowledge that situation as a theoretical possibility; and if that possibility is realized, then judges cannot, under these rules, assert either proposition as true or deny it as false. In any particular hard case, therefore, a judge may sensibly make, for that case, the same judgment as the philosopher seems to make for all hard cases.

TRS at 284. Ronald Dworkin goes on to say that such ties are extremely rare. He expands, but does not change, his position on objectivity in *A Matter of Principle* 119-177 (1985).

same status as answers in easy, straightforward cases.[36] Putting this objection in terms of threshold, position A states that for a judicial proposition to count as true or right it needs to have a certain threshold of supporting evidence. A judge may need to decide cases by making use of one or another of competing putative propositions, but his averral of one does not make it true. The chosen proposition enjoys a twilight status, in limbo until further evidence is marshalled to either allow it full status as true or knock it down as false. Position B states that such a proposition enjoys the same status as any other true proposition. Dworkin would endorse position B.

There seems to be no logical or conceptual reason position A could not be valid, and there is some evidence that it actually is held and used by some lawyers and judges. For it to be logically viable, one would, among other things, have to assign a different weight to best evidence below threshold propositions than to threshold surpassing propositions. Yet we can see evidence of this kind of distinction in common law precedent. Certain cases are given greater authority than others, while certain doctrines are, despite some case law enunciating them, considered tentative.[37] Some answers would be right or wrong, while others would enjoy a tentative, best candidate position, awaiting further review. The difference would be in how subsequent decisions were reasoned. A permanent (or less temporary in a strict continuum classification scheme) member of the set of true propositions would be either determinative or highly persuasive in settling the subsequent decision. A temporarily placed member could be more easily disregarded. Conversely, a temporary "right" answer could be overruled with less damage to the logic of the entire system.

There is a final objection Dworkin might make to the preceding criticism. We said that truth values could be assigned to

---

36 This is not their terminology, but it reflects the crucial distinction H. L. A. Hart, Joseph Raz, and Neil MacCormick want to maintain between easy and hard cases. See, generally, Chapter V.

37 Part of the reasoning behind the numerous and complicated techniques for handling past cases can be tied to this idea. See Karl Llewellyn, *The Common Law Tradition: Deciding Appeals* 62-92 (1960) for one description of the differential treatment of past cases in American jurisdictions.

judicial propositions only as a function of the convention of judicial reasoning. However, although conventions may be contingent in their construction, the choice of the applicable convention within a jurisdiction is hardly random. Dworkin might want to argue that there is a correct convention, a common enterprise that is right. What, however, could be the definitive criteria for correctness here? Dworkin rejects consensus when he introduces the use both of moral reasoning[38] and a theory of mistakes[39] in his theory of adjudication. The moral reasoning component requires that something more than social practices or a majority of beliefs be considered. A theory of mistakes suggests that independent criteria exist apart from judicial pronouncements for what the announced propositions ought to be. This set of criteria means that consensus alone cannot determine the results of judicial controversies, for consensus can be incorrect in meeting the independent criteria. If some set of beliefs rather than consensus is to be the test for convention, the problem remains: which beliefs? The truth or falsity of any proposition within a belief set is irrelevant to its being the correct belief set. In any actual society, no belief set is likely to be true without qualification, and verisimilitude might be a better measure. Yet even it fails. First, attitudes are as important as beliefs in detailing the parameters of a judicial convention, and these are without truth values.[40] Second, it is not the truth of a belief but the fact that it is held by a relevant individual which gives it its relevance. Beliefs in use form the basis of a convention. This is why Roman Law is nowhere law today while Nazi law was law in Germany between Weimar and the end of World War II.

The Logic of Judicial Views

We stated in Chapter II that judicial propositions which are the result of a judicial view's answering a first order question are able to be judged within the view for their consistency and

---

38 See *TRS* 123-130.

39 See *TRS* 118-123.

40 See Chapter II of this work for an elaboration of this point.

from outside the view for their rationality. If it is the conventional aspect which is most characteristic of a judicial view at its inception, once a view has been constructed, it must obey a certain, non-conventional logic. Put another way, when a convention is being constructed, there is a certain arbitrariness to its components. Once the construction exists, and once it is concomitantly held by some individual, then that individual is, to some extent, committed to the set of propositions involved in answering the original first order question or set of questions. Consistency and identity of view over time demand such a commitment.

The scope of this commitment is a function of the individual view. This works in two ways. First, the degree to which one's past answers affect future answers will vary among views. That is, within a view, there may be a lesser or greater reverence for a conclusion once made. A slight degree of reverence would suggest a view where conclusions are always tentative and subject to review. Third order propositions would be seen as vague and incompletely worked-out. Conclusions drawn from them would have only a slight effect on future determinations based on these (third order) propositions. A high degree of reverence would mean that solutions to previous questions would be determinative of virtually all future questions within their purview. The second parameter of scope function concerns the degree to which past cases are considered relevant to future decisions. Regardless of how much past outcomes are revered, one can imagine views where they are intended to have more or less relevance to the same or similar cases in the future. A view with third order propositions which emphasize stability of views will consider past outcomes more relevant than a view where some other principle (or set of principles) is dominant.

In fact, however, while it is interesting to speculate on the nature and scope of a view and what can be implied from it, this process of individuation of a static view can misrepresent the way actual views behave. The key to understanding the behavior of views lies in understanding the fit between the sets of answers a view implies and the set of answers given by individuals and institutions the view takes as authority. The fit is harmonious, for example, when the outcome of a case is just

the same as the outcome given by one's judicial view. The
tension for the fit will occur when the outcome of the case is
not that called for by the view, when, in other words, according
to the view, the case is wrongly decided. Let us imagine such a
case.

For the sake of familiarity, let us take a case often considered
to be wrongly decided, *Lochner v. New York*.[41] The issue there
was whether the New York State limitation of working hours
violated the Fourteenth Amendment to the United States
Constitution, by infringing the right to contract freely and
otherwise interfering with an individual's personal liberty. The
defendant Lochner had been convicted of violating the state
statute by permitting an employee to work in his bakery for
more than 60 hours in one week. Mr. Lochner was fined by the
state trial court. The United States Supreme Court held that
the statute violated the Constitution. The paternalistic aim of
protecting certain workers from long hours was a goal too
remote to be justified under the court's test requiring material
danger to the public for a state to be able to interfere in the
(private contractual dealings of the) workplace.[42] The court
appeared to embrace a social theory which limited governments
to their police powers, and explicitly denied them a role as

---

41 198 U.S. 45, 25 S. Ct. 539, 49 L.Ed. 937 (1905). Among those who
believed the case to be wrongly decided were the four justices in dissent.
A summary of the criticism of *Lochner* appears in P. Murphy, *The Constitution in Crises Times* 70-82, 99-110 (1972). Ronald Dworkin discusses this
case, among other places, in *Law's Empire* 374-375, 398 (1986).

42 The relevant portion of the Fourteenth Amendment of the United States
Constitution reads:

No state shall make or enforce any law which shall abridge the priv-
ileges or immunities of citizens of the United States; nor shall any
State deprive any person of life, liberty, or property, without due
process of law; nor deny to any person within its jurisdiction the
equal protection of the laws.

The test used in the so-called substantive due process cases was a "means-
ends" test. A statute was invalid in cases where the state interfered with
the general right of an individual to be free in his person and in his
power to contract his labor unless it had a direct relation to an appropriate and legitimate end. Needless to say, the test was extremely vague.

reformers of unfair contracts, either as redistributive agents or correcters of the wrongs of the unimpeded marketplace. [43]

> It seems to us that the real object and purpose (of the New York law) were simply to regulate the hours of labor between the master and his employees (all being men, sui juris), in a private business, not dangerous in any degree to morals or in any real and substantial degree, to the health of the employees. Under such circumstances the freedom of master and employee to contract with each other in relation to their employment, and in defining the same, cannot be prohibited or interfered with, without violating the Federal Constitution. [44]

Let us suppose that an individual, Z, supported a judicial view which, prior to *Lochner*, disapproved of judicial invalidation of economic regulations.[45] At the same time, Z had a high regard for the decisions of the Supreme Court, and Supreme Court opinions figured greatly in Z's judicial view. Z, *ex hypothesi*, believes *Lochner* is wrongly decided, but the fact of *Lochner* will alter Z's view.[46] That Z's view cannot remain as it was is clear.

---

43 This policy is discussed and criticized in A. Paul, *The Conservative Crisis and the Rule of Law* (1969); B. Twiss, *Lawyers and the Constitutions: How Laissez-Faire came to the Supreme Court* (1942).

44 This is taken from the majority opinion of *Lochner v. New York*, 198 U.S. 45, 25 S. Ct. 539, 49 L.Ed. 937 (1905).

45 A discussion of the case against *Lochner* can be found in Laurence H. Tribe, *American Constitutional Law* 456-473 (1978). Ronald Dworkin suggests that cases where judicial review are based merely on personal opinions are generally wrongfully decided. He includes *Lochner* in this group. See generally *A Matter of Principle*, Chapter 2 (1985).

46 There is an argument in American Constitutional law that court pronouncements on constitutional matters have a diminished or no effect on *stare decisis*, as any authority residing in the cases would lessen the authority of the written constitution. This position was most forcibly made by Justice William O. Douglas in "Stare Decisis", 49 *Col. L. Rev.* 735 (1949). The force of *stare decisis* in constitutional law has always been a mixed bag. One can compare the pro-precedential view of *Cooper v. Aaron*, 358 U.S. 1, 78 S. Ct. 1401, 3 L.Ed. 5 (1958) with the cases supporting the view of Justice Douglas, including *Smith v. Allwright*, 321 U.S. 649, 665, 64 S. Ct., 88 L.Ed. 987 (1944); *Glidden Co. v. Zdanok*, 370 U.S. 530, 543, 82 S. Ct. 1459, 8 L.Ed.2d 671 (1962). See, generally, Henry Monaghan, "Stare Decisis and Constitutional Adjudication," 88 *Col. L. Rev.* 723 (1988).

If Z rejects *Lochner*, the third order position which mandated respect and authority for the Supreme Court will be altered. If *Lochner* is accepted, then those propositions which, taken together, suggest that the courts should not strike down economic regulations must be changed.

This point can be made more generally. A wrongly decided case must invariably involve alterations in a judicial view. This is because any case is a legal form, and forms figure in view construction. A view bereft of the input of legal forms becomes a political theory only randomly likely to be related to any actual judicial system.

One question that may be thought to arise is this: as a view is constructed to work out answers to new first order questions, does it remain the same view? It can be seen that if one individuates a view at a given time, it is likely to be similar to but not identical with its predecessors and its successors. Identity is fleeting while similarity through view continuity is both likely and measurable.[47]

This does not appear to be Dworkin's theory on the matter, although his theory has some difficulty when encountering wrongly decided cases. Returning to *Lochner*, let us suppose that there exists a great deal of evidence for Z's position, and furthermore, that Z has engaged in a Herculean labor in constructing a political theory prior to *Lochner*. Z's political theory was selected from a large set of worthy contenders, for the legal forms were at once consistent and vague, and a

---

The entire issue of the force of precedent in constitutional cases is dependent, of course, on the third order propositions of a judicial view.

47   The view of identity here is the same as the one put forth by Derek Parfit in his papers "Personal Identity" in 80 *Philosophical Review* 3-27 (1971), reprinted in *The Philosophy of Mind* 142-162 (ed. Jonathon Glover, 1976); and in "Later Selves and Moral Principles" in *Philosophy and Personal Relations* 137-169 (ed. Alan Montefiore, 1973). The position endorsed is that of Derek Parfit's complex view of identity, that a thing identified is just the sum of its properties, and in losing some of them, becomes less of that thing as a matter of degree. No one property is essential for identity. Views over time are thus the same only as a matter of degree. Derek Parfit expands his views in ways outside the scope of this work in *Reasons and Persons* (1984).

number of theories justified them to some degree.[48]   One of the more important principles generated by Z's chosen political theory was one which stated that freedom of contract could be limited by legislation which protects the physical well-being of workers.   If Dworkin assumes that Z is correct in his political theory and its implications, the question arises as to what he would recommend that Z do after *Lochner*.   Dworkin's theory leaves him with only two choices.

One choice is to disregard *Lochner*.   It is wrongly decided, an aberration, and one's political theory will remain unaffected by it.   Such a choice has the advantage of not rendering imprudent or even useless the construction of a political theory.   The history of Anglo-American case law is rife with decisions which establish bold, new doctrines that were only to disappear shortly after adjournment, never to be followed or iterated again. (Lord Mansfield's dispensing with consideration in ordinary commercial contract cases in *Pillans and Rose v. Van Mierop and Hopkins*[49] is one well-known example of this phenomenon.) Keeping up with each new case, especially when such cases can put forth short-lived doctrines, might require more theory-building energy than even Hercules possesses.   Even if *Lochner* were not aberrational (as it certainly was not)[50] but a widely followed precedent, there are reasons for a Dworkinian to disregard it.   Dworkin wants moral reasoning to play a critical role in judicial discourse.[51]   If the wrongly decided cases generate malevolent principles—as *Lochner* might arguably do in

---

48   The ambiguities and vagueness of constitutional law are well-known. See Chapter VII of this work for further discussion and illustrations.

49   [K.B.] 1765, 3 Burrow 1663, 1669, 97 Eng. Rep. 1035. For one discussion of this case, its implications and demise, see C. H. S. Fifoot, *Lord Mansfield* 129-134 (1936).

50   *Lochner's* predecessors include the *Slaughter-House Cases*, 83 U.S. (16 Wall.) 36, 21 L.Ed. 394 (1873); *Loan Association v. City of Topeka*, 87 U.S. (20 Wall.) 655, 22 L.Ed. 455 (1875); *Munn v. Illinois*, 94 U.S. 113, 24 L.Ed. 77 (1877); and *Allgeyer v. Louisiana*, 165 U.S. 578, 17 S. Ct. 427, 41 L.Ed. 832 (1897). Its successors include *Adair v. United States*, 208 U.S. 161, 28 S. Ct. 277, 52 L.Ed. 436 (1908); and *Coppage v. Kansas*, 236 U.S. 1, 35 S. Ct. 240, 59 L.Ed. 441 (1915).

51   See *TRS* 123-130.

endorsing a Social Darwinism coupled with unregulated economic warfare[52]—then reasoning may occur, but it will not be of the type Dworkin wishes to label as moral.

Finally, given the overall degree of controversy in the judicial arena, there are likely to be a fair number of wrongly decided cases. The chance of dramatic and frequent reversals in the relevant political theory is thus great. Moreover, the reversals may make theory construction virtually impossible. *Lochner* occurred sixteen years after *Riggs v. Palmer*. *Lochner* encouraged the view that society is ruthless, and that unless explicitly barred by the narrow area of constitutionally permissible legislation, one was allowed to keep one's gains, whether morally or wrongfully attained. *Lochner* and its progeny struck down laws making the workplace more humane, including laws restricting child labor.[53] Dworkin suggests principles do not contradict one another, but have different weights in various situations; however, political theories can, in their implications, contradict one another. If *Lochner* were to be accepted, perhaps the *Riggs* principle—no man shall benefit by his own wrong—might have to be jettisoned. (The *Riggs* principle ought not to be read as condemning only criminal wrongs. It does not say that, and it is likely to be applied to cases of acts where no criminal liability attaches because of insanity, the statute of limitations, or a lapsed or a poorly drawn statute, while not applied in negligent manslaughter cases. There is clearly a strictly moral component to it). This would cause an ominous discontinuity of political theories before and after *Lochner*. If one tried to fashion a political theory in such a way as to allow for *Riggs*, *Lochner*, and the other major propositions the pre-*Lochner* theory demanded, one

---

52 The Social Darwinian aspect of *Lochner* is discussed in Laurence H. Tribe, *American Constitutional Law* 438-446 (1978). It was famously stated in Justice Oliver Wendell Holmes' *Lochner* dissent: "The Fourteenth Amendment does not enact Mr. Herbert Spencer's *Social Statics*." 198 U.S. 45, 90, 25 S. Ct. 539, 49 L.Ed. 937 (1905), (Holmes, J. dissenting).

53 In *Hammer v. Dagenhart*, 247 U.S. 251, 38 S. Ct. 529, 62 L.Ed. 1101 (1918), the Supreme Court held that Congress could not prohibit interstate commerce in the products of child labor. The court said that the purpose of attempting to raise the minimum age for children working in mines and manufacturing was constitutionally impermissible.

would end up with a debilitated theory, so circumscribed as to be of little use in providing answers in future cases.

One can see reasons, then, for Dworkin to exclude *Lochner* or wrongly decided cases generally from one's political theory, or in a different context, from the set of propositions true within the common enterprise. However, such a response has a fatal weakness. It allows the theory to drift from the legal forms indefinitely. The *Lochner* doctrine lasted about thirty years, but it might well have continued undisturbed indefinitely. Many shifts in legal doctrine have never been reversed. The individual who refused to agree with the evolution of case from trespass would, if she could somehow have enjoyed the longevity, have found herself increasingly isolated from the main body of property, contract, and tort law.[54] There is no room in Dworkin's theory for reconsideration of wrong cases once disregarded. If they are undeserving of initial entry into the set of input propositions, repetition of the mistake should have no effect. The only reason why such repetitions would count is because authority of itself would be a factor in the political theory. But such authority may as well reside in the initial decision, as the rather final pronouncement of the Supreme Court demonstrated in *Lochner* itself.

There is also the technical difficulty in discovering what the right answer would be in those intermediate cases after the initial wrongly decided case but before the hundredth affirmation and expansion of that case. When does the political theory shift, and to what extent does it change? If the initial case is without effect, how much effect has the second case? If two cases have more effect than one, the development of the political theory becomes a function of the random vicissitudes of continuing litigation. The fact that a series of cases arises at closely spaced intervals and gives courts an opportunity to affirm the mistaken case would be allowed to influence an

---

54 Case developed from trespass on the case, itself an offshoot of the ancient writ of trespass. From case came modern Anglo-American negligence and contract law. The development of case is traced through original sources in C. H. S. Fifoot, *History and Sources of the Common Law* (1949), though some of his own conclusions are now considered to be suspect.

entire political theory (or common judicial enterprise). The randomness of litigation alone could thus cause one theory to be abandoned in favor of a radically different theory.

Dworkin's second choice would be to embrace the wrongly decided case, to incorporate *Lochner* into a consideration of future cases. This position holds a number of attractions. The political theory would remain tied to actual past decisions and the element of commonality in the common enterprise would be stronger. This latter consideration is especially important, for it allows a residue of agreed upon easy cases to develop which will serve as the starting point for hard case analysis.

The problem lies in incorporating *Lochner* into a political theory which, without it, has an anti-*Lochner* outlook and anti-*Lochner* implications. It may be a Herculean task to square decisions which, if somewhat eclectic, are at least no more than marginally inconsistent. However, squaring p with -p is impossible, and finding a theory which will allow for Z's political theory and for *Lochner* requires a degree of individual choice as to what exactly must go and what ought to stay. For example, should the *Riggs* principle remain? Should certain restitutionary and promissory estoppel propositions advanced in contract cases—propositions which ensure that contracts must be fairly entered into without duress, with knowing consent, and by parties in similar bargaining positions—be exorcised? Should the Thirteenth Amendment to the United States Constitution barring slavery be interpreted so as to narrow the definition of involuntary servitude? Should the separate states be unable to intervene anywhere—to compel school attendance, to levy taxes for the support of the arts, to compete against private enterprise in the fields of energy and transportation—except in matters involving the police powers of public safety and health? Once the decision has been made to alter Z's pre-*Lochner* political theory, the ground for inclusion and exclusion of propositions can be limited by rationality, but given the initial contradiction, they cannot be definitively characterized.

One might wish to claim that the narrowest interpretation, involving the smallest degree of change for the initial theory, ought to be advanced. The strictly narrowest change, however, would limit *Lochner* to its facts. Then Z's old theory would apply except in the case of bakers working exactly sixty hours in New York City in contravention of New York State legislation. This will not do, clearly. The question as to whether *Lochner* upsets or does not upset notions of contract, due process, involuntary servitude, and states' rights then remains. One certainly cannot suspend judgment until post-*Lochner* cases settle, for the courts, the scope and reach of the initial decision. It is just for the purposes of being able to provide or judge a given solution to post-*Lochner* cases that the theory is formulated. Moreover, for Dworkin, there is always (at all places and times) a right answer based on the theory.[55] Waiting until the dust clears from the imposition of a seminal case allows for an impermissible hiatus.

The problem Dworkin has with wrong cases is a function of the tie between political theory and the legal forms. The intuitive image evoked by the mention of "political theory" is a grand scheme in the style of Plato, Hobbes, Montesquieu, Marx, or Rawls. The political theory Dworkin has in mind is of necessity more detailed, more practical, and more mundane than these. It cannot develop apart from the exigencies of court cases, and is highly circumscribed as it attempts to square the variety of these cases. It is really supervenient on the holdings of the cases and statutes.

The pluralist perspective largely avoids the problems of the wrongly decided case by allowing for a distance between legal forms and judicial views. Z may handle *Lochner* by assigning it a tentative status, by limiting it to a narrow holding or by altering his view. He is not committed to any one strategy *a priori*, nor does Z himself necessarily know what his post-*Lochner* view will be without some reflection. In part, this is due to the inexact determination of the judicial view by the set of third order sources of propositions, and in part to the question-originating workings of the propositional set. One consideration or caveat needs to be brought forward first. That is, any particular view may be more or less efficient and more or less rational. If a view were very inefficient, it would waver continually as new cases came forth, forcing constant and major reevaluations. If it were irrational, it would incorporate these cases without

---

55 This statement is subject to the limitations discussed earlier.

attempting any theoretical maneuvering to avoid systemic inconsistencies. No right answer exists for view manipulation in the face of troublesome cases, only better or worse (from the perspectives of efficiency and rationality, as well as ethics and politics) strategies.

When Z is constructing his pre-*Lochner* view, he notices that the case law is inconsistent and conflicting. The case law and other legal forms of themselves do not yield the basis of a consistent theory. However, Z notices further complications in this already unsettled picture. Many of the cases are themselves based on previous legal forms. The correspondence between previous forms and justified decisions is not one-to-one, but often many-to-one. Yet the many are themselves not always consistent. Thus, in sifting the legal forms, one might want to include the holdings of the justified decision, but one would be forced into a choice over selection of the proper justifying legal forms. This is an example of overdetermination, a phenomenon rampant in many judicial systems. Another complication involves the fact that other sources of propositions—political, ethical, social, and prudential—are likely to be inconsistent and overdeterminative of many of the results of past hypothetical cases. That such other factors as political ideas and preferences are unlikely to be fully worked out for individuals is hardly surprising, considering their difficulty and vastness. As a counterpoint to this overdetermination is the fact that many cases arise in which the individual appears to be unable to use his existing propositional set. This underdetermination is not the same thing as gaps in the law, for a view is reconstructed anew around the initiating judicial question, and an answer is guaranteed without a change in the decision procedure (discretion versus non-discretion). It is, rather, that the fact of underdetermination causes the individual to rework his view, by further empirical research and conceptual stretching. An answer may arise using what appears to be old concepts, but these concepts have been changed in their reworking to solve the instant case.

The imprecise determination recognized as a constant in the life of a judicial view makes it subject to continual change. The wrongly decided case will result in just another instance of the reworking of the view, a reworking which gives a certain tentativeness to the view generally. As consistency in all things is not a necessary proposition which governs view behavior, the wrongly decided case can be accommodated by allowing it as just another complication.

Inconsistency cannot remain if a judicial view is to be considered to be rational, but the fact that judicial views function around first order questions works to rid the views of inconsistency. A concept of judicial role is used to answer the issues which actually arise during adjudication. Z can be faced with answering a problem concerning substantive due process and the rights of states to regulate the workplace after *Lochner*, a possibility he may well never have imagined before *Lochner*. Yet such a possibility would have been apparent if he had worked out every detail of his pre-*Lochner* view. For, in that view, Z weighed heavily United States Supreme Court decisions, and that court logically could do what it empirically actually did: assert *Lochner*. Z worked out his view largely around the actual questions which had been raised by previous cases.

The status of judicial propositions comes to this. A first order proposition can be true or false within a view, if that view allows for a two valued logic, as virtually any rational view will. However, not only is the view itself conventional rather than objective, any particular individual is likely to alter the set of propositions within the view as new questions arise, and as the sources of third order propositions change. Continuity rather than identity is the relevant individuating property which matters. As views jettison more and more cases, or other legal forms, they do not become, at some point, wrong. No error is being committed, but they become less attractive as choices for understanding, predicting, and judging judicial reasoning. However, the acceptance or rejection of a judicial view is a matter of individual choice. This results in inevitable conflict between views, but such conflicts reflect deeper divisions in societies, and offer an outlet for societal tensions by allowing for the use of a shared institution for settlement. We shall now turn to the workings of this process in several specific judicial settings.

VII

Political Consequences of
Pluralist Adjudication

Unlike so many men
I cannot say Law is again,
No more than they can we suppress
The universal wish to guess
Or slip out of our own position
Into an unconcerned condition.
Although I can at least confine
Your vanity and mine
To stating timidly
A timid similarity,
We shall boast anyway:
Like love I say.
Like love we don't know where or why
Like love we can't compel or fly
Like love we often weep
Like love we seldom keep.

W.H. Auden

I have argued for a novel approach to the examination of judicial reasoning. I have suggested that the set of first order judicial questions, rather than a unified system of norms, offers a starting point and that personal judicial views rather than objective rule systems provide the grounds for answering questions. In the first part of this chapter, we shall look at how this procedure works on a single legal problem. In the second part of this chapter, I shall suggest briefly that pluralist theory furnishes clues to explain why judicial process and judicial reasoning so often have worked so well.

First, however, it needs mentioning that the idea of legal pluralist analysis, in its different guises, has generally been confined to discussions of constitutional law. There is, in this field, a belief held by some that every constitution has an extra-legal origin, and that constitutional law is not subject to addition or amendment in the same way as other branches of law.[1] Moreover, disputes about the content of constitutional law seem more intractable for a number of reasons: the authority to settle them is itself a matter of constitutional law and thus further dispute; most of the important questions are never litigated; judges' and officials' views on the subject are often believed to be tied to political allegiances; the area sees wide fluctuations on central questions rather than the constant narrowing of issues apparently produced in other areas of law. Constitutional questions are perceived to be "political," and have at times been labeled "essentially contested." [2]

The central problem with this position lies in its claim of exclusivity.   The difference between constitutional and other questions is in fact one of degree, rather than kind.   Of course, constitutional law is often concerned with the organization and authority of government, as well as the basic rules and standards which define the relation between the state and the governed. However, as areas such as due process, the right to a fair trial, free expression, suffrage, and protection of property and contract have entered into the constitutional arena, the definition of constitutional law as being concerned solely with that part of public law area prescribing the method of the proper administration of the state's affairs is no longer viable.   The more important the issue, the more likely it is to effect basic change throughout the political system or culture, the more

---

1 Some constitutions, such as that of the United States, require each amendment to undergo special procedures. Others, such as the British constitution, require only the rarest deviation in regular procedure to accomplish constitutional change, such as a hypothetical increase in the vote needed to enact legislation in Parliament from a majority to unanimity might require.

2 The term originated with W. B. Gallie, in "Essentially Contested Concepts," in *Proceedings of the Aristotelian Society* vol. 56 (1955-56); reprinted in *The Importance of Language* 121-46 (ed. Max Black, 1962). It refers to concepts shared by people with disparate assumptions which cause them to apply the concepts in conflicting situations. This idea is more fully worked out by William E. Connolly in his *The Terms of Political Discourse* 9-44 (1974).

general and universal its application, hence the more likely it will be called "constitutional." The fundamental nature of constitutional questions, rather than their subject matter, is often what sets them apart. They should be seen as indicators of different views, rather than inhabitants of some special, separate realm. Perhaps more instructively, because they are at once controversial and fundamental, their existence demonstrates that any consistent propositional set which includes answers to constitutional questions is apt to be eclectic. Because these basic questions are linked to so many other, smaller questions, slight differences in response can make for very different, propositional sets.

A Contract Law Illustration

One area of judicial subject matter traditionally thought to be stable is that of contracts. Contracts are by definition agreements freely entered into,[3] where certain expectations concerning and reliance arising from the fulfillment of the agreement are likely to be present. Unlike tortfeasors and their victims, contractors will be involved in the contractual behavior with the future consequences of their behavior uppermost in their mind. Businesses operate, sales are possible, employment is secure, services are rendered: each, in part, because the bargains struck between individuals or groups have, owing to their enforcement, a certain future. A component of that certainty includes a uniform treatment of contracts by the plethora of courts which act on them. Contract law has traditionally enjoyed a high degree of uniformity in Europe, to a degree even extended to common law England through courts of law merchant, equity, and the rulings of Lord Mansfield and his successors.[4] In America, it has achieved a unique legislative consistency

---

3 The voluntary nature of contract is what sets it apart from similar relationships which are compelled. This point was made in the nineteenth century by Henry Maine, *Ancient Law* Ch. IX (1861) and reiterated in Joel Levin and Banks McDowell, "The Balance Theory of Contracts: Seeking Justice in Voluntary Obligations," 29 *McGill L.J.* 24 (1983).

4 For an overview of this development, see Theodore F. T. Plucknett, *A Concise History of the Common Law* 657-670 (5th ed. 1956).

through the promulgation first of the Uniform Sales Act and then of the ubiquitous Uniform Commercial Code.[5] If any domain of propositions should be considered to be secure from widely varying, personally-based interpretations, it would appear to be that of contract law.

Certainly there have been American contract law theorists who have seen the area as clear, unified, and united. Both Oliver Wendell Holmes and Samuel Williston have written about contracts as if a grand theoretical framework explained all the major ramifications of bargains enforced by the courts; both have argued that such a framework must be definitive and unimpeachable in its interpretations.[6] When the American Law Institute in the 1920's wanted to restate the common law of contracts, it asked Williston to be the document's chief draftman. Williston surveyed the cases, looked to the purposes and results of specific contracts, and formulated the fundamental requirement for an agreement to be considered a valid contract. He wrote that in order for a contract to be enforceable in court, mutual consideration must pass between the offeror and the offeree.[7]

A small group on the drafting committee, although one which was later ultimately successful, believed that some notion

---

5 The Uniform Sales Act was drafted in 1906, the Uniform Commercial Code in 1953. The latter was eventually adopted everywhere in the United States except Louisianna, where portions of it were incorporated.

6 Holmes' position is found throughout *The Common Law* (1881), particularly in Lectures VII-IX. Williston's writings on contracts are voluminous. He was the chief draftman of the Uniform Sales Act and the first *Restatement of Contracts*. His most important work was his multi-volume *Contracts*, which came out in 1920-1922.

7 His formulation in Section 75 of the *Restatement of Contracts* (1932) reads:
   "(1) Consideration for a promise is
       (a) an act other than a promise, or
       (b) a forbearance, or
       (c) the creation, modification or destruction of a legal relation, or
       (d) a return promise, bargained for and given in exchange for the promise.
   (2) Consideration may be given to the promisor or to some other person. It may be given by the promisee or by some other person.

of promissory estoppel ought to be included in the *Restatement*. Led by Arthur Corbin, they believed that a promise giving rise to reasonable reliance could provide grounds for upholding a contract. Their view was adopted in Section 90:

> A promise which the promisor should reasonably expect to induce action or forbearance of a definite and substantial character on the part of the promisee and which does induce such action or forbearance is binding if injustice can be avoided only be enforcement of the promise.

The ambivalence thus introduced into the document is well-known, and the *Restatement* is peculiar in that it attempts to unite doctrines from different jurisdictions which share neither sovereignty, nor, always, traditions. Moreover, since the drafting of the *Restatement of Contracts*, the Corbin position has slowly but steadily been accepted both in diverse jurisdictions and among the legal writers.[8] The disunity and progeny of the *Restatement* have been widely discussed, as have the merits of the Williston and the Corbin positions.[9] What has somehow been overlooked is the fact that two opposing views regarding members of the judicial propositional set competed for a number of years openly and directly.[10]

Let us put aside the question of whether Williston or Corbin had better precedential evidence for their positions at the time the *Restatement* was drafted. Clearly, after the *Restatement*, and the publication of Williston's treatise,[11] the cases for some time were divided. Moreover, they were divided on the basis of the same precedents, the same scholarly writings, and the *Restatement*. The issues were segregated into neat categories, a fact

---

8 The cases and writings are too numerous to mention. See Stanley D. Henderson, "Promissory Estoppel and Traditional Contract Doctrine," 78 *Yale L.J.* 343 (1969); and Arthur L. Corbin, "Recent Developments in the Law of Contracts," 50 *Harv. L. Rev.* 449 (1937) for a discussion of some of the major cases.

9 The fullest discussion is found in Grant Gilmore, *The Death of Contract* (1974), a work which this section draws upon for its historical facts (although clearly not for its doctrinial or conceptual analysis).

10 The assumption was that the evidence would prove one position or another correct. Gilmore is typical in holding to this assumption.

11 See note 6.

which disguised the radical nature of the split. Suits were "on the contract" or "off the contract", in contract or in restitution, on a promise enforced or on a promise estopped, because of consideration arising or reliance occurring. All courts were seen to be allowing suits on the contract when consideration passed, and courts split on matters of reasonable reliance. This neat picture misconstrued what was actually happening, and it fails to tell why decisions in these matters were handed down the way that they were.

Two views were competing for ascendance in the realm of contract law. Evidence in the form of past decisions existed on both sides. However, any particular piece of evidence was likely to be weighed differently by each side. Cases were overdetermined in the sense that, within many prior cases, a number of different views would have yielded the same result. There was also underdetermination, in the sense that the prior decisions taken as a group were insufficient to cover numerous new cases which theorists, and eventually courts, worried about.

What is interesting about the conflict here is that it is not one drawn along traditional ethical or political lines. Contracts are certainly an area not exempt from purely political issues, as cases concerning illegal contracts,[12] irreversible contracts,[13] one sided and immoral bargains,[14] and generally the issue of duress vitiating consent[15] all demonstrate. The Corbin/Williston split

---

12   Such contracts commonly include those concerning gambling, marriage, and prostitution. A more political type of illegality concerns restraint-of-trade cases. See, generally, Arthur L. Corbin, *Contracts* Ch. 79 (1950).

13   "Irreversible" here is meant to stand for cases of indentured service and slavery, where the right to sell one's service indefinitely is often challenged.

14   Usury has usually been suspect, but other related types of contracts have usually been left to stand. See, for example, *Batsakis v. Demotsis*, 226 S.W. 2d 673 (Tex. Civ. App., 1949), where an unhappy court debated and then upheld a contract allowing for a $25 loan in Greek drachmae to be repaid as $2000 in American currency without considering the issue of usury.

15   The UNIFORM COMMERCIAL CODE has made explicit the duress problem for United States jurisdictions. Section 2-302 holds:

is not along the lines of these issues, nor along the fundamental issue of when the freedom to bargain ought to give way to the interest of just results. The conflict could be labeled as one occurring between an interest in achieving legal elegance and an interest in promoting the fulfillment of reasonable business expectations.

The interest in legal elegance was part of the impetus behind the *Restatement* itself: the desire to incorporate the diverse elements of a subject and bring them together in a unified whole. Achieving the neutrality and objectivity of science was intended, and ethical terminology was the residue of an outmoded era best swept away.[16] Large treatises were complied which emphasized fundamental themes, and law was seen to be evolving toward a modern objective state.[17] Holmes, a leader in this movement, wanted to cleanse everywhere the law of all traces of subjectivity.[18] In contracts, this meant that a promisee must express his intentions to the promisor solely

---

Unconscionable Contract or Clause. (1) If the court as a matter of law finds the contract or any clause of the contract to have been unconscionable at the time it was made the court may enforce the remainder of the contract without the unconscionable clause, or it may so limit the application of any unconscionable clause as to avoid any unconscionable result. (2) When it is claimed or appears to the court that the contract or any clause thereof may be unconscionable the parties shall be afforded a reasonable oportunity to present evidence as to reasonable opportunity to present evidence as to its commercial setting, purpose and effect to aid the court in making the determination.

What is unconscionable is left, typically, entirely open.

16 Oliver Wendell Holmes states this policy in "The Path of the Law" 10 *Harv. L. Rev.* 457 (1897); reprinted in Oliver Wendell Holmes, *Collected Legal Papers* 167-202 (1920).

17 For an instance of objectivism of law, see the opinion of Learned Hand, J. in *Hotchkiss v. National City Bank of New York*, 200 F. 287 (S.D.N.Y. 1911); for a judicial criticism fo this view, see the Frank, J. concurring opinion in *Ricketts v. Pennsylvania R. Co.*, 153 F. 2d 757, 760 (2d Cir. 1946). See Lawrence M. Friedman, *A History of American Law* 567-595 (1973) for a discussion of the attitudes and beliefs of the era.

18 "Subjectivity" here referred to state-of-mind subjectivity, rather than an objective meeting of the minds.

through the bargain: no later action can make a contract when none had arisen from the parties.

> It is said that consideration must not be confounded with motive. It is true that it must not be confounded with what may be the prevailing or chief motive in actual fact. A man may promise to paint a picture for five hundred dollars, while his chief motive may be a desire for fame. A consideration may be given and accepted, in fact, solely for the purpose of making a promise binding. But, nevertheless, it is the essence of a consideration, that, by the terms of the agreement, it is given and accepted as the motive or inducement of the promise. Conversely, the promise must be made and accepted as the conventional motive or inducement for furnishing the consideration. The root of the whole matter is the relation of reciprocal conventional inducement, each for the other, between consideration and promise. [19]

Williston took up this idea of the primacy of mutual assent, and constructed a multi-volume treatise based upon it:

> Doubtless the law is generally expressed in terms of subjective assent, rather than of objective expressions, the latter being said to be "evidence" of the former, as, for example, in the so-called parol evidence rule; but when it is established that this is no rule of evidence but rather a rule of substantive law, the whole subjective theory which is sometimes rather ludicrously epitomized by the quaintly archaic expression "meeting of the minds," falls to the ground. [20]

Certainly many cases fit within the view articulated by Holmes and Williston; and, within their scientific aspirations and model building inclinations, they extended the consideration doctrine to its logical extremity. They never, in print, asked whether such an extension would be economically advantageous, morally equitable to potential bargainers, or in line with ordinary business practices. These considerations—the concerns of the largest group of contractors, the business community—did concern Corbin. He saw the aggregate of past cases not in terms of movement from the subjective to the objective, but as a series of attempts to service the contracting community. As such, reasonable reliance, a concept of concern to this community, ought, in Corbin's mind, to play a role in settling

---

19   Oliver Wendell Holmes, *The Common Law* 230 (1881).

20   Samuel Williston, 13 *Contracts* 32-34, 36 Section 153b (1920).

disputes.[21] Williston had rejected reasonable reliance as a basis for establishing contractual liability, because it fell outside the scope of the bargained-for consideration theory which he thought served as the basis for the law of contracts.[22] For Williston, the bargain was central. Consequently, reasonable reliance and subjective assent were linked as possible challenges to the (objective) bargain theory, and both were to be disparaged. Model elegance was of little concern to Corbin,[23] just as the actual practices of the business community were of only slight importance to Williston.[24]

One may see signs of a larger schism here. Holmes and later Williston believed that, as a general principle, loss must be allowed to lie where it falls. Personal fault was a concept to be kept in the background, in tort as well as in contract. Once such a basic principle was established, moreover, it was necessary to see that it was applied throughout the case law. Objective manifestations, rather than the vague machinations of the mind, were primary. It becomes easy to understand the push toward unity of contract law once these principles were established. Holmes and Williston were professional legal theorists. They saw their job as pulling together the diverse strands presented by prior decisions into an elegant theoretical whole.

---

21 See Arthur L. Corbin, *Contracts* Ch. 8.

22 For references to Samuel Williston's view of the primacy of bargained-for consideration, see note 20.

23 Arthur L. Corbin says at one point "that one definition can rightly be set up as the one and only correct definition, and that the law of contract is an evolutionary product that has changed with time and circumstance and that must ever continue to change." For this quotation and Corbin's views on tidy categories and models generally, see his *Contracts* Section 109.

24 Lawrence M. Friedman exhibited scorn for what he saw as Samuel Williston's insularity. He wrote:

> Samuel Williston built a monumental fortress (1920-22) out of the law of *Contracts* volume after volume, solid, closely knit, fully armored against the intrusion of any ethical, economic, or social notions whatsoever.

Lawrence M. Friedman, *A History of American Law* 593 (1973).

The judicial process was teleological and a theorist's task was to understand where it was headed. Moreover, any lawyer had to make sense of the totality of cases. Judicial reasoning called for the reconciliation of past decisions, and the various lines of precedent needed rethinking to avoid anomalous discrepancies. The business community, on the other hand, wanted the case law to reflect business practice.[25]   It had little interest in conceptual unity, and even less sympathy, if it interfered with the daily expectations and reliance of trading partners. Businessmen generally wish to be as little burdened by form as possible, and routinely conducted transactions in an oral and incomplete manner, seeing the security of business expectations and reliance as an advantage against theory unity and category tidiness. This example is instructive in the general context of judicial decision-making, for it points to a conflict in beliefs concerning second order propositions that is likely to occur in any society.[26]

Two final points need to be reiterated. Williston and Corbin had widely differing views of contracts. Together, they demonstrate part of the spectrum of views[27] even among individuals

---

25 Businessmen increasingly use standardized contracts, and mail (or fax) form contracts back and forth without ever bargaining or even agreeing on any single contract, yet acting as though a contract exists. On the so-called battle of the forms see Otto Prausnitz, *The Standardization of Commerical Contracts in English and Continental Law* (1937); Nathan Isaacs, "The Standardizing of Contracts," 27 *Yale L.J.* 34 (1917); and S. Macaulay, "Non-Contractual Relations in Business: A Preliminary Study," 28 *Am. Soc. Rev.* 55, 58 (1963).

26 One explanation for the distinction between the English national courts and the early law merchant courts might involve this split. For the problem of the incorporation into English law of promissory estoppel, see *Central London Property Trust Ltd. v. High Trees House, Ltd.* [1947] K. B. 130; and *Combe v. Combe,* [1951] 2 K. B. 215. These cases are discussed in P. S. Atiyah, *An Introduction to the Law of Contracts* 86 ff. (2d ed. 1971).

27 There has recently been a resurgence of contract theory. Among the major works are Ian MacNeil, *The New Social Contract* (1980), Charles Fried, *Contract as Promise: A Theory of Contractual Obligation* (1981), Grant Gilmore, *The Death of Contract* (1974), P. S. Atiyah, *The Rise and Fall of Freedom of Contract* (1979).

who in many ways were similarly situated,[28] and whose views were far from drastic.[29] Yet it is clear that, although differences in this area of contract formation were great, not just any view would be acceptable. Any view could be constructed, but rationality, history, ethics, politics, and economics, just to begin the list, have imposed severe limits on putative contenders or candidates for acceptability. Views, moreover, are circumscribed by legal forms—statutes, decisions, codes, customs, constitutions, treaties, administrative regulations, and edicts—as well as by the expectations members of a society have concerning the content of judicial decisions. The individuality of judicial views ought to imply no license for mere random construction of those views. The Williston/Corbin debate demonstrates how particular positions are formed around basic beliefs and values rationally held in a society.

The more important point concerns the search for analogues or master rules to provide answers to first order questions. In the American legal system, one cannot say of some proposition p about the definition of or remedies for broken bargains that it is true or false. At the same time, for any individual knowledgeable about that system, whether judge, citizen, or anthropologist, it is possible to say that if she were asked whether or not p, then for her, p might be true or false. Moreover, once she states or denies p, her reasons for doing so become an issue. One can criticize that individual for averring p because of her judicial view, when that view is irrational, impolitic, immoral, uninformed, incomplete, or mistaken in certain of its premises. However, criticism because of failure of that proposition or that view to correspond to some objectively derivable,

---

28 Both were law professors at leading American law schools who spent their lives compiling massive contract treatises.

29 Their timidity is seen when viewed with those who see contract as economics, such as Posner, and those who see contract as tort, such as Atiyah. See Richard A. Posner, *Economic Analysis of Law* (2nd ed. 1977) (particularly Chapter IV), Richard A. Posner and Andrew Rosenfeld, "Impossibility and Related Doctrines in Contract Law: An Economic Analysis", 6 *J. Leg. Studies* 83 (1977), P. S. Atiyah, *The Rise and Fall of Freedom of Contract* (1979) and P. S. Atiyah, "Book Review," 95 *Harv. L. Rev.* 509 (1981).

contrary proposition or view is not possible. Responsibility for a decision or its endorsement thus always rests, in large part, with the individual. Answers are not somehow "there", platonic entities ready to be plucked when appropriate cases require their use. They are constructed, and as such, are always a function of the higher order propositions that justify them. Answers are thus better or worse. Even where there might be agreement among almost all knowledgeable observers about p, it is possible for that support to originate with individuals who have different views—as Williston and Corbin had different views about what constitutes a bargain and how important the bargain itself is in contractual relationships—because no proposition is likely to be unimpeachable. More importantly, no specific source of criticism is, *a priori*, illegitimate in the examination of that proposition. Thus, even where all have agreed on a proposition, if an examination of the judicial view supporting it reveals that the view ought to be changed, then that proposition is similarly liable to change.

Constitutional Questions

I have suggested that one can best understand judicial decision-making by using a pluralist analysis to explain the logic and content of actual judicial decisions. It is commonplace that law and judicial decisions are social phenomena and need always to be analyzed with the larger social picture in mind. I want, therefore, to look briefly at how the pluralist model partially explains both the prevalence and the popularity of courts as an almost universal conflict resolution tool in human societies.

Remarkably similar judicial systems are found in cultures with little else so specific in common. Common features of those judicial systems include the idea that both private and public disputes be referred to a third party, that this third party be either chosen or approved by the society generally, that the judge's decision is binding (enforceable and respected by other members of society) and impersonal, and that the standards employed for decision ought to be general, predetermined, reflective of conceptions of justice, and rational. Practice notoriously falls short of this idea, but what is interesting is how often practice coincides with the idea, how much more frequently the idea is advocated by governments with a history of failing to achieve that idea, and how widespread historically, geographically, and philosophically the idea is. One caught in some kind of veil of ignorance might not expect such diverse groups as Roman citizens, German burghers, Cheyenne Indian hunters, Scandinavian socialists, Franco fascists, Barotse tribesmen, Sinapur villagers and both fifteenth and twentieth century Englishmen to share a common ground of such a broad scope.[30]

Agreement between societies on these matters is mirrored by the convergence of beliefs within heterogeneous societies. The fact of impartial courts of law, employing independent, neutral judges and objective standards with authority backed by larger political sanctions remains a constant as one moves across the political, religious, and ethnic spectra.[31] A good illustration of this occurs when a *coup d'etat* or even a (so called) political revolution takes place. A new leadership with new elite may fashion a program explicitly contrary to that of the previous regime. It will, however, commonly allow the judicial system to remain, and will even make claims through that judicial system that the new governments actions are legal under the pre-existing and, therefore, continuously prevailing, judicial standards. [32]

It might be though that this practice of embracing the judicial model and its concomitant historical standards is explained by the close relationships often perceived to exist between law and

---

30 Insight into Barotse tribesmen can be found in Max Gluckman, *The Judicial Process among the Barotse of Northern Rodesia* (1955); into Sepapur villagers in Bernard S. Cohn, "Some Notes on Law and Change in North India", found in *Law and Warfare* 139 (ed. Paul Bohannan, 1967). A study of Cheyenne society can be found in Karl Llewellyn and E. Adamson Hoebel, *The Cheyenne Way* (1941).

31 While no universal study of this phenomenon exists, it is found, somewhat fragmented, throughout the anthropological literature.

32 Despite Kelsen's well-known statements about revolutions automatically terminating pre-existing legal systems, there are good conceptual and empirical reasons for believing otherwise. See John Finnis, "Revolutions and Continuity of Law," in *Oxford Essays in Jurisprudence*, Second Series 44-76 (ed. A. W. B. Simpson, 1973).

ethics, and between authority and morality. The very ambiguity of such terms as "law", "right", "principle", "*lex*", "wrong", "*droit*", "tort", "*recht*", "rules", "murder", "natural law", and "criminal" demonstrates the intimate ties between ethics and law.[33] The two areas overlap not only in shared concepts, but often in the acts they disapprove of, the reasoning (deontic or consequentialist) they employ, the goals they seek, and the authority for action each claims. Ethical language is often vague language, and ethical methodology operates without verification as to truth or observation as to starting point. Because ethics is so conflated with law, runs the argument, the two are difficult to separate and purify. Cases distill law on an *ad hoc* basis, while careful scholarly analysis does so on a wider and better ordered scale. Thus, individuals often embrace pre-existing judicial standards because they fail to understand them completely. They profess respect for the machinery of the judicial process— judges, advocacy and adversarial proceedings, sanctions—even when it is against their interest or contrary to their fundamental beliefs to do so, in part because the real workings of the system are obscured by ambiguous ethical language. (A general ignorance of complicated or voluminous decisions and legislation may also be a factor.) Good analysis would clarify this confusion. Judicial function and standards could be better appreciated while poorer ones could be weeded out.

There is some merit to this line of reasoning. Yet, the practice of turning to the judicial process to remedy all social wrongs is based in part on a confusion rooted in part on unclear and ambiguous language. It would be a mistake to think that certainty is either attainable or desirable. Much of this work has argued for the irreducibility of varying views of the judicial process. The resolution, briefly, is that the differing views are part of the attraction and the attractiveness of the judicial process.

Societies are typically composed of groups with conflicting ideologies, religions, and ethics. Within and among these groups are individuals with variant, derivative, and deviant

---

33 See H. L. A. Hart, *Theory and Definition in Jurisprudence* (1953) for a discussion of some of the difficulties imposed when such ambiguities are left unclarified.

beliefs and attitudes. Groups and individuals are in competition for resources and power. While much of the competition is ordered and useful, and the differences thus benign, conflict is ultimately a threat to the social fabric. When there is conflict, the great utility of the judicial process lies in its ability to resolve peacefully that conflict: the attraction of that process rests frequently on the various judicial views defining it. If judicial propositions were clear, precise, innumerable, and consistent, their appeal would be limited to those individuals who agreed with them.[34] If the judicial fog were owing merely to confusing language and the conflation of ethics with law, it could be dispelled by diligent analysis alone. The personal nature of judicial views guarantees that such analysis will not be successful. But the analytic failure may be seen as political success, for the ambiguity of judicial propositional sets allows the symbol of judicial process to remain vibrant among competing systems. One's commitment to the judicial system need not necessarily be a casualty of a singlely expressed view concerning the content of its standards.

The idea of shared symbols being cherished for different purposes is hardly new,[35] but the suggestion here is that there is no mistake being committed or illusion sighted when judicial reasoning is seen to rest on competing foundations. The great utility of this idea is that it allows us to see how social conflict is mitigated. Lack of a single authoritative statement concerning the propositional set allows competing groups to remain loyal to the same political institutions,[36] and to work out their differ-

---

34 It could be argued that a greater number of individuals would acquiesce in those propositions than those who agreed. Timidity and a desire to avoid conflict would account for this acquiesence. However, conformity is not agreement, and offered an alternative, these others would not remain loyal.

35 One good empirical study of the subject is Thurman Arnold, *The Symbols of Government* (1953). A more conceptual work is William E. Connolly's *The Terms of Political Discourse* (1974).

36 This idea is compatible with the first order political philosophy of factionalism espoused in Montesquieu's *The Spirit of the Laws* (1748) and Alexander Hamilton, James Madison, and John Jay, *The Federalist Papers* (1790).

ences through an ongoing court battle (or threat of a court battle). Still, judicial reasoning is not a transparent method. It leaves a mark on any dispute, for conflicts need to be framed in a new language and be carried on under a new set of rules when they come within the judicial process.

Two political examples of potentially belligerent groups employing courts to settle possible explosive matters of disagreement may be cited. Neither can be considered an unmitigated success for any party in the controversies, nor yet a victory for any set of ethical beliefs. Each began with first order questions posed within a society in which answers reflected widely varying views, and loyalty to an often frail and mediocre judicial system remained firm.

The first example involves a situation where stability remained during many years of fundamental sectional disagreement: the questions and cases arising in the years before the American Civil War. The well-known initial issue in a dispute drawing largely along geographical lines involved the concepts of slavery, chattelage, and citizenship. Were slaves citizens in states originally slave-owning, in states which prohibited slavery, or in states newly formed or still territorial in the American west?[37] The resulting issues included controversies over the scope of the rights of states to regulate human chattelage, the power of the states generally compared with the federal government, and the power of once independent states to withdraw from a political contract (union) into which they once freely entered.[38] Some of these questions came before the courts—most notably in *Scott v. Sandford*,[39] holding, among other things, that Negroes free or slave, were not citizens under the United States Constitution, and thus were without standing

---

Alexander Hamilton, James Madison, and John Jay, *The Federalist Papers* (1790).

37 For a detailed legal and historical discussion of these issues, see H. V. Jaffa, *Crisis of the House Divided* (1959).

38 Many of the issues, and the lower court cases which split on the solution of many of them, are discussed in an historial context by Eugene Genovese in *Roll, Jordan, Roll* (1974).

39 60 U.S. (19 How.) 393, 15 L.Ed. 691 (1857).

to sue in federal courts (which at that time required diversity of citizenship for jurisdiction). Others, including the ultimate question of the right of a contracting state to breach or terminate a contract of political union, were never litigated. What is interesting about the issues of this time is not merely their ethical starkness or the historical process by which they led to a gruesome war, but their consistency over a seventy year period. These issues were apparent at the time when the United States Constitution was drafted, during the early years of the republic, and through the years of western expansion. Myriad court cases during this period decided matters in conflicting ways. It was not until 1857 that *Scott v. Sandford* authoritatively decided even some of the these basic issues, and *Scott* was then held by many to be wrongly decided. Within American society, the elusiveness of any definitive principle which could be taken as authority allowed the various factions to believe that the Constitution supported them; and that whoever and whatever their enemies were, the set of valid constitutional propositions was not among them. Ambiguity allowed the competing sides to live with one another in relative peace and to keep their pride and their loyalty to the government, regardless of its actions. The South seceded because it felt the government had been captured by individuals without respect for constitutional law. On the other hand, the Confederacy claimed it had acted legally in secession and, more interestingly, it adopted an almost verbatim copy of the original federal Constitution for its own government.[40] Obviously, its judicial view was, even during rebellion, one it believed compatible with a correct view of the United States Constitution. The consequence of ambiguity was peace, of certainty, war.

The second example concerns the Pakistan Supreme Court case of *Bhutto v. The Chief of the Army Staff and The Federation of Pakistan*.[41] Petitioner Bhutto, the deposed Prime Minister, challenged the detention of himself and other leaders of the

---

40 For an overview, see Daniel J. Boorstin, *The Genius of American Politics* 99-132 (1953). For a detailed analysis, see Alexander H. Stephens, *Constitutional View of the Late War Between the States* (1870).

41 PLD 1977 SC 657.

Pakistan People's Party by the military government, and cited the Pakistan Constitution as authority for his contention. The respondents argued, among other things, that the constitution had been temporarily suspended on grounds of grave military necessity, and that the detention was allowable under valid edicts of the military government which succeeded the normal constitutional rule. Bhutto pointed out that the Constitution did not provide for military government under the doctrine of necessity at all. Respondents suggested that such a doctrine was either implied within the document or was a standard on a par with the written constitution and thus its peer in authority.

Here again, it is not the outcome of the case which is relevant. (In fact, Bhutto lost the decision and ultimately his life in a related capital criminal case against him, while the military government remained firmly in power). What is interesting is the faith both parties placed in the judicial process. It is possible to maintain that neither party had much choice: Bhutto because he was in jail, and the government because of the controversy and uproar concerning his detention. However, both sides recognized the courts to be a vehicle for securing their goals. Both could maintain viable arguments, ones which their supporters were able to rally behind. The military allowed the proceedings and risked defeat. The supporters of the People's Party appeared content to rally behind the detainees and restrict their other activities against the government. In any case, the battle lines were drawn around judicial propositions. Stability through the transition of government was maintained. Such stability would not have been possible if the fundamental principles of Pakistan constitutional law were capable of only one reasonable interpretation. At the least, face-saving and the precedent of orderly transition might have been endangered. At worse, rebellion and civil war might have resulted.

The central problem for those extolling legal virtue or defending legal power is how to separate legal command from mere political preference. Critics of a legal decision often claim foul, declaring that the law is no more than pretext for politics.

Legal skill is thought to reside in those who can clearly differentiate between the two, and judicial conservatism meant to apply to judges able to park their political agenda outside the courtroom, and decide cases according to the logic of statutes, prior decisions, *etc.* Scholars, both historians and anthropologists, study societies for signs that politics has departed from the law, and a mature legal order has become based in some objective, consensual, determinable, and discrete body of dogma or source for dogma.

The desire to differentiate law and politics permeates the judicial system in countless and crucial ways. The debates hovering around "the rule of law" and "governments of laws not of men" concentrate on the requirement of a minimal content of due process, and a legal system which excludes the political vagaries of arbitrary individuals and partisan debate. Wandering from this context is thought to be straying from law into politics. The debate regarding whether judges make or enforce law, between strict versus evolving constructivism, or between the competing virtues of judicial activism and judicial passivity are debates about the entry of politics into the legal system.

It has been one of the theses of this book that such a debate is fundamentally misguided. No distinction between law and politics is worth making, not because judicial decisions are mere fraudulent dressing for naked political power, but because the requirements of constructing a legal order involve an irreducible political element.

Part of the problem, surely, is that one concept (law) is being defined by association with another (politics), when that defining concept is itself problematic. Politics in the context of the jurisprudential debate covers tremendous ground. In the broadest sense of being concerned with the workings of the state or the science of government, politics includes law by definition.

In the narrowest sense of partisan interest for narrow constituencies, with the goal of attaining some tangible and parochial short-term end, law, or at least the judicial system, is hardly political. Basically, politics tends to imply partisanship while law is defended as universal and objective. In that neither description is accurate, and in that both issues and judges carry political baggage, debate appears impossible of resolution.

However, that is not the criticism set out here. Rather, because the basis for judicial decisions ultimately includes political preferences, the law and politics cannot be wholly divorced. Further, because it is the preference and not the correctly and fully explicated view which matters, there is a jarring note of subjectivity and individuality in judicial reasoning. This is only the beginning of an explanation. Judges customarily do not employ their preferences directly: they take on views of judicial conduct which demand that they behave as judges, and not as they otherwise would. Politics enters when determining and defining how judges should act: for example, basic notions of retribution versus mercy, executive versus legislative authority, deference to precedent, corporate intent, judicial ability, fairness, constitutional exegesis, jurisdiction—to name only a few—involve basic political questions. More fundamentally, what constitutes the proper role of a judge in a society is itself a political question.

The issue of politics is really an abbreviation for a myriad of other, parallel issues. Religion, ethics, custom, social goals, convention, manners, economics, even science: all bear on judicial reasoning through the ultimate criteria thought relevant and true for judges. Saying that one's religious or political beliefs shape the outcome of judicial decisions is misleading, unless we recognize the indirectness, remoteness, and generality of the shaping. A politically and economically conservative (supply side, monetarist, Posnarian, Libertarian, free market, or any other variety) judge might believe that a regressive federal corporate tax is bad judgment, bad economics, and bad government. However, none of that would, in the normal course, bear on a criminal conviction of a corporate tax evader or on a question of construing legislative intent in ascertaining a particular tax rate.

If all judicial issues have an indirect "political" (using this as a shorthand for other types of programs, beliefs and attitudes) component, the indirect and direct aspects at times mirror one another. Whether, in an apportionment case like *Baker v. Carr*, the court should become involved in putting a legislative house in order is a political question. It involves separations of powers, the right to vote, and the bounds of pure democracy. Assuming a system which separates power and universalizes the franchise, the issue of a rotten borough legislature unable effectively to reapportion itself is one which is not only political, it can easily become judiciable. Whether the court should hear such a case is certainly, in one sense, a political issue, and eventually, like other political issues may remotely shape an outcome. That shaping occurs through the concept of the judicial role.

We began with the observation that modern societies have become extremely litigious. As short opinions in scattered cases and *ad hoc* remedial statutes give way to definite and detailed court pronouncements and codified legislation, court loads have increased rather than decreased. We can see now why more decisions do not necessarily result in fewer future cases. We can also see how a theory justifying judicial authority might be sketched. In conventional social contract theories, the authority given the government is justified by some notion of consent, either actual or implied. Under older theories, the members of a society yield personal rights they enjoyed in a pre-civil state a (state of nature) in return for the guarantee that others do so, thus ensuring themselves a certain level of personal protection from those others and giving the state certain claims on their behavior.[42] John Rawls asked the members to design a just society from a position of ignorance of their own place in that society, and allowed the resulting society a certain moral authority from the consent which can be implied from those members' decisions.[43]

Actual societal members have generally, of course, not been consulted in, let alone consented to, the creation of their own societies; while the fact that one is forced to make a decision from behind a veil of Rawlsian ignorance about the shape of one's own society throws the fairness of the consent found by Rawls into doubt. The judicial pluralist analysis suggests a much weaker but still apparent justification for a part of governmental power: judicial authority. Judicial authority has a radically

---

42 The two best known contract theorists are Thomas Hobbes, *Leviathan* (1651) and John Locke, *The Second Treatise of Government* (1690). Their views are interpreted in a modern reconstruction in Leo Strauss' *Natural Right and History* (1953).

43 This is taken from John Rawl's *A Theory of Justice* (1971).

democratic component.   Certainly, legal forms cannot be ignored, and corrupt, petty, unjust, arbitrary, and discriminatory judicial systems exist; however, part of a judicial view includes notions of ethics and personal politics.   When one looks to propositional sets within a society, one must notice the contribution of individual segments of that society to their content.   To the degree that individual participation is implicated in judicial propositions, that degree of authority may be justified.   This is far from consensus, for the existence of disagreement is recognized.   Pluralism says, rather, that because a certain widespread participation is an integral part of judicial reasoning, that reasoning carries some moral justification. Participation permits varied contributions, most of them voluntary, into the judicial system, because it allows different views to receive a hearing and to influence society's rules.

Conclusion

Discussion of the status of judicial assertions has shown that such assertions are justified through the use of a judicial view, and that as regards truth value, each view is equally true.   Equality of truth does not imply equality generally, and individual views are subject to criticisms of other kinds, particularly moral, political and logical.

Oliver Wendell Holmes once objected to law being considered as "some brooding omnipresence in the sky".   In that first order propositions are ultimately the result of individual view construction, and rooted in personal beliefs and attitudes, Holmes' worry has been assuaged.   The fact that the conventional nature of judicial role provides the initial step in view construction belies any thought that judicial views are just a matter of free, individual preferences.   One's conception of a judicial role is, in large part, determined by public criteria.   For example, a judge may be thought to be obligated to make use of legislative enactments while not morally able to use the rules of his college fraternity.   If there is no brooding omniprescence, there may be a constant presence, in the form of the shared beliefs within a society.

This chapter looked at several examples of view disparity. In suggesting that judicial pluralism explains how societies with competing factions are held together through the capacity of courts to accommodate competing views, no endorsement of the results of such a process should be implied. Williston's view of contracts and the Southern view of the United States Constitution both allowed great inequities to exist, and perhaps different political institutions would have more readily and easily remedied them. The *Bhutto* case, moreover, demonstrates the ease with which it is possible for any group to carry out its beliefs under the authority of judicial process. Extreme and terrible examples of this are, unfortunately, everywhere in evidence.

The lesson drawn from pluralist analysis, then, is not one endorsing or disparaging any particular legal system or the process of adjudication generally. Rather, it is one which suggests that responsibility for judicial judgments lies in large part with the individual. Individual citizens judge what suffices as good justifications. The judgment contained in the judicial decision may be assessed and criticized just as any judgment would be assessed and criticized, except that a final determination of truth is impossible. This allows us to direct our focus more clearly on the ethical and rational aspects of adjudication, and to encourage them to flourish.

Index

How Judges Reason

"This is an enormously energetic exploration, employing powerful analytical techniques and an exceptionally rich familiarity with both social philosophy and the practice of the law. Philosophers of law and other social realities, teachers and practitioners of law, and above all judges will find in the argument, and in its abundant illustrations and annotations, much matter for reflection. The book brings to the debate a distinctive voice, offering an account at once descriptive and normative."

John Finnis
Professor of Law
and Legal Philosophy
Oxford University

"*How Judges Reason* leads the reader flawlessly through the thicket of legal realism and the modern schools of skeptical analysis. As such it is an essential supplement to the commonly read works of Holmes, Gray, Llewellyn, Dworkin, and Hart. It is the most important book on judicial theory in the last thirty years."

Daniel R. Coquillette
Dean and Professor of Law
Boston College
Reporter, Committee on Rules
of Practice and Procedure,
Judicial Conference of the
United States